LIBERATING EUROPE
D-DAY TO VICTORY
1944-1945

DESPATCHES FROM THE FRONT

The Commanding Officers' Reports From the Field and At Sea.

LIBERATING EUROPE D-DAY TO VICTORY 1944-1945

Introduced and compiled by
Martin Mace and John Grehan
With additional research by
Sara Mitchell

Pen & Sword
MILITARY

First published in Great Britain in 2014 by
Pen & Sword Military
an imprint of
Pen & Sword Books Ltd
47 Church Street
Barnsley
South Yorkshire
S70 2AS

ISBN 978 1 78346 215 5

Printed and bound in England
By CPI Group (UK) Ltd, Croydon, CR0 4YY

Pen & Sword Books Ltd incorporates the Imprints of
Pen & Sword Aviation, Pen & Sword Family History,
Pen & Sword Maritime, Pen & Sword Military, Pen & Sword Discovery,
Pen & Sword Politics, Pen & Sword Atlas, Pen & Sword Archaeology,
Wharncliffe Local History, Wharncliffe True Crime, Wharncliffe Transport,
Pen & Sword Select, Pen & Sword Military Classics, Leo Cooper,
The Praetorian Press, Claymore Press, Remember When,
Seaforth Publishing and Frontline Publishing.

For a complete list of Pen & Sword titles please contact:
PEN & SWORD BOOKS LIMITED
47 Church Street, Barnsley, South Yorkshire, S70 2AS, England
E-mail: enquiries@pen-and-sword.co.uk
Website: www.pen-and-sword.co.uk

CONTENTS

INTRODUCTION

The operation which was launched in the first week of June 1944, and led to the liberation of France and then Occupied Europe, was a success, even though it proved to be a far harder task than had been expected. It is frequently said that this success was in part due to the combined operation against Dieppe in 1942 where many lessons were learnt. Consequently an account of this raid, Operation *Jubilee*, forms the first despatch in this volume.

The despatch supplied by the Naval Force Commander, Captain J. Hughes-Hallett, whilst admitting to a number of mistakes (in what was in reality a disaster), claims that the operation, which achieved nothing "was well worth while provided its lessons are carefully applied when the time comes to re-enter France on a large scale". To regard the losses incurred in the raid – more than 3,000 killed, wounded or taken prisoner – as being "worth while" one would think that these lessons were truly revelatory. Yet what we learn from Hughes-Hallett is that very strong forces were needed to break through prepared defences and that a high proportion of troops should be held in reserve until it is known where to use them to exploit success. These are two of the most basic and fundamental aspects of military operations. To suggest that Britain's military commanders were unaware of these factors defies belief.

Nevertheless, when Operation *Overlord* was launched two years later, and whether Dieppe had taught the Allied leaders anything or not, it was with forces powerful enough to overcome the German defences. The second despatch in this volume, therefore, concerns the assault phase of the Normandy landings, Operation *Neptune*, and this is also supplied by a naval officer, in this case Admiral Sir Bertram Ramsay.

Operation *Neptune* was indeed a colossal enterprise, requiring, as Ramsay explains, "the co-ordination of the movement of thousands of ships and landing craft and aircraft and then of their fire power, the second the co-ordination of the activities of hundreds of thousands of men and women of all services, both in the United Kingdom and off the French coast, marshalling, loading, sailing, unloading and returning at least eight ship convoys a day in addition to ten or twelve landing craft groups".

It is interesting to note that though we view the transporting of some 150,000 Allied troops across the Channel in, or protected by, more than 5,000 vessels, whilst achieving almost complete surprise, as being the result of a high degree of careful planning and co-ordination, it is evident that Ramsay must have experienced a degree of difficulty dealing with the American Navy. In his despatch he states: "I am aware that the U.S. naval authorities had to exercise considerable restraint in submitting to a degree of control by superior authority on a level higher than that to which they were accustomed. In their reports the U.S. naval commanders have commented that in their view my orders extended to too much detail."

These are strong words. The Americans clearly did not like being told what to do by a British commander and *considerable restraint* had to be exercised.

Ramsay also reveals that there was disagreement amongst the force commanders. He states that after much discussion it was decided that the landings should take place in daylight. Even though this was agreed upon, at least two "vain" efforts were made to change it.

The third despatch in this compilation was written by Air Chief Marshal Sir Sholto Douglas in his capacity as Air Officer Commanding-in-chief, Coastal Command. His main task during Operation *Neptune* was to protect the ships and smaller craft from German submarines. It had been noticed from March 1944 that the Germans had been withdrawing their U-boats from their bases around the Bay of Biscay in order to concentrate them in the Channel in anticipation of the expected invasion.

To counter this, Douglas aimed to "flood an area of sufficient depth to kill or keep submarines submerged from the Western limits of the St. George's and Bristol Channels and the English Channel up to a point as near as possible to the route of our cross-channel convoys." Douglas called this his "the cork in the bottle" policy, meaning that he intended to use his aircraft as the cork which would keep the U-boats bottled-up beyond the invasion zone. Douglas also had responsibility for helping to provide aerial protection for the cross-Channel convoys and for this he was given eight Fleet Air Arm squadrons.

Air Chief Marshal Sir Trafford Leigh-Mallory provides the despatch concerning the main aerial support for the Normandy operations. In this respect, the air operations began as early as November 1943 with the objective of reaching a situation whereby the German air force was rendered incapable of effective interference with Operation *Overlord*. The second main objective was the disruption of the enemy's communications and channels of reinforcement and supply. Leigh-Mallory details how this was to be achieved in the preparatory bombing plan, which was designed to completely dislocate the railway network across northern France and the Low Countries.

Attacks were also to be delivered against coastal batteries, enemy naval and military targets and the enemy's Radar installations. It was necessary, Leigh-Mallory reminds us, that if all these attacks were delivered against the intended landing area this would be a fairly obvious indication where the assault was likely to take place. As a consequence at least two attacks were made on each type of target outside of the projected assault area to just one attack on a target within that area.

Other tasks allotted to Leigh-Mallory were:

1. To provide continuous reconnaissance of the enemy's dispositions and movements.

2. To support the landing and subsequent advances of the Allied armies.

3. To deliver offensive strikes against enemy naval forces.

4. To provide air lift for airborne forces.

Leigh-Mallory's despatch, which ends with operations up to 30 September 1944, is almost 50,000 words in length and is a highly detailed narrative of events during the period under scrutiny. The appendices and maps mentioned in the text by Leigh-Mallory were not, in fact, published.

A comparatively brief summary of naval operations following Operations *Overlord* and *Neptune* is provided by Admiral Sir Harold Burrough. It was written, Burrough claims, "with sufficient brevity that a busy man might find time to read it".

Burrough had to work under the command of US General Eisenhower, who was the Supreme Commander Allied Expeditionary Force. His final message sent to Eisenhower, when the Supreme Command was terminated, presents a somewhat different picture to that which we read about before D-Day: "Tomorrow, for the first time, the United States Ensign will not be flown over my Headquarters, and the hauling down of 'Old Glory' tonight will mark the end of one of the happiest associations in a Combined Command which has probably ever existed." The success that the soldiers, sailors and airmen of the two nations had experienced fighting together had, it would seem, brought greater appreciation of each other's efforts.

The final despatch is that of Field Marshal Bernard Montgomery. It covers the period from D-Day until the German surrender in May 1945.

Amongst the most interesting parts of Montgomery's despatch are his observations on the high quality of the medical care which he witnessed. He states that in the First World War two out of every three soldiers who were wounded in the stomach eventually died, whereas in the Normandy campaign two out of three that suffered such wounds recovered. He also observes that the healing of war wounds had been revolutionised by the use of penicillin. In this respect many men who in the First World War would have been permanent invalids, were fit and ready to go back to the line within a month of being wounded.

He also notes that as the troops swept through Germany they liberated many of the concentration camps, such as Belsen and Sandbostel where thousands of people were dying of typhus. Yet only twenty-five British soldiers contracted the disease and none died from it.

Whilst acknowledging the efforts of the doctors and medical staff, Montgomery also attributed the health of the troops, as well as their rapid recovery, down to morale. "Commanders in the field," he wrote, "must realise that the medical state of an army is not dependent on the doctors alone. Their efforts are immeasurably facilitated when morale is at its highest, and of all the factors which ensure a high state of morale, there is none more important than success."

Montgomery repeats this theme, concluding his despatch with these words: "I call morale the greatest single factor in war. A high morale is based on discipline, self-respect and confidence of the soldier in his commanders, in his weapons and in himself. Without high morale, no success can be achieved, however good may be the strategic or tactical plan, or anything else. High morale is a pearl of very great price. And the surest way to obtain it is by success in battle." This, quite possibly, is what Admiral Burrough had benefitted from.

*

The objective of this book is to reproduce those despatches as they first appeared to the general public some seventy years ago. They have not been modified, edited or interpreted in any way and are therefore the original and unique words of the commanding officers as they saw things at the time. The only difference is in the presentation of footnotes. Whereas they appeared at the end of each page in the original documents, these have been inserted at the conclusion of the relevant despatch and are indicated with numbers rather than symbols.

Any grammatical or spelling errors have been left uncorrected to retain the authenticity of the documents – for example Admiral Ramsay congratulated Rear-Admiral J. Wilkes, U.S.N. on his "splended" achievements and the success on D-Day was "greatily" helped by tactical surprise. The authors of the despatches also made frequent use of abbreviations, some of which may not be immediately obvious to the reader; consequently we have included in the book an explanation of these.

John Grehan and Martin Mace
Storrington, 2014

IMAGES

1   Burnt out tanks and landing craft lie strewn across the beach at Dieppe after the Allied withdrawal. (Courtesy of the War and Peace Archive)

2   In all, twenty-nine Churchill tanks, comprising of assorted Mark I, II and III examples, were disembarked during the Dieppe Raid. Of these, twenty-seven got ashore – two "drowned in deep water". Fifteen would make it to the esplanade – though not much further. (Courtesy of the War and Peace Archive)

3   A number of Allied prisoners under guard at Dieppe before being marched away to captivity. (Courtesy of the War and Peace Archive)

4   The Royal Navy's landing craft LCA-1377 transporting American troops across Weymouth Bay during preparations for the Normandy invasion, circa May–June 1944. (Courtesy of the Conseil Régional de Basse-Normandie/US National Archives)

5   At exactly 08.32 hours on 6 June 1944, Sergeant Jim Mapham of No.5 Army Film and Photographic Unit photographed this scene on "Queen Red" Beach, a sector in the centre-left of Sword Beach (the precise location is near La Brèche, Hermanville-sur-Mer). The shutter clicked just as the beach came under heavy artillery and mortar fire from German positions inland. One US newspaper which published this image in the aftermath of the landings described it as "the greatest picture of the war". (HMP)

6   US troops hit the shore on the morning of 6 June 1944. Titled "Into the Jaws of Death", this image was taken by Chief Photographer's Mate Robert F. Sargent. The landing craft seen here was crewed by US Coastguard personnel, and had set off for the Normandy beaches from the U.S. Coast Guard-manned USS *Samuel Chase*. (US National Archives)

7   A cameraman peers between men crowded in a landing craft to obtain this shot of the first wave going ashore as his own LCA nears the smoke-shrouded Omaha Beach. (Conseil Régional de Basse-Normandie/US National Archives)

MAPS

1

THE DIEPPE RAID 18-19 AUGUST 1942

The following despatch was submitted to the Commander-in-Chief, Portsmouth, on the 30th August, 1942, by Captain J. HUGHES-HALLETT, R.N., Naval Force Commander.

Portsmouth Combined Headquarters,
Fort Southwick.
30th August, 1942.

I have the honour to submit the accompanying report of proceedings for Operation "Jubilee" which was carried out on I8th/I9th August, I942.

2. Generally speaking I consider that the Naval Forces engaged in the operation carried out their role as well as was possible under conditions which became increasingly difficult as the operation proceeded. A number of minor mistakes were made, chiefly by myself, and find their place in the narrative. Fortunately none of these had any vital influence on the operation as a whole.

3. I am glad to be able to report that almost without exception the conduct of all Naval personnel was exemplary, and in accordance with the traditions of the Service. Recommendations for honours and awards are forwarded separately, but I have no doubt that many unrecorded acts of heroism must have occurred off the beaches and in vessels which were lost.

4. The fighter cover afforded by No. II Group was magnificent and the fact that a number of bombers got through was to be expected. It is considered that the loss of only one ship from bombing should be regarded as an unusually fortunate result.

5. I wish respectfully to pay a tribute to the Military Force Commander. No one could have been more helpful than Major-General J.H. Roberts. All our major decisions were jointly made in complete agreement.

6. I wish also to draw your particular attention to Major P. Young of No. 3 Commando, who with the troops from a single L.C.P. effectively diverted the attention of the coast defence battery at Berneval during an important part of the operation, thereby averting the exceedingly serious consequences which might have

resulted from the failure of the Yellow Beach landings. In my judgment this was perhaps the most outstanding incident of the operation.

7. Operation "Jubilee" differed fundamentally from any other Combined Operation that has been carried out by this country in modern times, in as much as it amounted to a direct daylight assault upon an important objective strongly held by the first army of Europe. From the point of view of its perspective in the war as a whole, it may perhaps be compared to the British offensives on the Western front during 1915. Although from purely a military point of view the results achieved were disappointing, and the heavy casualties sustained regrettable, it is considered that the operation was well worth while provided its lessons are carefully applied when the time comes to re-enter France on a large scale. The principal lesson appears to be, firstly, that much stronger military forces are required to break through the German coastal defences in any important area; secondly, that a very much higher proportion of the military force should be held in reserve until the progress made in the initial assaults is known, and that this reserve should then be employed in exploiting success. Unless this is done there is no guarantee that any of the beaches will be properly secured, and this is an absolute prerequisite of success whether the subsequent phases of the operation are to take the form of a withdrawal or a further follow-up.

8. A further point which was very clearly shown, is the strength of the German defensive system in the coastal regions, which confronts assaulting troops with the problem not dissimilar to that of the Western Front in the last war. Arising out of this is the need for far more effective methods of supporting the troops, unless it is quite certain that defences which dominate the landing places can be overrun by a surprise night assault. The methods whereby effective support can be given are not considered to include night bombing.

9. From the purely naval point of view the operation has taught us less, if only because the passage and landings went very largely according to plan. Although this was so, it is considered that the liberties that were taken in dispersing the force so widely on passage with so small a covering force, could not prudently be repeated. For example, the groups which sailed from Newhaven were vulnerable to attack from the east, and the L.S.Is. (Infantry Assault Ships) were exposed to a considerable risk from the time that they stopped to lower their boats until they returned to the English side of the Channel. The conclusion is that a substantially larger covering force should be employed in the future, because the enemy is less likely to be surprised again.

10. The Naval Forces were fortunate in as much as they sustained no damage from mines and no serious damage from coastal batteries. Until more experience is gained, however, it would be most unsafe to draw too firm a deduction from this for future operations.

11. The operation was interesting also as being perhaps the first occasion on which light naval forces (i.e., coastal craft and landing craft) manned almost entirely by the Royal Naval Volunteer Reserve, have been employed on a large scale and under conditions of extreme difficulty. They acquitted themselves well, but the small leavening of experienced officers of the Royal Navy who were employed in positions of control was an important factor in the results achieved.

I2. I consider that the chief lessons of the operation are:-

(i) It was shown still to be possible to achieve tactical surprise in a cross-channel operation of some magnitude.

(ii) The comparatively small naval forces which took part in the operation sufficed to prevent the enemy from offering any surface opposition whatever, apart from that resulting from the chance encounter of Number 5 Group with German armed trawlers.

(iii) If it should be necessary to attempt a frontal attack on strongly defended enemy positions again, it will be essential to provide far more effective means of supporting the troops. In this particular operation I am satisfied that a capital ship could have been operated in the Dieppe area during the first two or three hours of the operation without undue risk.

(iv) The enormous possibilities of this type of operation for bringing about a decisive air battle were demonstrated.

I3. Finally I venture to submit that, should it be decided to undertake further operations of this nature in the near future, my Staff and I may be afforded the opportunity to carry them out. While realising the force of the arguments in favour of giving other groups of officers a turn, I feel that in time of war the overriding requirement is to get results, and this is more likely to be achieved by those who have gained first-hand experience. While every effort has been made to record the lessons we have learned, there is so much which cannot be set forth on paper and which can only be properly grasped by those who have had the advantage of direct personal experience.

(Sgd.) J.H. HALLETT.
Captain, Royal Navy.
NAVAL FORCE COMMANDER.

OPERATION "JUBILEE."
NAVAL FORCE COMMANDER'S NARRATIVE.

The Passage.

I. Generally speaking the assembly of the force and the passage were carried out in accordance with the plan and without any major incident. After clearing the gate H.M.S. QUEEN EMMA (Captain G.L.D. Gibbs, D.S.O., R.N. (Ret.)) leading Groups I, 2 and 3, appeared to me to be proceeding at an excessive speed, and H.M.S. CALPE (Lieut.-Commander J.H. Wallace, R.N.) and the destroyers had some difficulty in taking station ahead. At 00I6 when H.M.S. CALPE was abeam of H.M.S. QUEEN EMMA a signal was made informing her that she was ahead of station and instructing her to reduce to I8 knots. After this the destroyers formed ahead, and shortly afterwards altered course for the Western passage through the minefield. The Dan Buoys and the M.L. marking the entrance to this channel were only sighted about 2 minutes before H.M.S. CALPE entered the channel, no signals from the type 78 Beacon being received on account of a breakdown of H.M.S. CALPE'S R.D.F.[1] However, H.M.S. CALPE and the destroyers of the 2nd Division successfully passed through the Western channel, but H.M.S. QUEEN EMMA with Groups I, 2 and 3 in company, lost touch with the destroyers and passed through the Eastern channel, overtaking H.M.S. FERNIE (Lieut. W.B. Willett, R.N.) and certain groups of L.C.Ts.[2] and L.C.Ps.[3] but fortunately without any collisions.

2. A word of praise is due to the 9th and I3th Minesweeping Flotillas (Commander H.T. Rust, R.N. and Commander L.S.J. Ede, D.S.O., R.N.) who carried out the task allotted to them with efficiency and precision.

3. After passing through the minefield H.M.S. CALPE stopped in accordance with the plan, and subsequently signalled her position to H.M.S. QUEEN EMMA, H.M.S. PRINCE ALBERT (Lieut.-Commander H.B. Peate, R.N.R.) and H.M.S. GLENGYLE (Captain D.S. McGrath, R.N.), as these vessels respectively came in sight. H.M.S. CALPE then proceeded and stopped about one mile to seaward of the position in which H.M.S. GLENGYLE with Group 4 had stopped to lower their boats.

4. At about 0350 gun fire was observed to the E.S.E. which it was realised must be in the immediate vicinity of Group 5. At the time I considered this might be caused by an E-boat attack, but with the knowledge that Polish Ship SLAZAK (R. Tyminski, Kmdr.-Ppov.) and H.M.S. BROCKLESBY (Lieut.-Commander E.N. Pumphrey, D.S.O., D.S.C., RN.) were within about 4 miles of Group 5 and that H.M.S. CALPE was the only ship in the immediate vicinity of H.M.S. GLENGYLE and Group 4, it was decided to keep Group 4 in sight.

5. Actually Group 5 had made a chance encounter with some armed trawlers, and although Commander D.B. Wyburd, R.N., in S.G.B.5 (Lieut. G.H. Hummel, R.N.R.) maintained a steady course and speed in order that his L.C.Ps. should remain in company, S.G.B.5 was soon disabled, and the L.C.Ps. disorganised. Commander Wyburd's persistence in remaining the guide of the slow L.C.Ps. while himself under heavy fire, showed great gallantry and determination. Nevertheless, I am of opinion that he would have done better to use the speed and smoke-laying capabilities of S.G.Bs.[4] in order to protect the L.C.Ps. L.C.F.(L) I[5] (Lieut. T.M. Foggitt, R.A.N.V.R.) also in company with Group 5, successfully engaged the German vessels, setting one on fire and claiming to have sunk a second. In the course of this engagement her fire control was unfortunately put out of action.

6. During the action O.R.P. SLAZAK with H.M.S. BROCKLESBY in company was approximately four miles to the N.N.E. but did not intervene. The Commanding Officer of O.R.P. SLAZAK has since informed me that he considered the firing came from the shore and therefore thought it best to continue with his patrol.

7. It will be convenient at this stage to complete the story of the Yellow Beach landings, which were frustrated by this encounter.

8. Five L.C.Ps. effected a delayed landing on Yellow I Beach.[6] Heavy opposition was encountered and the troops made no progress. Subsequent attempts were made

by the L.C.Ps. to withdraw them but it proved impossible to close the beach on account of machine gun fire, and eventually only the Naval Beach Party who swam off to the boats were taken off. During this period, a small German tanker was set on fire and driven ashore by M.L. 346 (Lieut. A.D. Fear, R.N.V.R.) whose conduct throughout the operation was outstanding.

9. One L.C.P. effected an unopposed landing at Yellow II Beach. [7] The troops on board, under the command of Major P. Young, M.C., succeeded in approaching the coast defence battery at Berneval and in sniping it for about two hours. Subsequently they were successfully withdrawn. I have little doubt that the failure of the coast defence battery at Berneval to play an effective part in the operation was largely due to the action of Major Young.

10. Subsequently on the extreme western flank, the PRINCE ALBERT'S Landing Craft, carrying No. 4 Commando, were successfully landed according to plan. This part of the operation, which was under the joint command of Lieut.-Commander H.H.H. Mulleneux, R.N., and Lieut.-Colonel the Lord Lovat, M.C., M.P., went through without a hitch from beginning to end. The troops were very fortunate in that they blew up an ammunition dump at their objective by a chance mortar hit early in their attack. They were subsequently withdrawn at approximately 0815 and returned to England without incident.

11. Reverting to the main landings, that at Green Beach[8] took place punctually and according to plan, and only encountered slight initial opposition. Subsequently Group 6, under the command of Commander H.V.P. McClintock, R.N., and carrying the Camerons of Canada, effected a landing at Green Beach according to plan but about 30 minutes late. The reason for the delay lay partly in the anxiety of the Senior Military Officer not to be landed ahead of time, and partly due to navigational difficulties occasioned by smoke during the final approach. This landing met with a certain amount of opposition, but the troops were successfully put ashore. It is interesting to note that at this stage the enemy fire on the approaches to Green Beach was slight, but steadily increased throughout the operation, and resulted in very heavy casualties being suffered during the eventual withdrawal. This was because the force landed did not succeed in occupying the high ground east of the beach.

12. The landing on Blue Beach[9] was delayed for 15 minutes, on account of time lost when the boats were forming up. This was due to M.G.B. 315 (Lieut. J.I. Lloyd, R.N.V.R.) (whose role was to remain with H.M.S. QUEEN EMMA and escort her back) going ahead and getting mixed up with the Landing Craft from H.M.S. PRINCESS ASTRID, who mistook her for M.G.B. 316 (Act Temp. Lieut.-Commander T.N. Cartwright, R.N.V.R.) whose role it was to lead in these landing craft. Although the landing subsequently took place according to plan, I fear that the 15 minutes' delay must have been partly responsible for the very heavy opposition which the troops immediately encountered after landing, and which apparently pinned them down on the beach area throughout the day. Subsequently H.M.S. DUKE OF WELLINGTON'S Flotilla of L.C.As. [10] landed additional troops on this beach according to plan. This landing took place at about 0545 and encountered no abnormal opposition. At about 0530 I was informed that a signal had been received

stating that no landing had taken place on Blue Beach, and I reported this in my situation report made at 0612. Actually there is some reason to suppose that this report was of German origin but the whole of the events that took place ashore at Blue Beach were obscure, although it was clear from the very outset that the troops were held up. There is little doubt that this was the chief cause of the failure of the Military plan, and in view of the uncertainty about what really happened, I have since requested the Commanding Officer, H.M.S. QUEEN EMMA to conduct a close enquiry with all the boat officers concerned. The resulting report has been forwarded separately.

13. Meanwhile the main landings on Red and White Beaches[11] took place punctually and according to plan, with the exception that the leading wave of three L.C.Ts. approached from too far to the westward and were about 10 to 15 minutes late in touching down.

14. The air support, and the smoke-making aircraft on the East cliff, were accurately synchronised, and the destroyer's fire, both on the houses along the front while the boats were going in, and subsequently on the East and West Cliffs, appeared to be as effective as could be expected. No losses of landing craft took place during the initial landing, but it did not appear to officer in charge that the troops were able to capture the strong points along the front after landing. However, the L.C.Ts. on going in encountered very heavy opposition, and I consider that theirs was a notable achievement in landing 28 out of 30 tanks dry-shod. The heavy damage and casualties in the L.C.T's. were undoubtedly due in a large measure to the relatively long periods they remained on the beach, waiting for the miscellaneous troops that they were carrying in addition to the tanks, to disembark.

15. The work of L.C.F. (L) 2 (Lieut. E.L. Graham, R.N.V.R.) in supporting the main landing, calls for special mention. This vessel closed in to provide point blank range, and gave most effective support. She was soon disabled, and her captain killed, but her guns were fought until one by one they were put out of action, and the ship herself was finally sunk.

16. Lieut.-Commander J.H. Dathan, R.N. (Senior Officer of Group 7) carrying reserve troops in L.C.Ps., reported on board H.M.S. CALPE within 5 minutes of the time laid down in the plan. At the request of Major-General Roberts, I instructed him to land his force on Red Beach, and the landing was successfully effected by 0700. This landing, which was shielded by smoke until the last moment, encountered very heavy fire just off the beaches, but all boats effected a landing, although in most cases the troops sustained heavy casualties immediately afterwards. Two out of the 26 boats were destroyed.

17. Up to this point the Naval part of the plan had proceeded very much as was intended, with the exception of the frustration of the Yellow Beach landing. Furthermore, there had been remarkably little opposition from shore batteries, and apparently none from enemy aircraft. Nevertheless it was clear that the military operations were not proceeding according to plan, and that the opposition ashore was considerably greater than had been expected. In view of the failure of the Blue Beach landing and hence of the plan to capture the East Cliff I felt doubtful whether H.M.S.

LOCUST'S proposed entry into the harbour would be either practicable or profitable. Commander R.E.D. Ryder, V.C., R.N., who was signalled to come on board H.M.S. CALPE at about 0645, shared this view, and informed me that H.M.S. LOCUST had already suffered damage and casualties whilst closing the East Cliff earlier on. Major-General Roberts was consulted and agreed that no attempt should be made to enter the harbour. It was decided instead to transfer the Royal Marine Commando to armoured landing craft and to land them as reinforcements. The General asked that they should be sent to White Beach, and this operation was entrusted to Commander Ryder, all L.C.F. (L)s. being ordered to close H.M.S. LOCUST and give support. Actually, owing to communication difficulties, only 2 L.C.F. (L)s. responded, but all the Chasseurs[12] backed them up and gave good support. The landing was effected in face of very heavy opposition at about 0840. Judging from the reports of the landing craft who took part it is doubtful whether the Royal Marines were able to achieve anything.

I8. About this time Commander Wyburd came aboard H.M.S. CALPE and informed me of what had occurred to the best of his knowledge to Group 5. He was instructed to embark in M.G.B.3I7 and to proceed to the vicinity of Yellow Beaches to round up what L.C.Ps. he could find.

I9. Lieutenant-Commander H.W. Goulding, D.S.O., R.N.R., also came on board about this time and informed me of the landing at Blue Beach, an account of which is given earlier. He was instructed to proceed to Blue Beach with 4 L.C.As. to endeavour to withdraw any troops which were there. Lieutenant-Commander C.W. McMullen, R.N., in an M.L. proceeded with him to provide support. I received a report later to the effect that Lieutenant-Commander Goulding was unable to close the Blue Beach owing to heavy opposition and that no one could be seen on the beach.

20. Commander McClintock also reported on board H.M.S. CALPE and I instructed him to proceed to investigate Green Beach and inform the Beachmaster that he should not evacuate the beach as it might be necessary to withdraw all the troops from Green Beach. Commander McClintock was unable to approach close to Green Beach owing to heavy and well directed fire of the enemy.

2I. At about 0750 I received information that I0 E-boats were approaching from Boulogne. Accordingly O.R.P. SLAZAK, H.M. Ships BROCKLESBY and BLEASDALE were ordered to proceed to the north eastward, and all available M.G.Bs. were also ordered to patrol to the eastward. (My signals timed 0752 and 08I6 refer). Nothing more was heard of the E-boats, and it is remarkable that at no time during the entire operation was there any organised opposition from German naval forces. While detached on this service, O.R.P. SLAZAK was damaged by near misses, and later had to return to England.

22. Throughout the period which followed, enemy fire from the shore steadily increased, and the destroyers were forced constantly to shift their positions in order to avoid damage and keep under cover of smoke. Periodically requests were received from the shore for supporting fire against strong points but in no cases was an F.O.O. [13] in a position to observe his fire. The requests were met by detailing destroyers in

succession, but I felt very doubtful of the efficacy of their support under the conditions which prevailed.

23. H.M.S. CALPE'S appearance during most of this period must have resembled that of a Fleet Flagship on regatta day, as there were seldom less than from six to ten craft alongside. They came to transfer wounded, bring reports, or seek instructions, and their presence was rather an embarrassment to the Commanding Officer when he wished to manoeuvre to avoid gun fire. Lieutenant-Commander J.H. Wallace, R.N. remained imperturbable, however, throughout the operation, and by his coolness set an excellent example.

24. My general impression during this phase of the operation from the Naval point of view, was a feeling of inability to give the troops effective support. The military situation was completely obscure, and the large quantities of smoke drifting inshore made it impossible to see what was happening. On the other hand, had it not been for the smoke, it would have been impossible for the destroyers and landing craft to remain as close inshore as they did.

25. Immediately after the landings, the landing craft had withdrawn to seaward of the destroyers. This was in accordance with the instructions they had received in the event of their finding that the approaches to the beaches remained under heavy fire. It was this fact, more than anything else, that indicated to me from the outset that things ashore were not going according to plan.

At about 0900 H.M.S. GARTH reported that her ammunition was nearly exhausted. I accordingly ordered her to escort H.M.S. ALRESFORD who had a damaged L.C.T. in tow, and Nos. I0 and II Groups, whose tanks and troops the General had decided not to land, back to England. (My signal 0903 refers.)

26. By 0900 it had become clear to me that the troops ashore were in difficulties and were unlikely to gain possession of the East and West cliffs which dominated the main beaches. I learned later that even some of the buildings on the front were still in enemy hands. It was obvious therefore that the military situation was serious, and that it was becoming steadily more difficult for ships and craft to close the beaches. Accordingly I advised the General that the withdrawal should take place with as little further delay as possible, and should be confined to personnel. I considered that I030 would be the earliest practicable time, as it was necessary to warn the Air Officer Commanding II Group and to pass instructions to the landing craft. The General agreed subject to confirmation nearer to time.

27. Accordingly Commander McClintock was summoned on board H.M.S. CALPE and it was decided that all A.L.Cs. [14] and M.L.Cs. [15] should be instructed to proceed into the same beaches as those on which they had originally landed and should ferry troops off on to L.C.Ts. who should remain about I mile from the shore. All possible support was to be given by destroyers and L.C.F.(L)s. (I considered it out of the question to send L.C.Ps. or L.C.Ts. inshore in view of the volume of enemy fire.)

28. To give effect to this plan, Commander McClintock proceeded in M.L. I87 and gave necessary instructions to the landing craft, and a signal, similar to that later sent at 0950, save that the time for the withdrawal was given as I030, was coded and

prepared for despatch. Later on, however, the General informed me that he would prefer to wait until II00. The signal thus amended was then despatched and Commander McClintock was informed of the later time. At about I022, the destroyers were ordered to form on a line to bear 070° to 250° and to follow the landing craft in. All vessels suitably placed were instructed to make smoke. The wind was onshore and slightly from the west, and an effective screen of smoke prevented the landing craft from being fired upon until they were close inshore. Unfortunately the smoke also hid the beaches from the destroyers and it was very difficult to see what was going on, or to offer effective support by gun fire. Nevertheless, without the smoke it is doubtful whether any withdrawal would have been possible.

29. During these events, H.M.S. CALPE steered for the western end of Green Beach, as it was thought that no supporting fire would be necessary in this area, and both the Military Force Commander and the Air Liaison Officer were extremely averse to H.M.S. CALPE'S guns being fired on account of the risk to the special wireless apparatus that had been installed. Actually, however, it soon became apparent that the western cliff at the end of Green Beach was held by the enemy, and H.M.S. CALPE came under small arms and machine gun fire necessitating her opening the range. It is interesting to record that when subsequently both H.M.S. CALPE and H.M.S. FERNIE were obliged to open fire with their main armament, much of the wireless apparatus remained intact.

30. It soon became virtually impossible to know how the withdrawal was proceeding, but at about II30 H.M.S. CALPE embarked two landing craft loads of troops, mostly wounded, from whom it was learned that there were still men waiting to come off at Green Beach. At about the same time the General asked for the ship to proceed to the main beaches and ascertain the position there. Accordingly M.L. I94 (Act. Lieut.-Commander W. Whitfield, R.N.R.) was hailed and instructed to round up the landing craft in the area and send them in again. At about the same time, a signal, originator unknown, was received to the effect that there were no more troops on Green Beach, and was immediately contradicted by my signal timed II47. H.M.S. CALPE then proceeded off the main beaches and closed L.C.T. 9, to whom troops were then being transferred by landing craft. Some of these troops were embarked in H.M.S. CALPE in order to save time. Slightly later I closed A.L.Cs. I85 and I88, who had just come off from the main beach. Both gave it as their opinion that the conditions ashore precluded further evacuation.

3I. At about I220 a signal was received from Commander McClintock indicating that no further evacuation was feasible. However, the Military Force Commander asked that a further effort should be made and although I felt that this might well result in greater losses to troops already embarked, than in the embarkation of additional troops, I decided to give Commander McClintock discretion whether to make a further effort. Accordingly the following signal was made:-

"If no further evacuation possible withdraw."

Actually the signal as reported to Commander McClintock omitted the word "if" and from that time onwards H.M.S. CALPE was unable to get into touch with him. I supposed at the time that his M.L. must have been sunk, but actually he was able to order the withdrawal of all landing craft, to a pre-arranged position, 4 miles 330° from Dieppe. Consequently A.L.Cs. 185 and 188, with H.M.S. CALPE were soon the only craft left close inshore, but owing to the low visibility, I was not aware of this at the time.

32. Throughout the whole operation, Commander H.V.P. McClintock, R.N., was of the greatest service in his capacity of "Boat Pool Officer." He was ably seconded by Lieut.-Commander J.H. Dathan, R.N., and Lieut.-Commander C.W. McMullen, R.N. The fact that over a thousand troops were evacuated under conditions which can seldom have been equalled, must be attributed largely to the work of these officers.

33. At about 1250 I decided to close the beach again for a final personal view and keeping A.L.C.s. 185 and 188 on either bow, H.M.S. CALPE steered for the eastern end of Red Beach at the same time opening fire from the foremost guns on the breakwaters, on which machine gun posts were reported to be preventing the troops on Red Beach from reaching the water. When about 9 cables from the beach, H.M.S. CALPE came under heavy fire, and no sign of troops or landing craft other than derelicts could be seen on the beach. Accordingly, H.M.S. CALPE manoeuvred to gain the cover of smoke, and I felt convinced that any further attempt to take off troops would be unlikely to succeed. Before finally giving up, however, I proceeded to seaward to close H.M.S. LOCUST and ascertain Commander Ryder's views, as it seemed possible that with H.M.S. LOCUST'S shallow draught, he might be more aware of the situation on the beaches. Whilst this interchange of signals was in progress, however, the General informed me that the larger body of the troops on the beach had surrendered. At almost exactly the same time H.M.S. BERKELEY (Lieut. J.J.S. Yorke, R.N.) received a direct hit with a heavy bomb. The ship's back was broken, her forecastle awash, and the engine and boiler rooms were flooding. Fortunately the loss of life was small, partly owing to the promptitude with which S.G.B.8 proceeded alongside to take off her crew and partly owing to the presence of A.L.C.s 185 and 188, who were able to pick up survivors in the water. I instructed H.M.S. ALBRIGHTON to sink her, which she did by torpedo fire. At much the same time a fighter attack was made on H.M.S. CALPE'S bridge, causing several casualties, including Air Commodore A. Cole, C.B.E., M.C., D.F.C., R.A.A.F., who was severely wounded. The destroyers in the vicinity of H.M.S. BERKELEY then proceeded to seaward to join the main convoy of landing craft and coastal craft who had formed up in accordance with instructions, approximately 4 miles to seaward of Dieppe and were now heading slowly north.

34. H.M.S. FERNIE was instructed to take Guide, and shortly afterwards I unwisely instructed H.M.S. CALPE to proceed to the eastward to pick up a British pilot who was reported in the water. This resulted in 2 bombing attacks, by dive bombers, on H.M.S. CALPE, both of which secured near misses causing damage and casualties.

35. Subsequently H.M.S. CALPE rejoined the convoy which proceeded without incident, other than some ineffectual air attacks, through the Western swept channel,

and to a position approximately 20 miles from Newhaven. At this point I was joined by Captain (D) 16 with H.M.S. MACKAY and H.M.S. BLENCATHRA and I requested him to escort the small craft into Newhaven, thus releasing H.M.S. CALPE and the other destroyers and H.M.S. LOCUST to proceed direct to Portsmouth with their wounded, who totalled over 500. The coastal craft and landing craft reached Newhaven without further incident, and the destroyers and H.M.S. LOCUST berthed alongside at Portsmouth shortly after midnight.

36. Before closing this narrative, a word of praise is due to the medical officers with the force. An exceptional strain was thrown upon them, partly by the very large proportion of casualties among the troops and partly because the organisation carefully prepared by Surgeon Commander W.B.D. Miller, D.S.C., M.B., Ch.B., R.N.V.R., was upset by the turning back of Group 12. This group, comprising four spare L.C.Ts., carried an important proportion of the available medical parties. It was a mistake on my part not to bring them on, despite the fact that they were no longer required for an evacuation as originally planned.

37. A detailed account of the work of the medical parties is reported separately, but the services performed by Surgeon Lieut. M.P. Martin, M.R.C.S., L.R.C.P., R.N.V.R., deserve special mention. This officer was embarked in L.C.F.(L) 2, and took charge of her when her other officers became casualties. Subsequently he was rescued from the water, after L.C.F.(L) 2 had sunk, and transferred to H.M.S. CALPE. Although himself injured, he was untiring in helping H.M.S. CALPE'S doctor, who had to compete with casualties to over a quarter of the crew plus 278 wounded soldiers.

Admiralty footnotes

1.   R.D.F. = Radar.
2.   2 L.C.T. = Landing Craft Tanks.
3.   L.C.P. = Landing Craft Personnel.
4.   S.G.B. = Steam Gunboat.
5.   L.C.F. (L) = A converted Landing Craft mounting anti-aircraft armament.
6.   Yellow I Beach = East of Dieppe, opposite Berneval.
7.   Yellow II Beach = East of Dieppe at Belleville-sur-Mer.
8.   Green Beach = West of Dieppe, at Pourville.
9.   Blue Beach = East of Dieppe, at Puits.
10. L.C.A. = Landing Craft Assault.
11. Red Beach = Eastern portion of Dieppe Sea Front, immediately to west of harbour entrance. White Beach = Western portion of Dieppe Sea Front.
12. Chasseurs = Free French Navy small A.A. escort craft, six of which were employed in this operation.
13. F.O.O. = Forward Observer Officer.
14. A.L.C. = Landing craft for assaulting troops.
15. M.L.C. = Landing craft for mechanised vehicles.

2

THE ASSAULT PHASE OF THE NORMANDY LANDINGS, 1944

The following Despatch was submitted to the Supreme Commander, Allied Expeditionary Force on the 16th October, 1944, by Admiral Sir Bertram H. Ramsay, K.C.B., M.V.O., Allied Naval Commander-in-Chief, Expeditionary Force.

> *Office of Allied Naval Commander-in-Chief,*
> *Expeditionary Force,*
> *London, S.W.I.*
> *16th October, 1944.*

Sir,

I have the honour to forward my report of the opening phase of Operation "Neptune," the period covered being from my appointment as Allied Naval Commander, Expeditionary Force, on 25th October, 1943, to the withdrawal of the Naval Task Force Commanders on 3rd July, 1944. The report is lengthy owing to the need to cover, if only superficially, the very many different aspects of what is acknowledged to be the greatest amphibious operation in history. Because the report is so bulky, I have decided to write this covering letter in a form which will enable those who wish to do so to obtain a bird's eye view of the operation as a whole, including the preparatory period and the build-up, without going into detail.

2.Because, in the event, the movements of over 5,000 ships and craft proceeded smoothly, and to plan, and because, despite bad weather, the Allied armies and air forces were landed and reinforced, if not quite as quickly as the optimum planning figure, at least more quickly than the enemy reinforced his forces by land, it may now appear that the size and complexity of the naval problem was somewhat exaggerated. This was not the case. That the operation proceeded smoothly and according to plan was the result of the hard work and foresight of the many thousands concerned in its preparation and of the determination and courage of the tens of thousands in the Allied navies and merchant fleets who carried out their orders in accordance with the very highest traditions of the sea.

Magnitude of the Operation and need for Close Control.

3. From the outset of detailed planning it was clear that success would be largely dependent upon the ability to exercise close and continuous control of the thousands of ships and craft taking part. This overall control would have to embrace control of loading of all types of shipping and craft, control of convoy sailing, control of tugs, and control of ship repairs. Without it time would inevitably be lost and the best use could not be made of the great resources given to the operation to establish our forces ashore and then to reinforce them as quickly as possible. As other services and authorities besides the navy were intimately concerned with many of the problems connected with the rapid reinforcement of the Expeditionary Force, it was found necessary during planning to set up new organisations to control various aspects of the operation during the vital first few weeks in which the tempo of the initial assaults had to be maintained at the highest pitch. TURCO, BUCO, COREP[1] and COTUG[1] accordingly came into being and were instrumental in the success achieved.

4. Because the assaults were to be carried out on a narrow front and because British and U.S. forces had to share port facilities in the Isle of Wight area, it was evident that co-ordination of naval plans in some detail would be necessary on my level as the Allied Naval Commander-in-Chief. This was effected smoothly due to the loyal support of both Task Force Commanders, but I am aware that the U.S. naval authorities had to exercise considerable restraint in submitting to a degree of control by superior authority on a level higher than that to which they were accustomed. In their reports the U.S. naval commanders have commented that in their view my orders extended to too much detail. No argument, however, that has been produced since the operation has led me to change my opinion that full co-ordination in detail was necessary on the highest naval level.

Development of the Plan.

5. An outline plan for the operation had been prepared by [2]C.O.S.S.A.C. in July, 1943, and was approved by the Combined Chiefs of Staff at the Quebec Conference. Its soundness was proved later in detailed planning as in no respect were its fundamentals altered, though its scope and range were extended. On the naval side, as the plan developed so the naval requirements grew, and for some months we were planning without being certain that our full demands would be met. This uncertainty was a constant anxiety to me and was only removed at the eleventh hour.

6. The naval problem that had to be faced can be briefly summarised as first the breaking of the strong initial crust of the coast defences by assault together with the landing of the fighting army formations; and secondly to commence, and continue without a pause for five or six weeks, their reinforcement at as high a rate as possible. The first required the co-ordination of the movement of thousands of ships and landing craft and aircraft and then of their fire power, the second the co-ordination

of the activities of hundreds of thousands of men and women of all services, both in the United Kingdom and off the French coast, marshalling, loading, sailing, unloading and returning at least eight ship convoys a day in addition to ten or twelve landing craft groups. Considerations of time and space did not permit the use of any unexpected manoeuvre to confuse the enemy: we had simply to drive ahead in great strength and to ensure that the organisation was as efficient as it could be, as the time factor was all important.

7. The one fundamental question on which there had to be early agreement was whether to assault during darkness so as to obtain the greatest measure of surprise on the beaches, or whether to assault after daylight and to rely on the greatly increased accuracy of air and naval bombardment under these conditions. The decision which was made, to make a daylight landing, was in accord with experience in the Pacific against strong defences, when the assaulting force possessed decisive naval and air superiority, and I am convinced that this is the correct answer under these conditions. When the decision was made there were no beach obstructions in place on the "Neptune" beaches. Their later appearance would almost certainly have caused the decision to be revised, had it been originally made in favour of darkness, and it was very fortunate that no change was necessary as all training, and, to some extent, development of weapons was affected. It should, however, be noted that there was by no means general agreement as to a daylight attack, and that even after the initial decision had been agreed between the three Commanders-in-Chief of the Expeditionary Force at least two vain efforts were made to change it.

Administrative Planning.

8. Administrative Planning for a major cross-Channel operation had been carried on in the United Kingdom since May, 1942, by a skeleton staff. As a result, preparations were far advanced before the operational plan took shape and the logistic requirements of the latter were able to be fully met.

Enemy Miscalculations.

9. Because the power of manoeuvre at sea was so limited the need for keeping the enemy uncertain as to our precise objectives was paramount. Characteristic wireless traffic accompanying training and movements of assault forces had to be controlled. I understand that the success of the radio measures taken was an important contributory factor in securing surprise. Other measures included the berthing of dummy landing craft in Dover and Nore Commands before D day and the parking of PHOENIX and WHALE Units[3] at Selsey and Dungeness. Arrangements were also made with the Admiralty for the large number of commercial ships that were destined for the Thames and ships for loading to sail in later "Neptune" convoys to wait in Scottish ports until the operation began. Thus the concentration of shipping automatically spread itself throughout the ports of the United Kingdom and although most congested on the South Coast, it was not confined to that area.

10. Tactically, a naval diversion employing light craft was carried out in the Straits

of Dover to support the air bombardment in this area simultaneously with the main assaults, whilst a similar diversion was made in the neighbourhood of Cap d'Antifer. In both of these and also off Cap Barfleur radio counter-measures were employed by aircraft and by the surface craft taking part to give an appearance to enemy radar similar to that presented by the real forces. We now know that these were very successful and were an instrumental factor in enabling our forces to continue for so long towards the enemy coast before their composition could be determined.

Security.

II. Complete security was maintained, and it is considered that the very highest satisfaction may be felt that, despite the many hundreds who were for months aware of all the details of the plan, so far as is known there was no leakage. Some anxiety was felt on one or two occasions over individual cases in which orders or maps were distributed or opened contrary to the instructions given, but no harm is believed to have come of these isolated incidents and, when the very large number of documents is considered, it is perhaps remarkable that so few grounds for anxiety existed before full briefing commenced.

MULBERRY Project.

I2. The suggestion that artificial harbours should be constructed in the assault area was, it is believed, first made by Commodore J. Hughes-Hallett, when serving as Chief of Staff (X) to Commander-in-Chief, Portsmouth, who suggested the use of sunken ships for this purpose. The original designs for such harbours, which were, however, to be constructed of sunken concrete caissons, were prepared by the War Office. It was apparent soon after taking up my appointment that much greater naval supervision of the preparations and an experienced naval staff to conduct the operation were necessary and I asked the Admiralty to appoint Rear-Admiral W.G. Tennant, to take charge of this matter. From the outset Admiral Tennant was uncertain of the ability of the concrete PHOENIX Units to withstand even a moderate gale; and their placing had been estimated under the most favourable conditions to take at least I4 days. It was on his suggestion that 70 obsolete ships were prepared as block ships, which could be placed in two or three days and thereby speedily provide some shelter over the 40 miles of beaches before the PHOENIX breakwaters could be built. His foresight was proved in the gale that blew from I9th to 22nd June, as these blockships alone gave some shelter to the hundreds of landing craft and barges on a lee shore and greatly reduced the number that was damaged, as well as making it possible to continue unloading on a small scale.

I3. The construction of the units for the MULBERRIES was an undertaking of considerable magnitude and coming at a time when all efforts were already centred on the preparations for "Neptune" proved difficult to complete to schedule. As the completion fell behind, the difficulties were accentuated by the shortage of tugs, as a regular phased programme was essential if all units were to be moved into their assembly positions before D-Day. Vigorous and continued representations for more and more tugs for "Neptune" were made, both in the United Kingdom and to the U.S.A., and, although there was still not a sufficiency to meet the full towing programme, by D day the MULBERRY units were in the main ready and in their assembly areas, thanks to the initiative and resource displayed by Admiral Tennant and his staff. A full report of the operations of the construction of the MULBERRIES and GOOSEBERRIES (craft shelters) has been compiled and has been forwarded under separate cover. In conception and execution these harbour shelters were unique. The damage wrought by the June gale to MULBERRY A, which necessitated the abandonment of the completion of this harbour, does not detract in any way from the value of the idea, for, had it been constructed similarly to MULBERRY B, there is reason to suppose that it might have survived to the same extent.

Pre-D-Day Reconnaissance.

I4. During planning it was necessary to carry out certain reconnaissances in the "Neptune" area to check the depths of water, both over drying rocks and also in the MULBERRY sites, and to examine the nature of the beaches, as geological estimate had reported unfavourably regarding the latter. This reconnaissance was carried out between November, I943, and January, I944, being confined to the dark moon period in each month. Combined Operations Pilotage Parties were employed, using first L.C.P. (Sy)[4], which were towed towards the French coast by M.L.s, and later X-craft[5]. Their missions were carried out successfully and skilfully, and, so far as is known, only on one occasion was a party sighted by the enemy. As diversions for these reconnaissances, operations were carried out between the Channel Island and the Pas de Calais (both inclusive). Initially these operations consisted of small scale raids, but were later replaced by offshore reconnaissance by L.C.P. (L)[6], similar to the "Neptune" reconnaissance. The diversion operations were planned by Combined Operations Headquarters and executed by the appropriate Home Naval Commands.

Administration of Ferry Craft.

I5. Previous operations have shown the great difficulties in administering the craft of the ferry service during the first few weeks before naval shore facilities are properly established. The problem in "Neptune" was greater than ever before, I,500 craft and barges and I5,000 personnel having to be provided for, but, although, there were individual failures and resulting hardship, reports show that in general the measures taken proved successful in maintaining the morale and efficiency of officers and men who perforce had to work long hours for days on end.

Salvage, Repair and Fuelling Organisations off beaches.

I6. As the plan envisaged the use of the beaches for a period of three months it was evident that provision would have to be made on a scale hitherto unknown for the salvage, repair, fuelling and watering of the great number of ships and craft that would be damaged or that would require fuel or water off the enemy coast. A considerable salvage fleet had to be assembled and special ships and landing barges were fitted for repair work and others to carry fuel and water. Naval parties were trained to assist in craft repairs ashore and were attached to the Assault Forces. Owing to the widespread damage caused by the four days' gale the salvage repair organisation was tested far beyond anything contemplated and, although it seemed at one time that it would be unable to compete, yet in the end it may be said to have triumphed, assisted as it had to be by additional resources from the United Kingdom.

Training and Rehearsals.

17. The training facilities and assault firing areas were originally provided for a three divisional assault, and the extension of the plan to include five assaulting divisions introduced some difficulties in providing adequate facilities for the two new divisions. But due to the great co-operation shown by all concerned, to the unselfishness of the Commanders whose divisions were already nearly trained, and to the initiative and drive of the Commanders of the new divisions who had to fit a six months' programme into three, all difficulties were overcome, and on the day Forces G and U (*see Chart below*) carried out their assaults with the precision of yet another rehearsal.

Force	Assembly Ports	Assault Area.
	Western Task Force (American)	
Assault Force U*	Torbay, Brixham, Dartmouth and Salcombe	Western flank of U.S. area (UTAH beach)
" " O	Weymouth, Portland and Poole	Eastern flank of U.S. area (OMAHA beach)
Follow-up Force B	Plymouth, Falmouth, Helford River and Fowey	U.S. area
First Build-up Divisions	Bristol, Channel ports	–
	Eastern Task Force (British)	
Assault Force G*	Southampton, Solent and Spithead	Western flank of British area (GOLD beach)
" " J	Southampton, Solent and Spithead	Centre of British area (JUNO beach)
" " S	Portsmouth, Spithead, Newhaven and Shoreham	Eastern flank of British area (SWORD beach)
Follow-up Force L	The Nore and Harwich	British area
First Build-up Divisions	Thames	–

* *These forces were additional to the original plan.*

18. It had always been felt that the enemy might react when large scale exercises were carried out in the Channel. He did not do so until exercise "Tiger," which was the final rehearsal for Force U, when during the night of 27th/28th April three groups of E-Boats penetrated the patrols covering Lyme Bay and delivered a successful attack on the last convoy to sail to the exercise consisting of eight L.S.T.[7] Two L.S.T. were sunk and one was damaged, and there was a regrettably high loss of life. Naval defensive measures on this occasion were undoubtedly on the weak side and this incident underlined the need for every available warship and craft to take part in the opening phases of "Neptune" when the enemy must be expected to attack our convoys with everything at his disposal.

19. The final rehearsals for the other four assault forces took place on 4th May under the code name of "Fabius". Opportunity was taken to exercise the simultaneous sailing from the Isle of Wight area of the three forces based there and also to try out the arrangements whereby A.N.C.X.F.[8] would assume control of all operations in the Channel. So far as the naval assault forces were concerned the exercises were satisfactory, but a freshening south-westerly wind in the afternoon of the first day caused the full programme to be curtailed to avoid damage to landing craft. Enemy reaction to "Fabius" was negligible, being confined to an aircraft attack on a destroyer in one of the covering forces. That it was not greater, and indeed that our naval preparations proceeded with so little interruption, must be largely attributed to the very high degree of air superiority achieved in the months before D day. Enemy air reconnaissance was slight and infrequent.

Mining.

20. Sea mining is carried on continuously by the Admiralty and by Bomber Command, but for some months before "Neptune" the mining programme was planned to afford direct assistance to the operation both as regards location and timing of each lay. Considerable success is known to have been achieved by mines laid during this period under plan "Maple," which was really an integral part of operation "Neptune."

Meteorological.

21. Early in planning it was appreciated that the decision which you as Supreme Commander would have to make to launch the operation would be one of the most difficult and far-reaching of the whole war. Not only was good weather necessary for the assaults, but also for the period immediately following them, to ensure a good start for the build-up. The meteorologists were doubtful of their ability to forecast the weather more than 48 hours ahead for certain, which was barely sufficient to cover the hour of the assaults, as Force U from Devonshire had to sail 36 hours before H hour.[9] To assist the forecasts, two additional U.S. and two British warships were stationed in the Atlantic to transmit weather reports for some days before D day. For security this procedure was also adopted before exercise "Fabius" and this, in

addition, served to practise the meteorological team concerned in making their deductions.

Availability of Landing Ships and Craft.

22. During planning there were frequent discussions as to what percentage availability of landing ships and craft should be taken for the operation. The original planning figures of 90 per cent. for L.S.T. and 85 per cent. for L.C.T. and L.C.I. (L)[10] were challenged by Washington who held that the U.S. Navy could achieve a higher standard of maintenance.

British Admiralty opinion, on the other hand, supported these estimates in view of the extremely heavy burden that would be thrown on all the repair facilities on the south coast shortly before the operation. Experience in the Mediterranean had shown that a greater number of ships and craft always offered for loading for an assault than had been expected, as the incentive of action had a clearly salutary effect on repairs previously deemed essential. While I therefore really expected the planning figures to be exceeded I was very loath to gamble on this and I only accepted higher figures for U.S. L.S.T. of 95 per cent. after Rear-Admiral A.G. Kirk, U.S.N. (Naval Commander, Western Task Force) had agreed them. In the event, due to the splended efforts of COMLANCRAB-ELEVENTHPHIB[11] (Rear-Admiral J. Wilkes, U.S.N.), and his staff, the record overall figure of 99.3 per cent. for all types of U.S. landing ships and landing craft was attained. The similar British figure was 97.6 per cent., and, in my opinion, the very highest credit is due to all concerned in the maintenance and repair organisations of both countries for this achievement, which is the more outstanding when it is remembered that the majority of the assault ships and craft had to be used continuously during months of training before the operation.

Increasing Enemy Naval Activity.

23. Although the enemy were slow to react to our much publicised invasion preparations from the end of April onwards, enemy naval activity in the Channel did increase. On 29th April in an engagement between two Canadian destroyers, who were covering a minelaying operation off Ile de Bas, and two Elbing class, one of our destroyers and one of the enemy's were sunk. Throughout the month of May enemy E-Boat activity in the Central Channel increased, and it was apparent that more E-Boats were being moved to Cherbourg and Havre. Our destroyers and light coastal forces operated by Commanders-in-Chief, Portsmouth and Plymouth, were, however, able to keep the enemy in check and to inflict casualties on him.

24. The first enemy U-Boat was reported in the Western Channel on 20th May, which necessitated a change in the dispositions of our covering forces. The Admiralty had some weeks earlier announced their intention of allotting four A/U Support Groups to Commander-in-Chief, Plymouth, to operate in the Western Channel and to co-operate with Coastal Command in sealing this approach to the "Neptune" convoy routes. The Air Officer Commanding-in-Chief, Coastal Command, had similarly made new dispositions to be effective some weeks before D day in

anticipation of the movement of the U-Boat battle to the Channel. Coastal Command threw themselves into the preparations for "Neptune" with as much enthusiasm as any unit in the Allied Expeditionary Force, and I personally and the whole Naval Expeditionary Force are deeply indebted to them for the efficiency of the measures they adopted, which was reflected by the very small scale of U-Boat attack that eventuated.

25. No weapon that the enemy might have employed before D day against our forces caused me more anxiety than the potentialities of minelaying. Mines were employed defensively on a considerable scale in the Bay of the Seine during the months prior to D day and caused the naval plan largely to be framed round the requirements for sweeping our forces through the enemy's minefields. In the six weeks before D day the enemy also considerably intensified his minelaying off the south coast of England, using aircraft on a scale which had not been attempted for over two years and introducing two new types of mine. This minelaying was confined to moonless periods. Had D day been in such a period it is doubtful whether the Portsmouth channels could have been cleared in time. As it was, no interruption was caused to the rehearsals nor to the assembly of our forces and it is considered that the enemy missed a great opportunity in not still further extending this form of attack. That he did not attempt more was yet another result of the air superiority we achieved before D day. Towards the end of May some aircraft minelaying was combined with night air bombing attacks on a light scale on south coast ports, but very few casualties were caused to ships and personnel.

D Day and H Hour.

26. No single question was more often discussed during planning than that of H hour. As H hour was linked to tidal conditions, D day was dependent on it. Until obstructions appeared on the assault beaches, the argument was largely confined to the determination of the ideal balance between a sufficiency of light for aimed air and naval bombardment and the minimum daylight approach, taking into consideration the number of days to which postponement in the case of bad weather would be acceptable in view of the different tidal conditions on later days. But as beach obstructions in some numbers were erected on the beaches, the need to deal with these dryshod, and therefore to land below them, overcame all previous arguments and H hour and D day were finally largely determined by the position of these obstacles.

27. As on the western (U.S.) beaches the obstructions were known to be in place further down the beach than on the eastern (British) beaches and as in Force J's sector near low water there were some rocks which would be a danger to the assault craft, it was finally necessary to select five different H hours, ranging over a period of one hour and twenty-five minutes. Anxiety was felt on two counts, first, that the earlier H hours in the U.S. Sector, coupled with their requirements to arrive in the transport area earlier relative to H hour than the British, might prejudice surprise in the west before it was lost in the east, and second, that so many H hours might confuse some

or many of the ships and craft taking part. In the event the lack of alertness of the enemy obviated the first and good briefing prevented the second.

28. Owing to the need to take account of the latest photographic reconnaissance showing the exact positions of the obstacles, the final decision as to D day and H hour was not made until I7th May when 5th June was selected, with postponement acceptable to 6th and 7th June.

Weather immediately before D Day. 24-hour Postponement.

29. You held the first meeting to discuss the weather forecast for D day a.m. on Ist June. The outlook was not very good and it deteriorated further during the next three days. At the meeting held p.m. 3rd June you decided to allow the movements of the Forces to commence, despite the unfavourable outlook, in view of the many advantages in launching the operation on the first possible day. But at the next meeting at 04I5 on 4th June it was clear that conditions the next day would not be acceptable and a postponement of 24 hours was ordered. By this time all of Force U from Devonshire and a proportion of Force O from Portland were at sea, and ships and craft had to reverse their course and return to harbour. Instructions for this eventuality were included in the Operation Orders and worked smoothly, except in the case of Force U2A,[12] who failed to receive the signal ordering the postponement. By 0900 this Force was about 25 miles south of St. Catherine's Point and still steering south. Two destroyers and a Walrus aircraft had to be sent at full speed to turn it round. Had this not been done it is possible that the Force would shortly have been detected by the enemy's radar and this would undoubtedly have resulted in his increased vigilance for the next few days.

30. The craft of Force U had a bad time punching into a head sea on their return westwards and, although the whole Force was ordered into Weymouth Bay, a number of craft never managed to enter it. Considerable anxiety was felt throughout 4th June both as to the need of a further postponement with all its resulting loss of efficiency of craft and assault troops, and whether Force U would be in a fit state to go forward again early the next morning should the decision be made to go on with the operation. At one time it was thought that Force U would have to return to Devonshire to re-form, but, when it was pointed out that this would almost certainly result in the postponement of the operation to the next moon period, Rear-Admiral Kirk, with characteristic verve, announced his readiness to proceed.

The Passage.

3I. When the assault forces again sailed early on 5th June the weather was still largely unfavourable for landing craft, but more suitable conditions had been forecast for the early hours of 6th June. Wind was W.S.W.[13] Force 5 veering to W.N.W. decreasing in force at times but with strong gusts; waves were five to six feet in mid-Channel. These conditions made the passage difficult, and considerable discomfort was experienced by the troops embarked in L.C.T.[14] and L.C.I.(L). Although some of the minor landing craft which were due to arrive p.m. on D day had to put back to harbour and others were delayed, the assault forces all drove on and almost without exception arrived off their beaches to time. The performance of the leading groups of Force U was particularly praiseworthy, since, as has been stated, some of these failed to enter harbour on the postponement, and by H hour their Commanding Officers had been on their bridges continuously for about 70 hours. Out of the 128 L.C.T. in Group U2A only seven failed to take part in the assault, and this figure took account of engine failures as well as the stress of the weather.

32. To ensure the correct positioning of the northern ends of the 10 approach channels that were to be swept across the known enemy minefields 10 F.H. 830 buoys had been laid by three H.D.M.L. of Force J during the night 31st May/1st June. The buoys were timed to transmit between the hours of 1400 and 2200 on six successive days, commencing on 4th June. At 1800 on 5th June, 10 H.D.M.L. took up position to point these buoys for the Assault Forces, and all reports show that this method was wholly satisfactory. A large number of ships was fitted with receivers to obtain positions from the Gee (Q.H.) and Decca (Q.M.) radio navigational systems, both of which worked fully according to expectations, and navigation was never regarded as a serious problem. The above additional measures were taken to guard against effective jamming by the enemy p.m. on D-I should surprise have been lost.

Achievement of surprise.

33. There was an air of unreality during the passage of the assault forces across the Channel curiously similar to that on D-I in "Husky" as our forces approached Sicily. The achievement of strategical surprise was always hoped for in "Neptune" but was by no means certain, whereas that of tactical surprise had always seemed extremely unlikely. As our forces approached the French coast without a murmur from the enemy or from their own radio, the realisation that once again almost complete tactical surprise had been achieved slowly dawned. This astonishing feat cannot be explained by any single factor and must be attributed in part to all of the following: the miscalculations of the enemy; the high degree of air superiority attained by our Air Forces, which, drastically reduced the enemy's air reconnaissance; the bad weather which caused the enemy to withdraw his E-Boat patrols to Cherbourg; and finally the radio counter-measures employed by our forces, which, coupled with the diversions against the Pas de Calais and Cap d'Antifer, left the enemy in doubt as to the points at which we would land even when he had become aware that the invasion was in progress. Although the unfavourable weather caused difficulties and damage to craft off the beaches later, the advantages gained by surprise were so striking that your decision to go on despite the weather was amply justified. A postponement of one more day, e.g. till 7th June, would, in the event, have proved disastrous owing to the conditions of sea off the beaches. The problems arising out of a postponement of 12 to 14 days to the next suitable period are too appalling even to contemplate.

Minesweeping during the Approach.

34. The sweeping of 10 approach channels for the assault forces represented the

largest single minesweeping operation that had yet been undertaken in war. The provision of the necessary minesweeping flotillas had only been achieved by drawing upon some which had little opportunity for practice, and, when my operation orders were written, it was realised that the successful completion of the minesweeping tasks would demand a high degree of skill from all concerned. Subsequently the late appearance of beach obstacles on the assault beaches further complicated the problem, as the alteration in the time of H hour relative to high water that resulted meant that it would now be necessary for all flotillas to change sweeps during passage to avoid sweeping with an unfavourable tide. Some flotillas had no opportunity to rehearse this manoeuvre at all, as it was not decided on until after exercise "Fabius," and the fact that all successfully achieved it is considered most satisfactory.

35. Sweeping was carried out in all cases according to plan, despite stronger tidal streams than had been allowed for and the unfavourable weather, which made very difficult the operation of the Mark 5 sweeps by M.L.s, and the minesweepers approached the French coast without interference. The early arrival of the Western Task Force flotillas had been a cause of some anxiety during planning but, because surprise was in the event achieved, it had no unfortunate result. The senior officers of the flotillas concerned expressed surprise in their reports that although the enemy coast at Cape Barfleur was sighted as early as 2000 on 5th June no batteries opened fire at them and the operation proceeded unopposed; in this connection it may be noted that minesweepers switched on R.C.M.[15] at 2130.

Naval Bombardment.

36. It had been planned that ships should be ready to open fire at their pre-arranged targets either from the time when the assault convoys came within range of them or from the time when it was light enough for the enemy to spot his fall of shot visually, which-ever was the later; but that, if possible, fire should be withheld until it was light enough for air observation. In the event, this proved possible with the exception of one or two ships in the Western Task Force, who found it necessary to open blind fire against certain batteries whose fire was more accurate than was the general case.

37. As Bombarding Force D arrived in position on the Eastern Flank at 0515, a half-hearted attack was made by four enemy E-Boats and some armed trawlers which had come out of Havre. The enemy were seen indistinctly against the land and were almost immediately obscured by the pre-arranged smoke screen laid-by our aircraft, from behind which they fired torpedoes. The heavy ships managed to comb the torpedo tracks but the Norwegian destroyer SVENNER was hit and sunk. One enemy trawler was sunk and one damaged; and the attack was not renewed. The danger to friendly forces of smoke laid to a pre-arranged plan was plainly exemplified.

38. The fire from enemy batteries, which was never severe, was directed initially against bombarding ships only, and was largely ineffective. This is considered to have been due to the combined success of the pre-D day bombing programme, the heavy air bombardment in the early hours of D day, and the measures taken to prevent the enemy from ranging and spotting; and it demonstrates that duels between ships and coastal batteries are in certain eventualities feasible provided such precautions are

taken. It must be remembered, however, that the scale of coast defence in the assault area was the lowest on this part of the coast and the results would have been very different for instance, in the Pas de Calais. Much of the success of naval bombardment must be attributed to the work of the single-seater fighter spotters, who carried out their tasks tirelessly and gallantly. Communications between bombarding ships and spotting aircraft suffered a number of failures at the start owing mainly to the novel nature of the technique, but they improved rapidly with successive waves of aircraft.

39. Warships and gun support craft took part in the drenching of beach defences immediately prior to the assault. This fire appeared accurate, and was of sufficient weight to neutralise and demoralise the defenders, except on OMAHA Beach where the total failure of the day heavy bombers, due to low cloud base, contributed to the much stiffer opposition than was found elsewhere. Of the support craft the L.C.G.(L)[16] deserves special mention. This craft, which achieved only partial success in the Mediterranean due to lack of training and shortcomings in its equipment, was particularly effective and further demonstrated the value in assault of high velocity guns at close range. Since D day it has continued to provide effective direct and indirect fire support.

The Assaults.

40. The choice of the "lowering positions" (U.S. "transport areas")[17] had been a matter of considerable discussion, the conflicting factors of being outside the range of the enemy's shore batteries and south of the known mined area having to be balanced. The Eastern Task Force (British) finally chose their "lowering positions" about 7 to 8 miles off shore, whilst the Western Task Force (U.S.A.) decided to place them further to seaward, 10 to 11¼ miles out. In the rough weather that obtained when the assault forces arrived in the "lowering positions," the longer passage inshore for the assault craft from the Western Task Force appeared to add appreciably to their difficulties.

4I. To mark the approaches to the beaches for Forces S and J two X-craft were employed as it was very important that Force S should not be too far to the eastward, and the coast in Force J's sector was not distinctive in outline. These craft had sailed on the night of 2nd/3rd June, being towed for part of the passage. Each submarine received at 0I00 5th June a message that the assault had been postponed 24 hours, and, in spite of the difficulties of navigation for a craft of very slow diving speed in a cross tidal stream, had maintained their positions off the enemy coast until daylight on the 6th June when they flashed lights to seaward from the surface in their correct positions as a guide to the oncoming assault craft. It is considered that great skill and endurance was shown by the crews of X.20 and X.23. Their reports of proceedings, which were a masterpiece of understatement, read like the deck log of a surface ship in peacetime, and not of a very small and vulnerable submarine carrying out a hazardous, operation in time of war.

42. Weather conditions off the assault beaches immediately before H hour were as follows:-
Wind – Westnorthwest – force 4.[18]

Sea – Moderate – waves 3/4 feet.
Sky – Fair to cloudy with cloud increasing.

These unfavourable conditions interfered to some extent with the release of the assault craft and also with the launching of D.D. tanks,[19] but nevertheless the majority of the leading waves of the assaults touched down at the right place and at approximately the right time throughout the length of the front. The following is a brief summary of how each Assault Force fared.

Force S (British).

43. The leading groups passed through the "lowering positions" and approached the beaches generally on time. Enemy opposition was restricted to shell fire at craft off the beaches from light batteries ashore. D.D. tanks were successfully launched but were overtaken by the L.C.T. (A.V.R.E.)[20] which touched down at the right time and place. Beach obstacles presented some difficulty but landing craft were, when necessary, driven through them relentlessly. Opposition ashore was initially only moderate, and for some hours the chief difficulty in this sector was that of congestion on the beaches, as only two exits could be brought into use.

Force J (British).

44. The first touch down was from I0 to I5 minutes later than planned, and moderate opposition was experienced on landing. On account of the weather D.D. tanks were not launched but were discharged directly on to the beach. By I000, however, all beach objectives had been gained and the Army were advancing steadily, if slowly, inshore against opposition. Several major landing craft were damaged in this sector by beach obstacles and TELLER mines.

Force G (British).

45. The assaults landed dead on time but the left group of L.C.T. (A.V.R.E.) touched down slightly to the eastward. D.D. tanks were not launched here on account of the weather but were later beached inshore. Considerable difficulty was experienced in developing JIG beach on the left, which was enfiladed from the outset by two strong points, and it was not until I600 that the situation became stabilised on that beach. Here also a large number of major landing craft were damaged by TELLER mines and beach obstacles.

Force O (U.S.A.).

46. Considerable difficulty was experienced in this sector due to the state of the sea. Assault craft on their way inshore had a bad time, a number of craft were swamped and the assaulting infantry in the remainder in general arrived on the beach in rather poor shape. D.D. tanks were launched three miles offshore as planned on the left flank but regrettably all but two or three foundered. Thus the initial attack here had to be carried out with little tank support. On the right flank D.D. tanks were landed

directly and successfully on to the beach, but were quickly put out of action by enemy fire. Enemy opposition at the beach exits was severe. The first waves of the assault touched down five minutes late at 0635, but due to the weather, the loss of the D.D. tanks and the failure of some L.C.T.(A)[21] to keep their position the order of landing was somewhat mixed. Due to the heavy surf, the difficulty in clearing the beach obstacles, and the persistent enemy fire directed on the beaches, the programme of landing troops and vehicles quickly fell behind in time. For about two hours assault troops were pinned to the beaches. During the rest of the morning penetrations were made inland but only slowly and by relatively small groups. All naval personnel who witnessed the battle were unanimous in paying tribute to their determination and gallantry. The supporting destroyers and gun support craft stood in close inshore during the period of fiercest fighting on the beach and rendered great support to the troops. At one time it was considered that it might be necessary to land part of Force O through the Force G beaches, but this proved unnecessary, as the First U.S. Division fought its way off the beach towards the end of the forenoon and the beach exits could then be developed. A considerable number of craft were sunk or damaged in this sector due to enemy action and the weather. Beach obstacles and mines proved particularly troublesome. The Assault Force Commander has reported that the preliminary air bombardment planned for this area had struck too far inland to affect the beach defences. Its absence was severely felt when the landing commenced and fierce opposition was met.

Force U (U.S.A.).

47. Almost complete surprise appeared to be achieved in this sector. Despite the late arrival of some groups in the transport area, due to the weather, assault waves were generally landed on time and against only slight enemy opposition. Due to the early loss of two control vessels the landing was made 2,000 yards to the south-east of the planned position. This proved fortunate, as the obstacles and defences there were found to be less formidable than those farther north. D.D. tanks were launched and landed successfully, but did not arrive until H + 20 minutes. Beach obstacles were relatively easily dealt with. There was less sea at UTAH than elsewhere and very good progress was made in landing troops and vehicles throughout the day.

General Remarks on D Day.

48. The outstanding fact from the naval point of view was that, despite the unfavourable weather, in every main essential the plan was carried out as written. Tactical surprise, which had not been expected, was achieved and greatly eased the problem of getting ashore in every sector except at OMAHA. Losses of ships and landing craft of all types were much lower than had been expected, but damage to L.C.T. and smaller craft, aggravated by rough weather conditions, was higher than had been allowed for. Only one or two minor air attacks were made on our shipping and on our landing beaches during the day. This was a remarkable demonstration of the degree of air superiority that had been attained before D day. By the end of D day

immediate anxiety was felt on only one count – whether the weather would improve sufficiently quickly to enable the build-up to start as planned.

Commencement of the Build-up.

49. The build-up was planned to commence immediately on D + I with the arrival of eight ship convoys on that day. The convoys all arrived to time but unloading was severely restricted due to the unfavourable weather, wind being force 5 from the north at midday. Anxiety had been felt regarding the passage through the Straits of Dover, p.m. on D day, of convoy E.T.P. I, consisting, of nine large personnel ships from the Thames. They were the first large ships to pass the Strait for four years, and arrangements were made with Coastal Command for F.A.A. aircraft to assist M.L.s in laying smoke screens for this and subsequent convoys. The enemy batteries opened fire on an M.T. ship convoy that was preceding it and sank one ship. I decided, however, that the risk of a daylight passage must be accepted and convoy E.T.P. I, then ahead of time, was accordingly turned back until the smoke screening M.L.s had had time to replenish. A most effective smoke screen complementary to the shore-based R.C.M. cover was finally laid and convoy E.T.P. I passed through the Straits at I700, 6th June, without any enemy interference. This was the only personnel ship convoy to be sailed from the Thames during the build-up.

Arrival of blockships.

50. The first convoy of 45 blockships arrived in the assault area at I230 on 7th June and the sinking of these ships was commenced at once according to plan. All five GOOSEBERRY shelters were completed quickly and conformed broadly to the planned design. The early completion of this project was later found to be of the greatest benefit to the ferry craft off the beaches and the skilful manner in which this operation was conducted reflected great credit on all concerned.

Air Attacks.

5I. Air attacks on the beaches and the shipping lying off them were carried out during the night of 7th-8th June. The attacks were not serious and only minor damage and casualties were caused, but, unfortunately, one of the early attacks soon after midnight coincided with the arrival of some of our troop-carrying aircraft with airborne reinforcements. These Dakota aircraft were fired on by ships of the Eastern Task Force and at least one of them was shot down. This most unfortunate incident, which was a repetition, though happily on a small scale, of our experiences in Operation "Husky", emphasises the danger of routeing our own aircraft over our own naval forces. This had been pointed out repeatedly during the planning but the naval objections had to give way to the demands of the Air Force plan.

First Enemy Light Craft Attacks.

52. During the night of 6th-7th June, enemy R-Boats came out from Havre and E-

Boats from Cherbourg. Both were intercepted by our coastal forces and the enemy were forced to retire after suffering damage. Similar sorties were made almost nightly from Havre and Cherbourg during the next few weeks but the measures taken by the Task Force Commanders nearly always prevented the enemy from penetrating the protecting screen. By inflicting casualties on the enemy forces on most nights that they came out, their offensive spirit was blunted and the potential threat from them thereby reduced.

Casualties due to Mines.

53. The enemy scored a measure of success with his mines on D + I when a number of ships were sunk or damaged. In some cases this resulted from ships either not following, or being forced out of, the swept channels; and showed clearly that the policy of sailing ships in convoy, which I had insisted upon, was very necessary during the opening phases of the operation.

Prevention of U-Boat Attack.

54. The concentration of effective U-Boats in the Biscay ports that had been made before D day showed that it was the enemy's intention to launch a full scale submarine offensive against our invasion shipping as soon as we had become committed to a major landing. The plan of the Admiralty and Headquarters Coastal Command was accordingly to flood the western approaches to the Channel with aircraft in order to keep the U-Boats submerged for as long as possible and also to operate a number of A/U Support Groups in this area. Initially four of these groups worked under the command of Commander-in-Chief, Plymouth, while five more took part in operation "C.A." under the orders of Commander-in-Chief, Western Approaches, in conjunction with escort aircraft carriers. A/S conditions were generally poor in the Channel area but a number of promising attacks were made by these Support Groups during the first four weeks of "Neptune", including some kills. Coastal Command also increased their offensive patrols in the "northern transit area" off the Norwegian coast prior to D day. From I6th May until 3rd July, there were 44 sightings in this area, 38 of which were attacked and I3 probably sunk. These operations were of direct value to the anti-U-Boat operations in the Channel and were a material factor in the defeat that the enemy undoubtedly suffered here during the opening weeks of "Neptune".

55. The first move by the enemy was when it was reported that five U-Boats had sailed from Brest on the 6th June. On this night there were no less than II U-Boat sightings by Coastal Command aircraft, six of which were attacked. The next night there were I0 more sightings, seven being attacked. After this vigorous action the enemy tried to approach the assault area with submarines using Schnorkel but it was some days before U-Boats penetrated into the area of the cross-Channel convoy routes.

56. Within the period of this report the success achieved by U-Boats in the Channel was extremely slight. This was primarily due to the offensive operations of Coastal Command and of the A/U Support Groups covering our convoy routes. Between the

Ist June and 3rd July, I944, Coastal Command aircraft had 96 sightings in the Bay of Biscay and the Channel and its approaches, 59 attacks were made, six U-Boats were known to be sunk, and many other attacks were promising.

Build-up Improvement in Better Weather.

57. From p.m. D + I until D + 8 better weather enabled the rate of build-up to be progressed, despite some shortage of ferry craft due to casualties from the first two days. Convoys sailed from the U.K. and arrived in France on time. As had been anticipated, some difficulties naturally arose initially in the assault area with regard to the great volume of shipping that had to be unloaded and sailed back to England. This resulted in a slower turn round than had been planned, and for a period there was some shortage of ships to be reloaded in the U.K. When the conditions which obtained at the outset on the French coast are further considered, however, it is thought that what was achieved by the Task Force Commanders and their subordinates was in fact very creditable.

Increased Enemy Action.

58. Once it was apparent that our landings constituted invasion on a major scale, it was to be expected that the enemy would attempt to interfere with our build-up convoys and with the shipping off the beaches with all means available to him. Increased enemy shelling of the beaches, particularly on the eastern flank, was experienced from D + 2 onwards, but no great success was achieved by the enemy, although unloading in the SWORD sector was retarded. Our bombarding forces were kept busy countering enemy shelling of the beaches and also in assisting the army ashore. It was evident that the enemy was reinforcing his E-Boats in Havre and E-Boat sorties were made nightly from Havre and from Cherbourg. Indications of the enemy's intentions to lay mines in the assault area first became apparent on 9th June when Naval Commander Western Task Force reported attempts to restrict the movements of his bombarding ships by laying a mine barrier on his northern flank. During the first week, Task Force, Assault Force and Assault Group Commanders were fully occupied in combating the various forms of attack which the enemy tried to bring against the assault area, whilst at the same time developing their organisations, first afloat and later ashore, in order to speed up the unloading and turn round of shipping and craft. Enemy attacks were very largely beaten off, except in the case of air mine-laying which later proved almost impossible to prevent. The similarity of the defence plans for both Task Force Areas, which was the result of close co-operation between the Task Force Commanders during planning, was an important factor in ensuring the overall security of the anchorages.

Destroyer Action off Ile de Bas.

59. In the early morning of 9th June, Force 26, consisting of eight destroyers operating under the orders of Commander-in-Chief, Plymouth, made Contact with four enemy destroyers 20 miles north-west of the Ile de Bas. A spirited action followed, which

resulted in two of the enemy being destroyed and the other two being damaged. This action virtually ended the threat to "Neptune" convoys from attack by enemy destroyers.

Construction of MULBERRIES.

60. MULBERRY tows commenced sailing on D day so that the first PHOENIX, WHALE and BOMBARDON units arrived on the Far Shore early on 8th June (D + 2). The laying of the BOMBARDON moorings and the sinking of the PHOENIX breakwaters began at once. The construction of the MULBERRIES proceeded as quickly as had been expected, and in general all units were accurately placed. The weather was on the whole not favourable for cross-Channel tows, and a number of WHALE roadway tows was lost on passage, the total losses being in the region of 40 per cent. of these units, including damage sustained on the Far Shore. On a number of occasions WHALE roadway units having sailed in reasonable conditions were overtaken by bad weather halfway across. By D + 5 the CORNCOB breakwaters in both harbours were completed and by D + 8 the PHOENIX detached breakwaters were half completed.

Increased Enemy Mining.

61. It was soon apparent that the most serious threat to our shipping in the assault area would be enemy minelaying, as this was carried out at night by both E-Boats and aircraft. Defence against the latter proved extremely difficult as had been expected, as low-flying aircraft were not picked up in sufficient time by radar and so avoided our night fighters. The enemy introduced two new types of mine, both of which were actuated by the reduction of pressure caused by a ship passing over them. One of these could not be swept under any conditions and the other only in certain weather conditions, and a number of casualties was early sustained amongst ships and craft of all types. The problem of sweeping ground mines in the congested anchorages off the beaches proved very difficult as the tails were continually liable to foul other ships and craft. The uncertainty of the distance from the sweeper that an acoustic mine would detonate also proved a constant menace to neighbouring ships.

Bombardment Support of the Land Advance.

62. From D Day onwards, Battleships, Monitors, Cruisers, Destroyers and L.C.G. (L) engaged enemy targets ashore until our armies had advanced beyond the range of their guns. Ships and craft on both flanks engaged coast defence batteries when these fired on our shipping or at the beaches. A large but carefully controlled amount of ammunition of all types was expended; replenishment at the home ports was carried out rapidly, due to the excellent provision made at the ports concerned, and to the efficient organisation evolved by the Admiralty departments responsible for planning and executing the very complicated arrangements for supply of ammunition and exchange of ships' guns. Spotting by fighter spotters, Air O.P.s, S.F.C.P.s, and

F.O.s.B.[22], was very successful, though there were some failures in communication between F.O.s.B. and ships, particularly in the early stages. Improvement in F.O.B. communications is still required, but failures were in part due to the natural tendency to land F.O.B. parties too early in the assault, which caused damage to their equipment and also a high percentage of F.O.B. casualties. By common consent shooting was uniformly good and it is considered that the initial advances inland of our armies were helped in no small measure by the naval supporting fire.

Build-up Difficulties and Delays.

63. As mentioned in paragraph 57 above, delays in the turn round of ships and craft occurred initially in the assault area due to the abnormal conditions obtaining there. There were also difficulties in the United Kingdom, particularly in the Isle of Wight area and in the port of Southampton, due to the large amount of shipping to be handled in a congested area. The initial congestion in the Isle of Wight anchorage, which was caused by a variety of reasons, led to ships that should not have been there staying there for two or three days, and there were also some naval delays in getting ships up to Southampton to reload. The problem in the Isle of Wight area was far more difficult than anywhere else due to the physical characteristics of the anchorage, and it is not considered that the delays which occurred, although irritating to the army, were in any respects unreasonable. Energetic measures were taken to clear the Isle of Wight anchorage, and after the first ten days or so, there were no major delays in the United Kingdom. The figures of the rate of build-up show the great quantity of shipping that was sailed to France each day. When these are examined any serious adverse criticism of the naval organisation, either in the United Kingdom or in France, would seem unwarranted.

Wide scope of the Operation.

64. It is extremely difficult in a letter of reasonable length to deal with any completeness with the many aspects of the operation as it progressed from day to day. On the majority of the early days there were perhaps three or four incidents that in any previous operation would have been considered of outstanding interest, and it is only possible here to give my general impression of the naval operations as they developed. With 16 convoys and about the same number of landing craft groups at any one time at sea in the Channel, exposed to attack by enemy mines, E-Boats, aircraft and U-Boats, with the enemy active on both flanks with his light naval forces and his shore guns, with nightly air minelaying and sometimes air bombing, it was obvious that each day a number of actions of different types would be fought against the enemy forces and that our ships would suffer casualties and damage. The salient fact, however, was that no matter how the enemy attempted to sink our ships, he was fought, and generally with success. The casualties that we sustained were relatively light when the very large number of ships taking part is considered. The build-up proceeded quickly. By D + 9 half a million men had been landed in France and 77,000

vehicles. The millionth man was landed on D + 28, one day after the end of the period covered by this report.

Operations by our Coastal Forces.

65. Our coastal forces operating both from the United Kingdom and from the assault area had many successful encounters with enemy E-Boats. Because it was appreciated that it would not be possible to provide shore radar cover for the cross-Channel convoy route and the covering patrols on its flanks, Commander-in-Chief, Portsmouth, decided to extend the radar cover by using frigates fitted with American S.L. search radar to control units of M.T.B.s attached to them. Four frigates were allocated for this duty and proved very successful in controlling interceptions in over 30 actions. Great spirit was shown by all the Coastal Force Commanding Officers concerned, the majority of whom it should be noted were civilians a few years ago.

Difficulties of Aircraft Recognition.

66. The S.H.A.E.F.[23] rules for restrictions to flying and to A.A. fire are considered to have worked well, but unfortunately casualties to our own aircraft were caused by naval gunfire in the early stages of the operation, particularly in the U.S. Sector. Fire discipline and aircraft recognition in such a diverse fleet of ships and craft as was at any one time in the assault area was obviously extremely difficult to achieve; and the situation was much aggravated by the extremely low cloud base which prevailed on most days, and which, by forcing aircraft to fly very low, gave the minimum of time for their recognition. It is strongly recommended that in other theatres of war where cloud base may normally be expected to be much higher than in the Channel operations, the restricted height for aircraft should be such as to keep them outside the effective range of close range weapons. The appointment of Royal Observer Corps personnel to merchant ships to assist in aircraft recognition, which was a novel experiment, proved most successful and undoubtedly did something towards helping in this matter.

Buoying and Minesweeping of Channels.

67. Minesweeping was carried out continuously from D + I and during the first few days of the operation channels were widened and permanently established from England to France and along the French coast in the assault area. A very large number of light buoys had to be laid to mark the channels as quickly as possible and this was expeditiously carried out by the Trinity House vessels. The greatest co-operation was given by Captain Barber, Superintendent of Trinity House, Cowes, to whom considerable credit is due. The difficulty of keeping to a swept channel with a strong cross tide had always been foreseen before D day and the attention of all concerned was drawn to it in my Operation Orders. As feared, however, the light buoys were roughly treated during the opening phases of the operation and a very large number of these was sunk.

Heavy Air Attack on Havre.

68. By I4th June there was a considerable concentration of enemy E-Boats in Havre and at my request Bomber Command carried out a heavy attack on the port just before dusk with the object of immobilising the enemy craft. This attack was extremely successful and I0 E-Boats and three torpedo boats are known to have been sunk, in addition to many other minor vessels.

Visit of H.M. The King.

69. His Majesty The King visited the British assault area on I6th June in H.M.S. ARETHUSA. This visit gave the greatest satisfaction and encouragement to all British naval personnel on the Far Shore. On the other hand it is worth remarking here that I had to make strenuous efforts to reduce the overall number of official visitors to the assault area during the first few weeks of the operation. The number of persons of greater or less importance who produced good reasons for proceeding there was alarming, observing that, during their stay, of necessity they occupied the time and attention of officers who should have been engaged in other more useful work.

The Northerly Gale.

70. From D day onwards the weather was never what one expected for June in the Channel and from I4th June onwards it deteriorated steadily apart from a temporary improvement during the night I7th-I8th June which raised false hopes of better conditions. Low cloud very largely deprived our army of their close air support and a moderate to strong wind made conditions generally unfavourable for the optimum rate of discharge of shipping off the beaches and for the cross-Channel MULBERRY tows. On I9th June a north-easterly gale, unexpected and unforecast, began and at once stopped all unloading to the beaches. Conditions deteriorated rapidly and a large number of landing craft was soon in difficulties. Steps were taken to stop the sailing of further build-up convoys, but some of those already at sea had to continue, to prevent congestion in U.K. anchorages. Additional tugs were despatched to the Far Shore to assist ships and craft in difficulty until the weather moderated. Casualties were suffered by MULBERRY tows that were already at sea and all further sailings of these had also to be stopped. By 20th June a large number of ferry craft had been stranded by the onshore wind and had received serious damage. All unloading was on this day suspended, although a quantity of stores had been discharged the two previous days in the shelter of MULBERRY B (Arromanches). To meet this situation it was decided to dry out, regardless of risk of damage, a number of stores coasters and all L.S.T. awaiting discharge.[24] It had previously been considered that L.S.T. should not dry out except in an emergency, but the operation was so successful when attempted on a large scale that thereafter this became the normal method of discharge. Coasters were also beached successfully and only a few of these ships suffered damage. By 2Ist June it was apparent that the continued high seas were seriously damaging the MULBERRIES. The BOMBARDONS protecting both harbours broke

adrift and sank and generally proved useless to withstand weather with wind force 6^{25} and above. The damage to blockships and the PHOENIX breakwaters was far more severe at MULBERRY A (St Laurent) than at Arromanches. GOOSEBERRY I also lost all protective value. The WHALE piers in MULBERRY A were completely wrecked, chiefly by landing craft being driven down on to them. The gale eased slowly on 22nd June, but the sea did not finally go down until the next day.

7I. The results of the gale were to confront the Task Force and Assault Force Commanders with a very critical situation just at the time when their organisations were finally settling down and when it was hoped that they and their staffs might be withdrawn. It is very difficult to estimate the total effect of the gale on the operation as a whole. An army estimate was made which suggested that from I9th to 24th June inclusive the unloading loss due to the gale was in the neighbourhood of 20,000 vehicles and I40,000 tons of stores. The effect of the gale on the arrivals of shipping and craft in France during these days is shown in the attached Table A. From the naval point of view the most serious result was the stranding of about 800 craft of all types, most of which were damaged and neaped, as this caused an immediate shortage of ferry craft on the far shore. It was soon also apparent that the damage done to St. Laurent harbour was very largely irreparable, and, shortly afterwards, you decided that this harbour would not be completed but that all remaining resources would be devoted to the strengthening of Arromanches to withstand winter conditions.

72. As a result of the gale it was decided that the Task Force and Assault Force Commanders would have to remain in the assault area until conditions were again normal. Energetic measures were taken to salve all the damaged craft possible, and new equipment and blockships were sent over for the MULBERRIES. About 250 additional hull repair ratings drawn from the Home Fleet and Home Commands were brought forward as planned for such an emergency, and an additional repair ship and a reserve port repair party were moved over to the assault area. The full salvage organisation was mustered. Due to the energy and resource of all concerned about 600 stranded craft and a few coasters and other small vessels were temporarily repaired and refloated at the next spring tides, on 8th July. A further I00 were refloated a fortnight later.

Landing Craft Repair Situation.

73. The numbers of damaged landing craft returning after the assault were much greater than expected and the repair of craft was proving difficult in the Portsmouth area before the gale. After it, it became clear that this area alone would be unable to compete even with all the short-term repairs. Directions were accordingly given by COREP (Admiralty) to increase the number of repairs that were undertaken in yards in the southwest and on the east coast. Throughout the period of this report the number of unserviceable L.S.T. and L.C.T. increased slowly day by day and the number available for the build-up accordingly slowly decreased. This was disappointing to the army who at times demanded that more vigorous measures should be taken by the naval authorities responsible. I made a number of representations regarding this to the Commander-in-Chief, Portsmouth, and to the Admiralty, but except for minor

improvements they were always able to show that all that could be done was already being done. The COREP organisation had been specially set up to meet the heavy demands of "Neptune" and it is clear that without it the distribution for, and early completion of, the repairs of hundreds of ships and craft would have been entirely impracticable.

Release of Warships.

74. COMINCH[26] and the Admiralty began to press about 20th June for the release of a considerable number of warships and landing craft from the operation. Some of these were required for Operation "Anvil" (later "Dragoon")[27] and some for service in the Far East. Vessels were released progressively as they could be spared but no large withdrawal of bombarding ships was possible until after Cherbourg had been captured. Previous experience in this war had shown the danger of withdrawing ships from an area before an operation had fully succeeded, and I was careful not to agree to the release of ships before I was really satisfied that they could be spared.

Naval Bombardment of Cherbourg.

75. General Bradley[28] had asked for naval bombardment of the defences of Cherbourg to synchronise with his final assault by land. A Task Force consisting of three battleships and four cruisers with screening destroyers and two minesweeping flotillas was formed under the command of Rear-Admiral M.L. Deyo, U.S.N. (C.T.F. I29), and was withdrawn to Portland, a few days before the operation for planning and briefing. The initial plan provided for a preliminary bombardment at a range of 28,000 yards to neutralise the long-range batteries, after which ships were to close in to about 14,000 yards and engage targets designated by the Army. The long-range bombardment was, however, cancelled at the request of the army after the ships had arrived in their initial positions, presumably due to the uncertainty of the position of our forward troops at the time. The bombarding ships then closed in to their close-range positions before they opened fire. The enemy batteries opened fire with extreme accuracy whilst the force was turning at slow speed from the approach channel into the fire support area. To avoid heavy damage destroyers had to make smoke and the heavier ships to manoeuvre at increased speed and, in some cases, without regard to keeping inside swept water, in order to maintain manoeuvring searoom. Fire was opened with all speed on the army's targets but in many cases had very soon to be shifted to the batteries which were straddling our ships. Despite the accuracy of the enemy's fire, by frequent use of helm and alterations in speed the force managed to avoid any but minor casualties and damage, whilst at the same time continuing accurate fire on the enemy's defences. The bombarding force withdrew 3½ hours after it first came in, by which time it was reported that all batteries save two had been silenced. This operation was carried out with skill and determination by Rear-Admiral Deyo, but it is considered unfortunate that it was not found possible to adhere to the original plan, which provided for the initial neutralisation of the enemy long-range batteries as, had better fortune attended the enemy gunners, they might well

have inflicted heavy damage to our ships at the relatively close range at which they were firing.

Increased Casualties due to Mines.

76. By about 24th June casualties to our ships due to enemy mines were becoming serious. This was apparently as much due to the ripening of mines that had already been laid as to new lays that were made by enemy aircraft at night. Special measures were taken to reduce all traffic and the speed at which it proceeded within the assault area to a minimum. As soon as these regulations were rigidly enforced, casualties were reduced to small dimensions. Our sweeping was also largely successful. By 3rd July it was estimated that, including spontaneous detonations, nearly 500 mines had been accounted for by our minesweepers, and at this date, although the threat had not been completely mastered, it was felt that the worst was probably over and that the build-up and our operations generally would develop as desired in spite of mining.

Increasing Air Attacks in Assault Area.

77. Enemy aircraft were more active at night during this period and, in addition to continued minelaying by low-flying aircraft, attacks by composite aircraft and by torpedo aircraft were also reported. It is possible that the enemy were aware that craft on the eastern defence line were restricted from A.A. fire because aircraft sometimes came in very low over them. The restriction of ships' gunfire at night in order to give full scope to night fighters will always remain a most vexed problem, as low-flying enemy aircraft cannot be successfully countered by night fighters whilst, in this case, A.A. fire is often most effective.

Capture of Cherbourg.

78. The completion of the capture of Cherbourg was effected p.m. 27th June and no time was lost in commencing a reconnaissance of the port and deciding upon salvage operations. The first naval report on the state of the harbour showed that severe damage had been done to the docks and the arsenal, whilst the entire anchorage had been heavily mined. All types of mines were swept during the next few days in Cherbourg harbour – moored contact, ground contact, fired on a snag line, moored magnetic, ground magnetic, and ground acoustic. A great number of ships had been sunk in the harbour, and full scope was given to the genius of Commodore Sullivan, U.S. Navy, in effecting the clearance of the port, which in the event took nearly 90 days.

Sound Army Administrative Position.

79. During the first few weeks of the operation frequent representations were made by your staff and those of your Army Group Commanders whenever the build-up appeared to fall any distance short of the plan. This was natural and their desire for the maximum rate of reinforcement and of landing stores was fully shared by me.

Sometimes I felt, however; that their protests were not entirely related to facts as, so far as I know, the position of the Expeditionary Force was never in doubt from D + 2 onwards. The naval view had always been that the build-up plan should be an optimum plan at which we should aim but that its attainment was most improbable, if only by reason of the naval difficulties inherent in the continuous turn round of such a large volume of shipping. In the event, not only naval difficulties were experienced during the first few weeks, but also a considerable number of military ones, especially with regard to loading in the port of Southampton, and the programme did fall behind as we had expected that it would. It was very satisfactory, therefore, to me that your Chief Administrative Officer was able to report at his meeting held on Ist July, that the "Commanders in the field had complete freedom of action so far as the administrative arrangements were concerned". This, it was considered, confirmed our view that the Navy had in fact met the Army's requirements for their reinforcement and maintenance.

Withdrawal of Task Force and Assault Force Commanders. Transfer of Naval Command ashore.

80. During the last few days of June the British and U.S. Assault Force Commanders were successively withdrawn from the assault area when conditions in their sector permitted. On 25th June, Rear-Admiral J.W. Rivett-Carnac established his Headquarters ashore as F.O.B.A.A.[29] and Rear-Admiral J. Wilkes similarly hoisted his flag as F.O. West on 27th June. Rear-Admiral Sir Philip Vian left the British Assault Area on 30th June when the Command was assumed by F.O.B.A.A. Rear-Admiral Alan Kirk withdrew from the U.S. Assault Area on 3rd July, when F.O. West assumed command. The withdrawal of all these officers and the transfer of the two naval commands to the shore marked the stabilisation of the naval position in the assault area and the conclusion of the first phase in the capture of the lodgment area by our armies. Both during the training and planning period, and during the operation, the Task Force and Assault Force Commanders and their subordinates rendered the very highest service to the operation and thus to the Allied cause. The experience that the majority of them had gained in other theatres in previous amphibious operations proved invaluable. They afforded me the greatest possible measure of support and assistance and I could not have wished for more loyal or helpful commanders.

Comments and, Recommendations of Task Force Commanders.

8I. A large number of comments on the operation and recommendations arising therefrom are included in the reports of Naval Commanders Eastern and Western Task Forces. It is clear that Naval Commander Western Task Force and his staff had considerable difficulty both during the preparatory period and during the operation in working in a foreign country and with a command system which was unfamiliar to them. The fact that they overcame these difficulties so well reflects great credit on them all. It is obvious that the general organisation and procedure to be adopted for any joint operation must be that of the nation from whose country it is launched.

Although British and American methods are by no means similar, we are now becoming accustomed to each other's working, and with the mutual trust and goodwill which has obtained in the past there should be no undue difficulties in this respect in the future.

My Relations with the Home Commands.

82. The introduction of a Flag Officer as Allied Naval Commander-in-Chief to conduct an operation of the nature and extent of "Neptune" naturally called for a careful consideration of the system of command and division of responsibilities as between myself and the respective Home Commanders-in-Chief in whose stations I was called upon to plan and to operate. It was clear that whilst I was charged with the preparation of the naval plan and with the formation and training of the naval assault forces, and later with the chief naval command of the operation, the executive implementation of the plan must very largely remain in the hands of the Home Commanders-in-Chief. From the very outset it was my policy to make them my agents for this operation and to employ existing organisations, where these existed, rather than to institute new ones. This policy worked admirably.

83. Some resentment might well have been felt by the Commanders-in-Chief, Home Commands in the Channel, at receiving directions from an authority other than the Admiralty, especially as all three were senior to me. I cannot speak too highly, however, of the unselfish manner in which they accepted the situation and I would particularly mention Admiral Sir Charles J.C. Little, Commander-in-Chief, Portsmouth, on whose Command fell the main burden of the operation on the naval side. Admiral of the Fleet Sir John C. Tovey (Commander-in-Chief, The Nore) and Admiral Sir Ralph Leatham (Commander-in-Chief, Plymouth) together with Admiral Sir Henry D. Pridham-Wippell (Admiral Commanding Dover) also threw themselves wholeheartedly and unselfishly into our preparations, quickly grasping the problems ahead of them and reorganising their Commands to deal admirably with the particular requirements of "Neptune". During the operation the co-ordination between the Commands was perfect and the intricate machine worked as if it had been running for years.

Condition.

84. I am greatly indebted to my staff, so admirably led by Rear-Admiral G.E. Creasy, for their magnificent work and outstanding devotion to duty throughout the long planning period and later during the operation. No Commander-in-Chief has ever been better served and I count myself fortunate in having had the services of so fine a company of officers.

85. I desire also to record my complete satisfaction and admiration for the manner in which the ships of our Allies have carried out their arduous duties, and which has contributed so much towards the liberation of their countries.

86. Finally, I cannot close this letter without expressing my deepest admiration for the manner in which the efforts of the many Commands of all Services and of

both our countries were directed and co-ordinated by yourself as Supreme Commander. I deem it a very great honour to have commanded the Allied naval forces in this great operation under your inspiring leadership, which more perhaps than anything else has been responsible for the success achieved.

I have the honour to be,
Sir,
Your obedient servant,
(Signed) B.H. RAMSAY,
Admiral.
GENERAL DWIGHT D. EISENHOWER, U.S. Army,
Supreme Commander,
Allied Expeditionary Force.

TABLE A
ARRIVALS OF MERCHANT SHIPPING AND LANDING CRAFT IN FRANCE

7th June – 30th June, 1944, inclusive
(Subsequent to Initial Lift of Assault Forces.)

Date	Liberty Ships	Coasters	L.S.T.	L.C.T.	Personnel Ships	L.C.I. (L.)"
7th June	I7	I7	4	5I	9	-
8th June	29	29	6	II0	II	3I
9th June	35	37	I5	50	I0	I8
I0th June	29	44	3I	8I	I0	28
IIth June	30	25	39	80	9	I6
I2th June	I7	68	55	57	II	I8
I3th June	I9	30	56	73	8	30
I4th June	30	25	53	95	9	29
I5th June	34	44	52	76	8	I7
I6th June	25	52	62	48	8	I8
I7th June	27	29	42	79	7	I7
18th June	30	26	48	89	II	29
I9th June	39	37	48	75	8	32
20th June	20	22	3	-	2	-
2Ist June	-	-	-	-	-	-
22nd June	-	30	38	-	I3	-
23rd June	-	33	60	I65	9	I4
24th June	I4	39	37	22	3	5
25th June	23	50	29	39	7	I5
26th June	26	38	55	72	3	I3
27thJune	28	27	38	59	7	9
28th June	35	33	48	-	8	-
29th June	33	29	4I	-	4	I6
30th June	30	24	45	I2I	5	I7
	570	**788**	**905**	**I,442**	**I80**	**372**

Note:- Following vessels not included:-

(*a*) Tankers.

(*b*) Hospital Carriers.

(*c*) Salvage ships and other auxiliaries.

Admiralty footnotes
1. T.U.R.C.O. – Turn Round Control Organisation;
B.U.C.O. – Build-Up Control Organisation;

1. *C.O.R.E.P. – Control Repair Organisation.*
1. *C.O.T.U.G. – Control Tug Organisation.*
2. *C.O.S.S.A.C. – Chief of Staff, Supreme Allied Commander, General Sir Frederick Morgan.*
3. *PHOENIX and WHALE Units were components of the artificial (MULBERRY) harbours.*
4. *L.C.P.(Sy) – Small personnel landing craft fitted for survey duties.*
5. *X-craft – 2-men submarines.*
6. *L.C.P.(L) – Landing Craft Personnel (Large).*
7. *L.S.T. – Landing Ship, Tanks.*
8. *A.N.C.X.F. – Allied Naval Commander-in-Chief, Expeditionary Force*
9. *H hour – The hour at which the first flight of landing craft "touch down" on the beach in an assault. Formerly known as zero hour.*
10. *L.C.I. (L) – Landing Craft, Infantry (Large).*
11. *COMLANCRABELEVENTHPHIB – Commander Landing Craft and Bases, IIth Amphibious Force.*
12. *Force U2A, which was a large and slow assault convoy of Force U, was composed of 128 L.C.T. with their escort.*
13. *Force 5 – Fresh breeze (16-20 m.p.h. at sea level).*
14. *L.C.T. – Landing Craft, Tanks.*
15. *R.C.M. – Radio Counter-Measures.*
16. *L.C.G.(L) – Landing Craft Gun (Large), a type of "support craft" not actually used for landing men or material.*
17. *These positions or areas are those in which the ships carrying assaulting troops and craft stop to lower these craft and disembark the troops into them.*
18. *Force 4 – Moderate breeze (11-15 m.p.h. at sea level).*
19. *D.D. tanks are tanks fitted with flotation gear to enable them to swim ashore when disembarked outside their wading depth.*
20. *L.C.T. (A.V.R.E.) – Landing Craft carrying tanks fitted with special obstacle clearing equipment used by R.E.*
21. *L.C.T. (A) – Tank Landing Craft strengthened to allow the self-propelled artillery which they carried to fire whilst still embarked, thus providing an addition to the naval close support fire.*
22. *Air O.P.s – Air Observation Posts.*
 S.F.C.P. – Shore Fire Control Party.
 F.O.B. – Forward Observer, Bombardment.
23. *S.H.A.E.F. – Supreme Headquarters, Allied Expeditionary Force.*
24. *On some beaches the practice of drying out L.S.T. had been resorted to as early as D + 2 day.*
25. *Force 6 – Strong breeze (21-26 m.p.h. at sea level).*
26. *COMINCH – C.-in-C. U.S. Fleet, Navy Department, Washington.*
27. *ANVIL (later DRAGOON) – The landing on the South Coast of France.*
28. *General Bradley – In command of U.S. Troops employed in this sector.*
29. *F.O.B.A.A. – Flag Officer, British Assault Area.*

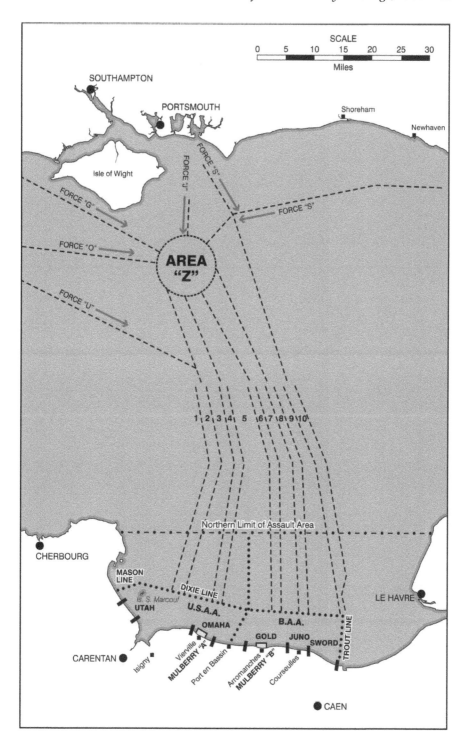

3

LIBERATION OF EUROPE (OPERATION "OVERLORD")

OPERATIONS OF COASTAL COMMAND, ROYAL AIR FORCE, FROM MAY TO AUGUST, 1944.

The following despatch was submitted to the Secretary of State for Air on November 1st, 1944, by Air Chief Marshal Sir Sholto Douglas, K.C.B., M.C., D.F.C.,

Air Officer Commanding-in-chief, Coastal Command, Royal Air Force.

I have the honour to submit a despatch on the preparations for and results of operations by my Command for the period May to the end of August, 1944. By September the successful progress of our Armies during the three months that they had been established on the Continent had denied the enemy the effective use of the Bay of Biscay ports as submarine bases from which to conduct his war against our shipping. This marked the end of an important phase in the U-Boat war.

PLANNING AND PREPARATION.

Preparations by the Enemy and Ourselves

2. At the end of March, 1944, there were signs that the enemy was reducing the number of U-Boats operating in the Atlantic, presumably with the intention of conserving his forces for the forthcoming assault. This was confirmed in April, when the number operating in this area was very small. The lull continued during May, with large concentrations of U-Boats in the Bay of Biscay ports. This policy of the enemy's, while it reduced our opportunities for killing U-Boats, permitted an intensive training programme for the Leigh Light squadrons in the United Kingdom – which I had started at the end of March – to proceed without hindrance. The urgent

need for Leigh Light aircraft over the past two years had meant that aircrews turned over to this role had had insufficient time to devote to training, and the standard of homing and Leigh Light manipulation was not as high as it might have been. Ten weeks' intensive training was carried out by the U.K.-based Liberator and Wellington searchlight squadrons, and when D-day came the standard was much improved.

Directive for "Overlord"

3. In April, 1944, I issued to my Groups a directive which set out the tasks of each Group for the OVERLORD operation that was shortly to take place, and outlined the action that the Admiralty anticipated would be taken by the enemy.

ANTI-U-BOAT.

Appreciation of Enemy Intentions

4. On the assumption that the enemy would direct his U-Boat offensive principally against our cross-channel convoys, the Admiralty appreciated that the bulk of his U-Boats would operate from the Bay ports and endeavour to penetrate the S.W. Approaches to the Bristol, St. George's and English Channels, and that he would maintain only comparatively small forces in the Atlantic to hamper the passage of our convoys. The main focus of our anti-U-Boat operations was therefore to be in the S.W. Approaches, and the effort directed to protecting Atlantic convoys would be drastically reduced. It was also necessary to provide to some extent against the passage of U-Boats through the Northern Transit Area and also against the possibility of the movement of U-Boats through the North Sea. These areas had however to be regarded as of secondary importance when compared with the S.W. Approaches, and it was not intended to provide permanently for more than thin cover in the Northern Transit Area. The North Sea area would be covered only if the situation demanded it, and my plans allowed for four anti-U-Boat squadrons to be drawn from those allotted to the S.W. Approaches and to be transferred to bases on the East coast should the necessity arise.

Tasks of Coastal Groups

5. The tasks of my various Groups in the United Kingdom in the anti-U-Boat role were briefly as follows:-

19 *Group (Plymouth).*

(i) To provide adequate air cover in the S.W. Approaches to protect the flanks of the Allied Assault Convoys.

(ii) To provide cover or close escort to Allied Assault Convoys in the S.W. Approaches.

(iii) To hunt and destroy enemy U-Boats attempting to attack Allied Assault Convoys in the S.W. Approaches.

I6 *Group (Chatham).*

(i) In the event of a threat by U-Boats to the Eastern flank of the Allied Liberation Forces by way of the North Sea, to hunt and destroy enemy U-Boats attempting to enter the English Channel from the east.

(ii) To provide cover or close escort by Fleet Air Arm Squadrons allocated to the Group to Allied Liberation Convoys on passage between The Nore and Beachy Head.

I5 *Group (Liverpool).*

(i) To provide cover to threatened Atlantic Shipping.

(ii) To cover the entrances of the North Channel against the passage of enemy U-Boats.

(iii) To provide A/U cover in the Northern Transit Area.

I8 *Group (Rosyth).*

(i) To provide A/U cover in the Northern Transit Area.

(ii) To provide aircraft for Fleet Reconnaissance duties.

The Main Threat

6. In the main area of the S.W. Approaches, the first principle adopted was that of "the cork in the bottle", the object being to flood an area of sufficient depth to kill or keep submarines submerged from the Western limits of the St. George's and Bristol Channels and the English Channel up to a point as near as possible to the route of our cross-channel convoys. The patrols were so calculated as to provide a cover of thirty minutes density in the area. By this plan I expected a high percentage of kills if the U-Boats came through on the surface, or, alternatively, it would force upon them maximum caution tactics throughout their passage. In the latter event there would be a zone to the East of the flooded area in which U-Boats would be forced to surface for prolonged periods to recharge their batteries, and in which they could be attacked and hunted by air and surface forces with good prospects of success. Moreover, individual patrol areas were so designed as to be readily removable from one part of the main area to another, so that one portion could be immediately strengthened at the expense of another in the light of the situation as it developed. Further, the "cork" could be pushed home or withdrawn at will. In this way the plan preserved flexibility without detriment to the principle upon which it was based.

The Need for Fighter Cover

7. The extent to which the "cork" could be inserted was considered dependent upon the degree of fighter cover that could be provided by A.E.A.F., since the Southern

boundaries of our patrols ran close in to the coast of France along which the enemy was expected to move his U-Boats under cover of his fighters and shore defences. Once the assault was launched it was expected that the enemy fighters would be heavily engaged in the area of the main battle and that no substantial numbers of S.E. fighters would be able to be spared for the protection of U-Boats. The commitment for providing fighter cover was not therefore likely to be a prolonged or heavy one, but it was reasonable to expect from the enemy some early reactions to the preparations in progress and also to any exercises which took place before D-day. One such exercise, known as FABIUS, was considered sufficient in scope to make it possible that the enemy might believe the assault was starting. Should this happen, I considered that it might be necessary prematurely to implement the plans of my Command in full, and in this case the requirement for S.E. fighter cover would become much more serious. I considered, however, that at this stage our fighters would not be heavily committed, elsewhere, and Air Commander-in-Chief, A.E.A.F., confirmed that full scale fighter support could be provided any time up to D-day. Provision for the protection of A/U aircraft against enemy long range fighters (Ju 88s) was to be met by allotting Mosquito and Beaufighter aircraft of my own Command for this task.

Convoy Cover

8. In addition to flooding the selected area, plans were made for the protection of our cross-channel convoys sailing along the South coast of England. I allotted this task principally to the Fleet Air Arm Squadrons (eight of which were placed under my operational control for "Overlord"), backed by such 19 Group aircraft as I could spare from their main task.

Operation of Surface Hunting Groups

9. Surface hunting groups were to be operated under the control of the Naval Commanders-in-Chief, Plymouth and Portsmouth. Co-operation between these Groups and aircraft was arranged between A.O.C. 19 Group and C-in-C Plymouth, who co-ordinated his own requirements and those of C-in-C Portsmouth.

ANTI-SHIP OPERATIONS.

Tasks of 16 and 19 Groups

10. It was expected that the enemy would launch an offensive with destroyers and light surface craft against our convoys sailing to and from their assembly ports and on passage across the Channel. Air operations to meet this threat were to be conducted by 16 and 19 Groups, whose tasks were as follows:-

19 *Group.*

(i) To hunt and destroy E-Boats and destroyers in the S.W. Approaches and Western Channel.

(ii) To provide anti-E-Boat and destroyer reconnaissance in conjunction with Naval Surface Forces operating in the area in (i).

I6 *Group.*

(i) To hunt and destroy E-Boats and destroyers in the Southern North Sea.

(ii) To provide anti-E-Boat and destroyer reconnaissance in conjunction with Naval Surface Forces operating in the Southern North Sea.

Form of Operations

II. It was correctly appreciated that anti-ship operations would take place mostly at night and at dawn and dusk, and these were to take the following forms:-

At night.

(i) Operation of Albacore and Swordfish under G.C.I, control of I0 and II Groups.

(ii) Reconnaissance by Wellington flare-dropping A.S.V. aircraft operating under I6 and I9 Groups, and the subsequent direction of Naval Surface Craft and/or Coastal Command Beaufighters to the target.

At dusk and dawn.

Beaufighter sweeps with the object of destroying enemy Light Surface Craft when leaving harbour at dusk or returning from patrol at dawn.

I2. As in the case of anti-U-Boat measures, I was prepared to implement these plans as a result of enemy reaction to exercises such as "Fabius", or to any other event which might have led him to believe that the assault was imminent.

Main Battle Zone

I3. In agreement with the Admiralty and the Air Commander-in-Chief, A.E.A.F., I demarcated an area between the lines Portland to Jersey on the West and North Foreland to Calais on the East, as the main battle zone. Coastal Command aircraft were to operate primarily on the flanks of this area and only to a limited extent within it. This was an important point. I expected such a concentration of shipping of all sorts in this zone that even by day I considered it would be difficult to distinguish friend from foe, and at night almost impossible. As it turned out, however, it became possible, by special briefing at Area Combined Headquarters, for my anti-shipping aircraft to operate within the Battle Zone outside the central area containing the cross-channel shipping lanes.

Order of Battle

I4. The Order of Battle, as it stood on 6th June, I944, shows that, in order to make the flooded area in the S.W. Approaches effective, I deployed no less than 2I of my A/U squadrons together with 4 Fleet Air Arm squadrons in this area. My anti-shipping Striking force consisted of seven Beaufighter squadrons, of which I allotted initially five to the east of the main battle zone where the threat of E-Boats was considered greater, and two to the west.

CONDUCT AND RESULTS OF OPERATIONS.

U-Boat Operations in the North

I5. Intensive operations for Coastal Command began in mid-May, although only the Anti-U-Boat squadrons in the North were involved. At this time the enemy decided hurriedly to reinforce his U-Boat flotillas in the Bay of Biscay by moving a number of his Norwegian-based boats into the Atlantic and thence southwards to the Channel and French West Coast ports. The U-Boats were presumably in too much of a hurry to proceed submerged, and their Commanding Officers were apparently confident in the efficiency of their anti-aircraft defences, for they remained on the surface and shot it out with the aircraft to their own detriment. Every opportunity was taken to bring to bear on the enemy the fullest weight of attack without reducing the forces preparing for the vital struggle which was shortly to take place in the S.W. Approaches, and I therefore moved detachments of squadrons from Iceland and Northern Ireland to airfields and flying boat bases in northern Scotland and the Shetlands, to supplement the aircraft at the disposal of the A.O.C. I8 Group. All through June and July these Northern operations went on, and towards the end of July they had extended into Arctic waters, where the enemy seemed to be trying to work round into the Atlantic out of aircraft range. This meant that operations were being conducted at no less than 850 miles from the aircraft's bases. At the end of June, however, I had moved the whole of the VLR[1] Liberator squadron from Iceland to Tain, and this squadron bore the brunt of the operations conducted in these very far Northern regions.

I6. During June perhaps three or four boats in all got through to the Bay of Biscay. The rest were either destroyed or damaged and forced to put back to Norway. In those Northern latitudes at that time of year there was no darkness, and, at the beginning of the battle at any rate, few of the Northern U-Boats had been fitted with "schnorkel". These two factors were largely responsible for the opportunities for so many attacks.

I7. During the period mid-May to the end of July, we sighted seventy-five U-Boats in Northern Waters and attacked fifty-one. Of these sixteen were sunk or probably sunk and twelve damaged. These successes were not achieved without cost. I62 Canadian Squadron sank four U-Boats and lost three Catalinas in June alone. Two Victoria Crosses were awarded to officers taking part in these operations, one posthumously to the Captain of a Catalina of the afore-mentioned 162 (R.C.A.F.) Squadron, and a second to the Captain of a Catalina of 210 Squadron.

U-Boat Operations in the South

18. Despite the importance of these far away operations, it was inevitable that the main attention should be concentrated on the beaches of Normandy and the English Channel. The preparations for the assault and the large scale exercises during the last few days of May and the beginning of June did not produce any reactions from the enemy, and on 6th June the majority of the enemy's operational U-Boats were still assembled in the Biscay ports. They were not offensively deployed on that date, so there can be no doubt that the enemy had been unable to discover the date of our landing. On D-Day however, he reacted swiftly. It soon became clear that the U-Boats were making for the assault area with the utmost speed – that is, on the surface whenever possible. The air patrols which had been planned to counter this move were already being flown and successes soon materialised. Off the Brest Peninsula and in the mouth of the Channel, thirty-six U-Boats were sighted by Coastal Command in the first four days of the assault and twenty-three were attacked. Six were destroyed and four seriously damaged. Sixteen of the attacks were at night. Two of the U-Boats destroyed were sunk on one sortie within 20 minutes by a Liberator of No. 224 Squadron, piloted by Flying Officer, Moore. In almost every case the enemy fought back desperately with his anti-aircraft armament, for in those four days the U-Boats were in too much of a hurry to be able to proceed submerged. They inflicted a high proportion of casualties on our attacking aircraft, but very few got through. Prisoners of war from the U-Boats have told us that the penetration of the Channel was a nightmare.

19. After D plus 4 the enemy was forced to change his tactics. During their sojourn in the Bay ports almost all the U-boats had been fitted with the exhaustible air intake (Schnorkel), and from the fourth day of the assault until the end of June sightings mainly consisted of periscopes and "Schnorkels" of U-Boats trying to get through by remaining submerged continuously and by relying on "Schnorkels" to ventilate the boat and charge batteries. The "Schnorkel" is a most difficult target for airborne radar, and it cannot be denied that the enemy's recourse to this cautious method of approach reduced his losses. At the same time, however, the effect of remaining submerged had an adverse effect on the morale of the U-Boat crews and their achievements were notable by their absence. Between D plus 4 and the end of June forty-seven sightings of U-Boats were made by Coastal Command in southern waters and twenty-four were attacked. During this period at least one more U-Boat was sunk by aircraft and two kills were shared with ships of the Royal Navy, who were taking an ever increasing part in the policing of the Channel and its approaches. In addition, aircraft damaged another four U-Boats and shared with the Navy in damaging a fifth.

20. In July the picture was the same. The enemy was still trying to get in amongst our shipping by making the fullest use of his schnorkel device. In all, twenty-two sightings were made and fifteen U-Boats attacked during this month, of which two were sunk and another damaged.

2I. By the end of July there was no doubt that the enemy's threat had been beaten. Only a small number of U-Boats had got through to our shipping lanes, and in the three months from D-Day to the end of August, of the thousands of merchant ships taking part in the Channel operations, only nine were sunk by U-Boat action.

22. Finally, the steady progress of our armies made it obvious to the enemy that he would soon lose the use of the Bay ports. He therefore began to evacuate them during August and to send U-Boats northward to his Norwegian bases. During the month some ferocious actions were fought in the Bay of Biscay almost within sight of land with U-Boats trying to escape, and six were accounted for by Coastal Command aircraft, three of these being shared with the Navy. By early September, the Biscay U-Boat force had withdrawn and was making its passage, underwater nearly all the time, to the Norwegian ports.

23. In the whole battle in the North and the South from mid-May to the end of August, Coastal Command sank twenty-seven U-Boats, damaged another so badly that when it reached its base it was paid off, shared in five more sunk, and damaged another twenty-nine, including two shared with the Royal Navy.

24. In these operations, where skill counted as much as courage, and where both were indispensable, we lost thirty-eight anti-U-Boat aircraft by enemy action and another twenty-two through the hazards of maintaining our patrols in fair weather and in foul. A high proportion of these aircraft were four-engined heavies with large crews.

Anti-Shipping Operations.

25. While the U-Boats were being defeated in the south-west and the north-east, Coastal Command was also in action against enemy surface forces. Soon after the assault began, the enemy tried to reinforce his surface craft in the assault areas by bringing up three destroyers from the Gironde. These vessels were attacked by our aircraft while still south of Brest on 6th June, but the damage inflicted did not prevent the enemy from making port. Two days later the ships tried to round the Brest Peninsula, but were brought to action by the Royal Navy. One Seetier class destroyer was driven ashore, the Tjerk Hiddes was sunk, and the second Seetier was forced back to Brest. The beached destroyer was later attacked by Beaufighters with rockets and bombs, and became a total loss. After this the enemy made no further attempts to reinforce his surface craft from the west, and the only serviceable Seetier and Elbing destroyers were withdrawn to the Gironde.

26. In the early stages, as was expected, the enemy operated his light forces on quite a considerable scale against our assault forces in the assault area. E-Boats were the main weapons. Some thirty of these vessels were based between Boulogne and Cherbourg, but the number was later reduced by air attack, by surface action, and by the outstandingly successful attacks by Bomber Command against Le Havre and Boulogne.

27. The operations of Coastal Command against these light forces consisted mainly of continuous anti-shipping patrols in the Channel. Albacores, Avengers, Swordfish, Beaufighters and Wellingtons made a great many attacks, mostly at night, against E-

Boats, R-Boats, "M" class minesweepers and trawlers. Wellingtons did a great deal of reconnaissance work, dropping flares and directing naval forces to their targets. Results were naturally extremely difficult to assess, but we know from prisoners of war that hardly an E-Boat put to sea without being spotted and attacked from the air. In the darkness and in the face of flak from other vessels it is almost impossible to investigate the result of a bombing attack on an E-Boat flotilla, but there is no doubt, that the menace of the enemy's light forces was held in check by the operations of the Royal Navy and Coastal Command.

28. The enemy made no use of his major units in the Baltic. Moreover, with the exception of one or two flotillas of E-Boats, he never attempted to reinforce the Channel from the East, in spite of the fact that he had a number of heavy destroyers and about twenty torpedo boats available in the Baltic. It is probable that he realised our combined sea and air defences made the Southern North Sea and the English Channel a very unpleasant area for operations by the German Navy. In any case, it is certain that, despite the few positive results of our night attacks, the enemy was so harassed by them that he was unable seriously to interfere with our "Overlord" shipping.

29. This success meant that, from the end of June, my anti-shipping aircraft were able to devote more of their time to the second of their two tasks – the interruption of German coastal shipping. In June, I directed the greater part of my effort to the naval targets in the Channel, and only a few attacks were made on convoys. These, however, included some very successful engagements, the most important of which occurred on 15th June north of the Dutch island of Schiermonnikoog, when Beaufighters sank a merchantman of 8,000 tons, a naval auxiliary of 4,000 tons and a minesweeper, besides damaging four more of the escort vessels.

30. In July I kept up the Channel protection, but diverted all but one of the Beaufighter Squadrons to convoy strikes off the coasts of Southern Norway and the Low Countries. There is no doubt that these strikes proved most harassing to the enemy, and he was obliged to divert to this purely defensive task numbers of minesweepers and naval escort craft which he urgently required elsewhere.

3I. The beginning of August saw a new phase open in the shipping war. As our tanks swept through North-Western France, enemy coastal craft broke for the comparative safety of the North Sea ports; one night alone saw 70 of them attacked from the air. Moreover, the enemy in the Brest Peninsula was cut off by land. He was therefore obliged to squeeze yet more work from his seaborne supply services. Every available ship in Western France from Brest to Bordeaux was pressed into service to keep the beleaguered garrisons supplied. Coastal Command made the best of this opportunity. Mosquitoes based in Cornwall, Halifaxes, previously operating in an Anti-U-Boat role, and a Wing of Beaufighters which I transferred from the East Coast convoy routes, operated all along the Biscay coast. Merchant ships, sperrbrechers, minesweepers and coasters of all kinds were sunk, and a fitting climax was reached on 24th August when the last of the larger German warships in this area, a Seetier and an Elbing class destroyer, were sunk in the Gironde by the rockets of the Beaufighter Wing.

32. At the beginning of September, the area of anti-shipping activity had moved eastward in the wake of the Allied armies. There were no more attacks in the Bay of Biscay or in the Channel. As the enemy-occupied ports fell into our hands, the night patrols of the Beaufighters, Avengers and Wellingtons moved eastwards along the coast. This happened so quickly that there were no attacks off the Belgian Coast after 7th September, and our attention was turned completely to the intensification of the offensive against the enemy's shipping operating off the Dutch and Norwegian coasts.

33. Thus concluded three months of intensive operations in which the German naval units and merchant shipping in Western Europe had been hammered unmercifully.

CONCLUSION.

34. I wish to end this despatch by paying tribute to all personnel in Coastal Command who by their tireless endeavour and concerted efforts helped to bring about the victory over the enemy sea opposition to the liberation of Europe. In addition to the operations of my Anti-U-Boat and Anti-Shipping aircraft, whose activities have been recounted, the photographic reconnaissance squadrons, the meteorological squadrons and the air/sea rescue air and surface craft all carried out their arduous tasks with skill and resolution.

35. I would like to mention particularly the Fleet Air Arm Squadrons which were incorporated in my Command for operation "Overlord". They performed their varied duties with outstanding keenness and precision.

36. A tribute must also be paid to the Liberator Squadrons of the U.S. Navy, under Commodore Hamilton, U.S.N., which, working under the operational control of I9 Group, did invaluable work, particularly during the "cork in the bottle" operations.

37. Two Norwegian Squadrons, a Czech and a Polish Squadron were also distinguished for their gallantry and enthusiasm in the combined team.

38. Finally, it will not be forgotten that the successes of our operations could not have come about but for the skill in planning and organisation of the Command and Group Staffs who –with the invaluable and enthusiastic co-operation of the Staffs of the Naval Commands –worked long and hard to perfect our preparations; and but for the ceaseless energies of the ground personnel at Stations who provided our aircrews with the means to reap their victories.

I have the honour to be,
Sir,
Your obedient Servant,
SHOLTO DOUGLAS,
Air Chief Marshal,
Air Officer Commanding-in-Chief,
Coastal Command, Royal Air Force.

Footnote
1.Very Long Range.

4

AIR OPERATIONS BY THE ALLIED EXPEDITIONARY AIR FORCE IN N.W. EUROPE

FROM NOVEMBER 15TH, 1943 TO SEPTEMBER 30TH, 1944.

The following despatch by the late Air Chief Marshal Sir Trafford Leigh-Mallory, K.C.B., D.S.O., Air Commander-in-Chief, Allied Expeditionary Air Force, was submitted to the Supreme Allied Commander in November 1944.

On relinquishing my command of the Allied Expeditionary Air Force I have the honour to submit the following Despatch, covering its operations under my command during the period from 15th November, 1943 to 30th September, 1944.

Since this Despatch covers the air support of the assault of Europe and the subsequent land operations, it necessarily includes reference to the strategical operations of the United States Eighth Air Force and the Royal Air Force Bomber Command in addition to the operations of these two Air Forces and the Royal Air Force Coastal Command directed to the tactical support of the assault.

As the period covered by the Despatch extends over ten and a half months of the most heavy and concentrated air war in the history of the world, I have not attempted to deal with the events on a day-to-day basis. Rather I have taken the tasks undertaken in the preliminary and preparatory phases and in the assault and post-assault phase and have attempted to show how these tasks were fulfilled, as well as briefly indicating what I feel are some of the outstanding features of these air operations.

PART I – COMMAND AND CONTROL.

Formation of A.E.A.F.

By a Directive (reference COSSAC (43) 8I) dated I6th November, I943, issued by your Chief of Staff, I was informed that the Combined Chiefs of Staff had appointed me Air Commander-in-Chief of the Allied Expeditionary Air Force under yourself as the Supreme Allied Commander, and that I was to exercise operational command of the British and American tactical air forces supporting the assault of Western Europe from the United Kingdom. I was also informed that a United States General would be appointed Deputy Air Commander-in-Chief, Allied Expeditionary Air Force. Major-General William O. Butler was the first General Officer to hold this post. He served in this capacity from Ist January, I944, to 25th March, I944, and was succeeded by Major-General Hoyt S. Vandenberg who occupied the position until 8th August, I944. Major-General Ralph Royce then held this appointment until the disbandment of A.E.A.F. on I4th October, I944.

Forces available.

2. The forces under my command comprised the Royal Air Force Second Tactical Air Force, the United States Ninth Air Force and the forces of the Air Defence of Great Britain. The Royal Air Force Second Tactical Air Force and the formations of the Air Defence of Great Britain passed to my command on I5th November, I943; the United States Ninth Air Force passed to my operational command on I5th December, I943, but was not released from its commitment to assist the United States Strategic Air Forces in "Pointblank" operations until I0th March, I944.

3. You will recall that a definition of the role of the strategic air forces was not covered in the original Directive to me, but was deferred to a later date. However, my plans were made on the assumption that I should be able to count on the full support of the strategic air forces when it was required.

4. On I7th November, I943, I issued a Directive to the Air Marshal Commanding, Royal Air Force Second Tactical Air Force and to the Commanding General, United States Ninth Air Force, in which I informed them of my appointment as Air Commander-in-Chief and of the respective dates on which their units came under my operational control. I further directed that these forces should proceed, without delay, to prepare for operations in support of two British and two American Field Armies in an assault on the Continent. I also issued a Directive to the Air Marshal Commanding, Air Defence of Great Britain, setting out the functions and organisation of the Air Defence of Great Britain, following on its conversion from Royal Air Force Fighter Command.

5. On 6th December, I943, I issued a further Directive to the forces under my command, outlining the "Overlord" plan and defining the control that I would exercise as Air Commander-in-Chief. A table showing these forces and the chain of command is at Appendix "A" (not reproduced).

Operation *"Pointblank".*

6. During the preliminary period of preparation for the assault, in late 1943 and early 1944, the medium and light bomber forces of the Allied Expeditionary Air Force continued to lend support to Operation "Pointblank." This was the name given to the combined bomber plan of the strategical bombing forces which had as its aims, first, the reduction of the fighter forces of the G.A.F., second, the general reduction in the war potential of Germany, and third, the weakening of the will of the German people to continue the struggle. The co-ordination of these operations was effected through a Combined Operational Planning Committee, which was a joint British/American Fighter and Bomber Committee responsible for planning daylight operations when the United States Army Air Force heavy bombers took part. During this preliminary period, the operations by Allied Expeditionary Air Force medium and light bombers in conjunction with, and in support of United States Eighth Air Force were given precedence over any other daylight operations. A second Committee, known as the II Group Planning Committee, co-ordinated operations of the medium and light bombers of the Allied Expeditionary Air Force other than those in the support role mentioned above. The activities of the fighter forces of the Allied Expeditionary Air Force as escort to, and in support of, bombing operations were also co-ordinated through these Committees.

Ninth Air Force Released from "Pointblank" Commitments

7. On 10th March, 1944, I forwarded a Directive to Commanding General, United States Ninth Air Force, advising him that you, as the Supreme Allied Commander, had decided that the time had come for the operations of the Ninth Air Force to be directed towards the preparation for Operation "Overlord" and that it would, therefore, operate exclusively under the Allied Expeditionary Air Force and be released from the commitment to assist the United States Eighth Air Force in "Pointblank" operations. As an exception to this ruling, such fighters of the United States Ninth Fighter Command as were suitable and available continued to operate as escort to the United States Eighth Air Force when required.

8. At this time also, I advised the forces under my command that the most important assistance the Allied Expeditionary Air Force could give the Army during the preparatory phase would be by attacking the enemy's rail communications, with the object of so disorganising his railway system that he would find it difficult to supply his divisions in Northern France when the fighting started and still more difficult to bring reinforcements into the lodgment area. Selected rail centres were, therefore, put in the first priority for attack.

Role of Strategic Air Forces

9. Until March, 1944, strategic air forces comprising the United States Eighth Air Force and Royal Air Force Bomber Command, continued to be employed on Operation "Pointblank" under the direction of the British Chief of Air Staff acting as

a representative of the Combined Chiefs of Staff. In March, 1944, as the completion of the preparatory tasks for Operation "Overlord" became more urgent the Combined Chiefs of Staff directed that "Overlord" should have priority over "Pointblank" and that the direction of strategic air forces should pass from the British Chief of Air Staff to yourself as the Supreme Allied Commander, on 14th April, 1944.

10. You instructed your deputy, Air Chief Marshal Sir Arthur W. Tedder, G.C.B., to exercise for you general supervision of all air forces, particularly in the co-ordination of the efforts of heavy bomber forces to be employed on operations "Pointblank" and "Overlord". I was responsible to you for all air operations in connection with the latter plan and I accordingly passed to Air Chief Marshal Tedder my requirements for heavy bomber effort both in the preparatory and assault phases. During May, 1944, the Deputy Supreme Allied Commander decided that all air operations could be more easily planned and laid on at a single headquarters, and the Air Operations Planning Staff of Supreme Headquarters was moved to my Headquarters. The Deputy Supreme Allied Commander and the Commanders of the strategical and tactical air forces then regularly attended my daily conferences at Stanmore, thus enabling all operation orders covering all air forces occupied with "Overlord" tasks, to be co-ordinated and given rapidly to the forces to be employed.

Formation of Advanced A.E.A.F.

11. In order to achieve the most economical and effective employment of the air forces at my disposal for the assault and its subsequent development, I considered it essential that the air operations in immediate and direct support of the land battle should be specially co-ordinated and directed. I, therefore, decided to establish a small operational organisation to be known as Advanced Allied Expeditionary Air Force. Under my general direction, the Commander Advanced A.E.A.F. was given the task of directing and co-ordinating the planning for and operations of such forces of the United States Ninth Air Force and Royal Air Force Second Tactical Air Force as were allotted to him from time to time.

12. Air Marshal Sir Arthur Coningham, K.C.B., D.S.O., M.C., D.F.C., A.F.C., was appointed Commander, Advanced Allied Expeditionary Air Force, and he undertook this responsibility on detachment from the Second Tactical Air Force. The Commander, Advanced A.E.A.F. was the one air commander with whom the Commander-in-Chief, 21st Army Group dealt in his capacity as Commander-in-Chief, Land Forces, during the initial phases of the operation. The Commander, Advanced A.E.A.F. had the necessary authority to implement the requests for air action made by the Army, referring to me any requests for air support beyond the resources of the two tactical air forces. Headquarters, Advanced A.E.A.F. was set up at Uxbridge on 1st May, 1944. Its War Room, where meetings to coordinate operations of the tactical air forces were held daily, was adjacent to the Combined Operations Room and the Combined Control and Reconnaissance Centres referred to below.

Machinery of Control of Tactical Air Forces.

I3. Throughout the preparatory and assault periods, the control of the fighter bombers and the light and medium bombers of the two tactical air forces was exercised through a Combined Operations Room located at Uxbridge. This Operations Room was staffed by representatives of the United States Ninth Air Force and the Royal Air Force Second Tactical Air Force. Also under the direction of the Commander, Advanced A.E.A.F., a Combined Control Centre was set up and operated by the Air Officer Commanding No. II Group, Royal Air Force, with the full collaboration of the Commanding General, United States IXth Fighter Command and with authoritative representation of the United States Army VIIIth Fighter Command. This Combined Control Centre was manned by a British/American staff and was, in effect, the Operations Room of No. II Group, Air Defence of Great Britain, with the complete static signals system of the old organisation developed over a long period and augmented by additional communication facilities. This Centre planned, co-ordinated and controlled all fighter operations in the initial phases of the operations; it was also responsible for issuing executive instructions for the fighter bombers.

I4. A Combined Reconnaissance Centre was also operated under the command of the Commander, Advanced A.E.A.F. to co-ordinate and direct the visual and photographic reconnaissance efforts of both the British and United States reconnaissance forces, during the initial phases.

I5. At Appendix "B"[1] is a diagram, setting out the chain of control and the locations of various Headquarters at the time of the Assault. Modifications in this chain of control were made later as they became necessary. Headquarters, Royal Air Force Second Tactical Air Force and Headquarters, United States Ninth Air Force moved overseas on 4th August, I944, and Headquarters, Advanced A.E.A.F. moved to the Continent on 9th August, I944; to economise in communications, this Headquarters was located alongside Headquarters, United States Ninth Air Force. It continued in the field alongside this latter Headquarters (which was located next to I2th United States Army Group), in the advance from the Cotentin Peninsula to the Paris area, where it was located at Versailles. Main Headquarters, A.E.A.F. moved from Stanmore to the Continent on 8th September, I944, and was located alongside your own Headquarters at Julouville. Communications at that place were quite inadequate to meet the needs of a headquarters of the size concerned, and Main Headquarters A.E.A.F. moved with Supreme Headquarters to Versailles on I9th September, I944.

I6. Plans had been drawn up for the further move of Advanced Headquarters, A.E.A.F. with Advanced Headquarters Ninth Air Force to Verdun. In view of impending developments, chiefly the absorption of A.E.A.F. into S.H.A.E.F., these plans were not put into operation. Headquarters, Advanced A.E.A.F. was therefore merged into Headquarters Main A.E.A.F. at I200 hours on 23rd September, I944.

PART II – POLICY AND PLANNING.

(a) Operations prior to D-Day.

Operation "Overlord".

17. Operation "Overlord" was part of a large strategic plan designed to bring about the defeat of Germany by heavy and concerted assaults on German-occupied Europe from the United Kingdom, the Mediterranean and Russia. A Joint Study and Outline Plan for Operation "Overlord" was completed in July, I943. This plan was elaborated in more detail under the title "Neptune" – Initial Joint Plan and Maintenance Project/Administrative Plan – by the Allied Naval Commander-in-Chief, the Commander-in-Chief, 2Ist Army Group and myself. Operation "Neptune" provided for the launching of an assault from the United Kingdom across the English Channel, designed to secure a lodgment area on the Continent, from which wider offensive operations could be developed.

I8. To cover the operations of all air forces allotted to Operation "Neptune", an Overall Air Plan was evolved, which set out briefly the Joint Plan, the command and control of air forces involved, the principal air tasks and their development through the preliminary and preparatory phases, the assault and follow-up, and air operations subsequent to the assault and securing of the lodgment area. The main features of the Overall Air Plan are more fully dealt with in paragraphs 25 and 26 below.

I9. To supplement the Initial Joint Plan for Operation "Neptune", joint instructions and memoranda were issued by the Commanders-in-Chief of the Naval, Army and Air Forces.

Administrative and Signals Planning.

20. To supplement the Overall Air Plan, additional Operational and Administrative Instructions were prepared and issued. In particular, comprehensive Administrative plans were issued for the Royal Air Force formations in A.E.A.F. and the United States Ninth Air Force. These Administrative plans, which were issued separately, were based on three previously agreed fundamental decisions:-

(*a*) The relative administrative responsibilities of the Army and Air Forces in the field. The division laid down was closely followed and, in practice, worked excellently.

(*b*) Since the United States Army Air Force and the Royal Air Force respectively depended on separate administrative systems, no attempt to combine them should be made, except where advantage was clearly to be gained.

(*c*) The main base was to be the United Kingdom, and the principal administrative units were not to be moved to the Continent until it was clearly advantageous to do so.

2I. These Administrative Plans were supplemented from time to time by additional Administrative Instructions issued by my Headquarters.

22. The completeness of these administrative plans and the accuracy of forecasting which was used enabled the air forces involved to fulfil all of the commitments laid upon them, and in the midst of their heaviest operations, to move across the Channel without any diminution of their effectiveness. This, I feel, constitutes a major triumph of organisation. Some details of the problems involved and overcome in this planning and administration are given in Part IV of this Despatch.

23. A comprehensive Signal Plan for Operation "Neptune" was also issued by my Headquarters. This plan was implemented with success on the whole. I deal with certain features of Signals Communications in Part IV of this Despatch.

24. To supplement the Overall Air Plan as necessary, Air Staff Policy and Operational Instructions were also issued by my Headquarters. Operational Memoranda and Administrative Memoranda were additionally issued by your Headquarters in cases where two or more of the Services were affected.

Overall Air Plan.

25. In the Overall Air Plan I set out the under-mentioned principal air tasks for the forces under my command and for the allotted effort of the strategical air forces and Royal Air Force Coastal Command. These tasks were decided upon after discussions with yourself and the respective Commanders-in-Chief as to the requirements of the Army and the Navy from the air forces:-

   (*a*) To attain and maintain an air situation whereby the German Air Force was rendered incapable of effective interference with Allied operations.

   (*b*) To provide continuous reconnaissance of the enemy's dispositions and movements.

   (*c*) To disrupt enemy communications and channels of reinforcement and supply.

   (*d*) To support the landing and subsequent advances of the Allied armies.

   (*e*) To deliver offensive strikes against enemy naval forces.

   (*f*) To provide air lift for airborne forces.

26. The co-ordination of the Air Plans with those of the other services was achieved by weekly meetings between the other Commanders-in-Chief and myself, together with our respective Chiefs of Staff and Chief Planners. These meetings, held alternately in the office of the planning centre of each of the three Services, ensured that each service was kept informed of the relative development of planning.

Objects of Preparatory Bombing.

27. I considered that the primary objective of preparatory bombing should be to impose the greatest possible delay in the movement of the enemy reinforcements and supplies, and to this end, the railway bombing plan was designed. The object of this plan was to produce a lasting and general dislocation of the railway system in use by the enemy. By so doing the capacity of the system as a whole would be greatly reduced, and the task of dealing with isolated movement once the battle was joined would be made all the easier. Accordingly, the primary targets planned for attack were the railway centres where the most important servicing and repair facilities of Northern France and the Low Countries were located; the secondary targets were the principal marshalling yards, particularly those which possessed repair facilities. The selection of targets was made difficult in some cases by the necessity of avoiding heavy civilian casualties or damage to historic buildings. Where railway centres were situated in thickly populated areas (as at Le Bourget, for example), alternative centres were chosen in order to isolate them. A further limitation was imposed by the necessity to pinpoint the attacks on these targets; this demanded visual bombing conditions for day attacks and clear weather during moon periods for night attacks. The possibility of unreliable weather, particularly round about D-Day, was one of the major factors which dictated an early commencement of this plan; in fact the weather did seriously hamper its execution. The development of the railway plan and some indication of its success are set out in Part III of this Despatch.

28. Complementary to the railway plan, a further plan was made, covering the destruction of road and rail bridges. This plan which called for the cutting of the Seine bridges below Paris and the bridges over the Loire below Orleans was put into operation at D -30.

29. In the formulation and adoption of these plans to cause the maximum overall interference with enemy movements, it was fully appreciated, that the more successful were our attacks, the more embarrassing it would be to the Allied Armies when they came to move through the same area. This disadvantage though serious, was felt by the planners to be outweighed by the advantage of preventing the enemy from bringing in to the assault area sufficient reinforcements to contain the Allied bridgehead. I have dealt with this subject further in the section dealing with post-assault operations in Part III of this Despatch.

30. Other preparatory bombing plans included attacks on coastal batteries, enemy naval and military targets and the Radar chain. It was necessary to remember when making these plans that the enemy should not be given any indication of the area selected for the assault. The principal effect of this on the preparatory air operations was that at least two attacks were made on each type of target outside of the projected assault area to one attack on a target within that area.

Estimation of G.A.F. Capabilities.

3I. I was confident that the German Air Force would constitute no serious threat to our operations on land, sea or in the air. However, I could not dismiss the possibility that the enemy was conserving his air forces for a maximum effort against the Allied assault forces. A bombing plan was therefore prepared which aimed at driving the G.A.F. fighters on to bases as far from the battle as were the Allied fighter forces, by destroying its bases within I30 miles radius of the assault area. Enemy bomber bases even further inland were also scheduled for attack.

32. Moreover, as I considered it possible that an intense air battle might last for anything up to a week following the launching of the assault, it was necessary to have on hand a strong enough force of fighter aircraft to ensure that the enemy would be completely mastered in any such battle. I refer to the constitution and use of this fighter force in Part III of this Despatch.

"Crossbow" Operations.

33. Throughout the whole of the preliminary and preparatory phases of the operation, I had to take into account the need to maintain a sufficient weight of bombing attacks on "Noball" targets. "Noball" was the code word used to designate the sites being prepared by the enemy for attacks on the United Kingdom with flying bombs and rockets. The operations against these sites carried out under the title of "Crossbow" had begun as early as 5th December, I943, and constituted a considerable diversion of bomber effort. This bombing, while it did not, of itself, succeed in completely eliminating the menace of the flying bomb, was fully justified, in view of the fact that the original scheme had to be abandoned by the Germans. Details of the effort involved and an indication of the results achieved are given in Part III of this Despatch.

34. The diversion of bombing effort on to "Noball" targets, however, was not wholly unprofitable, even if judged from the point of view of "Neptune" alone. The medium and light bomber crews gained invaluable experience in finding and attacking small and well concealed targets and inevitably improved their standard of bombing accuracy. Moreover, much of the flying in these winter and spring months was carried out in very bad weather conditions. Again the crews gained invaluable experience in instrument flying through bad weather. These were all gains that were to stand us in good stead later in the battle.

(b) Operations during the Assault.

35. My plan for the use of air power in direct support of the assault called for the fulfilment of the following principal air tasks:-

(*a*) To protect the cross-channel movement of the assault forces against enemy air attack, and to assist the Allied naval forces to protect the assault craft and shipping from enemy naval forces.

(*b*) To prepare the way for the assault by neutralising the coast and beach defences.

(*c*) To protect the landing beaches and the shipping concentrations from enemy air attack.

(*d*) To dislocate enemy communications and control during the assault.

To accomplish these tasks, detailed plans were produced and a record of the manner in which these plans were put into operation appears in Part III of this Despatch.

(c) Operations Subsequent to D-Day.

36. The planning of air operations during the post-assault phase of the battle was along two lines. The first part included the continuation and expansion of attacks designed to interfere with the movements of enemy supplies and reinforcements, in addition to other detailed plans covering the operations of the heavy bomber forces in close support. These plans were produced at my main headquarters. The second part of post-assault planning covered the changing needs of the ground situation and this day-by-day planning was co-ordinated and controlled through the headquarters of Advanced A.E.A.F.

37. In the foregoing paragraphs I have set out briefly the main principles which guided the planning of air operations before, during and after the assault. A general picture of these air operations as planned is given in the attached map.[2] More detailed descriptions of the individual plans evolved to implement these principles will be found in Part III where such descriptions fit in more logically. In the final part of this Despatch I have included some considerations governing our general planning.

38. I should like to emphasise that my Planning Staff, like my Operations Staff, was Allied in the true sense of the word, and that both the American and British components worked together most successfully under the direction of my Senior Air Staff Officer, Air Vice Marshal H.E.P. Wigglesworth, C.B., C.B.E., D.S.C.

PART III – NARRATIVE OF OPERATIONS.

(a) Preliminary Period.

Air Superiority essential.

39. Air superiority was the principal prerequisite for the successful assault of Europe from the West. The winning of air superiority was therefore the cardinal point of air planning. Air operations to ensure that the requisite degree of air superiority had been gained by D-Day were begun in the preliminary phase and continued during the preparatory phase. On D-Day itself a series of concentrated attacks was made on the G.A.F. airfields in the pre-selected area; but as a result of the earlier operations, I was confident that the necessary degree of air ascendancy had been gained sometime

before D-Day and advised yourself, the Allied Commanders and the Chiefs of Staff to this effect. In the event, the German Air Force was more impotent than I expected.

40. I have set out in the following paragraphs some of the efforts of the strategical bomber forces directed to securing air superiority during the preliminary period. The medium and light bomber forces of the A.E.A.F. were throughout this period engaged in support of the stragetical bomber programme and in meeting the commitment for attacks on flying bomb and rocket sites.

4I. The long-term strategic bombing plan directed against enemy centres of production and assembly of aircraft and aircraft components, principally by the United States Eighth Air Force and also by Royal Air Force Bomber Command, and the United States Fifteenth Air Force operating from the Mediterranean, inflicted crippling blows on the supply and maintenance organisation of the German Air Force. Moreover, the heavy daylight raids of the United States Eighth Air Force into Germany achieved a steady attrition of the German fighter forces.

Attrition of the G.A.F.

42. How crippling these blows were on German aircraft production is illustrated by information obtained from intelligence sources. A comprehensive picture of the effects of direct air attack in terms of enemy single-engine fighter production during the five months from Ist November, I943 to Ist April, I944 can be gained from the estimates below:-[3]

	Planned	*Achieved*
November	1,280	600
December	1,335	600
January	1,415	650
February	1,480	600
March	1,555	500
	7,065	**2,950**

43. The difference between the production planned and achieved totals 4,II5 aircraft, an average loss to the enemy of more than 820 single-engined fighters per month.

44. These figures ignore the heavy losses sustained by German Air Force fighters in air attacks on their airfields and in combat; also the effective attacks on the factories producing twin-engined fighters must be taken into account.

45. Parallel with the attacks on production centres by the strategic air forces, a campaign of day and night intruding against enemy airfields, designed to hamper enemy training schedules as well as to destroy the enemy in the air, was carried out by aircraft of A.E.A.F. with very great success. In addition, many heavy attacks were made in the preliminary period on the enemy's airfields, which achieved considerable destruction of airfield facilities.

46. It became evident during this period (November, I943, to May, I944) that the

High Command of the German Air Force was pursuing a policy of conserving its air forces for the defence of vital targets only. This policy made it extremely difficult to get the G.A.F to fight. Even large scale fighter sweeps failed to produce any serious reaction. However, in the period from I5th November, I943, the date of the formation of A.E.A.F., to the 5th June, I944, the eve of D-Day, the Allied forces accounted for the following enemy aircraft in air combat alone (*Subject to modification in the light of information subsequently received*).

47. This enormous attrition of G.A.F. strength is based on claims of enemy aircraft destroyed in combat alone; no account is taken in these statistics of aircraft destroyed on the ground. Of the figures given above no less than 2,655 enemy aircraft were destroyed by Allied Air Forces operating out of the United Kingdom during what I have termed the preparatory period of the assault, namely Ist April to 5th June, I944. I deal with the planned attacks on the G.A.F. and its bases in France during this preparatory period in para. I29 et seq.

(b) Preparatory Period.

Method of Presentation.

48. Since the war began all attacks against enemy targets have, in some measure, influenced the situation prevailing on the eve of the assault. The commencement of the preparatory phase for this Despatch I have, however, fixed at Ist April, I944, except in so far as detailed co-ordinated plans for attacks on targets of specific importance within the framework of the "Neptune" plan were in operation earlier. In these cases, I have included all the attacks made in accordance with the complete plan.

49. For convenience of presentation, I have dealt with these preparatory operations under the headings set out below. These headings cover the various operations planned and carried out to fulfil the tasks laid on to the air forces (see paragraph 25):-

Dislocation of Enemy Lines of Communication, including Destruction of Bridges.
Neutralisation of Coastal Defences.
Disruption of Enemy Radar Cover and W/T facilities.
Attacks on Military facilities.
Harassing of Coastwise Shipping and Sea Mining.
Attacks on Airfields.
Air Reconnaissance.
Protection of the Assembling Assault Forces.
"Crossbow" Operations.

	Probably Destroyed	Destroyed	Damaged
A.E.A.F.			
Aircraft on offensive operations	711	79	308
Aircraft on defensive operations over the United Kingdom and Channel areas	167	23	39
	878	**I02**	**347**
Guns of Anti-Aircraft Command	73	5	22
Eighth Air Force:			
by Bombers	2,223	696	1,188
by Fighters	1,835	202	705
R.A.F. Bomber Command	201	52	267
R.A.F. Coastal Command	28	3	22
Grand Totals	**5,238**	**1,060**	**2,551**

Strength of A.E.A.F. at Ist April, 1944.

50. Details of the composition of the forces at my disposal at Ist April, I944, are given at Appendix "C".[4] The number of operationally available aircraft on hand at that date in these Commands was as follows:-

Type	Ninth Air Force	Royal Air Force
Medium Bombers	496	70
Light Bombers	96	38
Fighter and Fighter Bombers	607	1,764
Transport Aircraft	865	225
Gliders	782	351
Reconnaissance Aircraft	63	156
Artillery Observation Aircraft	–	164
	2,909	**2,768**

Dislocation of Enemy Lines of Communication.

5I. Next to the winning of air superiority, the dislocation of the enemy's lines of communication was the most important task set the Air Force (see paragraph 27). The basic intention of my plan for attack on the enemy lines of communication was to force the enemy off the railways, initially within an area of I50 miles from the battle front. There were two broad plans for doing this; one was a short term policy which involved attacks on certain rail centres during the period immediately before D-Day; the other was a longer term plan of destroying the potential of the railway system in North-Western Europe.

52. The short term policy involved attacks on I7 specially selected rail focal points, plus an extra 7 points as cover. It was claimed for this plan that if the attacks were made immediately before D-Day, the enemy's reinforcements by rail would be adequately delayed. Further, it would allow the bomber forces to continue attacks on "Pointblank" and other strategic targets until just before D-Day. Complete success

would, of course, have been necessary, with all the 17 primary targets to achieve the desired result; more over, several of the targets chosen were unsuitable for air attack, either by virtue of their location or their nature as bombing targets. Other disadvantages of this plan were that any failure to achieve complete success on the primary targets would have meant that the enemy could direct traffic through such gaps as would be left; the attacks would have to be made at a time when other demands on the available bomber forces were strongest; the successful outcome of a programme covering such a short period would depend entirely upon favourable bombing weather conditions – such conditions could never be guaranteed even in the summer.

53. The longer term plan involved attacks on a large number of repair and maintenance centres designed to reduce the movement potential and the motive power of the railway system, supported by complementary action in cutting railway lines and bridges on the canalized routes nearer D-Day. There were, however, limitations to this longer term plan. It would take longer to implement and would involve a greater diversion of the total effort of the bomber forces. If successful, it would hamper the Allies as effectively as it did the enemy, when the Allies came to move over the same territory. It was, however, a much more certain way of achieving the primary object stated above in paragraph 51, and was less dependent upon a period of good weather near D-Day.

54. In March, 1944, in consultation with the British Chief of Air Staff, Marshal of the Royal Air Force Sir Charles Portal, G.C.B., D.S.O., M.C., the Commanders of the Strategical Air Forces and the representatives of the land forces, you accepted the longer term plan, and the targets selected for attack were allocated to the respective forces (see paragraph 57).

55. Later, the initial plan was amplified and the area selected for attack was greatly expanded. In fact, finally it had little limitation.

56. Attacks by heavy and medium bombers on railway centres were maintained up to and after D-Day. From D - 7 they were supplemented by attacks designed to cut the lines and halt or destroy such traffic as could still be moved. In these tasks, fighter bombers played the major part, although the medium and heavy bombers also cooperated. The principal targets in these attacks were bridges, junctions, cross-overs and tunnels, as well as locomotives and rolling stock. I deal with these attacks in paragraph 74 onwards; but in view of special features involved in the attacks on bridges, I deal with those attacks separately, for the sake of clarity, in paragraph 83 onwards.

57. *Allocation of Targets.* A total of eighty rail targets of primary importance were scheduled for attack by A.E.A.F., Royal Air Force Bomber Command and the United States Eighth Air Force. These targets were finally allocated as follows:-

> A.E.A.F. 18
> R.A.F. Bomber Command 39
> U.S. Eighth Air Force...................................23

58. In addition to these targets, the United States Fifteenth Air Force were allocated

fourteen targets in Southern France and nine targets in Germany. However, this Command did not operate against these targets in Southern France until 25th May, I944 and then only for three days. The targets allocated to them in Germany were not attacked.

59. A number of railway centres not included in the Directive were also lightly attacked, but I have not included these in the general survey of results which follows.

60. By D-Day, of the eighty targets allocated, fifty-one were categorised as being damaged to such an extent that no further attacks were necessary until vital repairs had been effected; twenty-five were categorised as having been very severely damaged, but with certain vital installations still intact, necessitating a further attack; the remaining four were categorised as having received little or no damage, and needing a further attack on first priority.

6I. The proportion of successes in this respect was as follows:-

Force	*Cat "A"*	*Cat "B"*	*Cat "C"*
A.E.A.F.	14	2	2
R.A.F. Bomber Command	22	15	2
U.S. Eighth Air Force	15	8	–

62. In the period of the operation of this rail plan, i.e., 9th February to D-Day, a total of 2I,949 aircraft operated against the eighty selected targets and dropped a total weight of 66,5I7 tons of bombs. The scale of effort was as follows:-

Force	*Sorties*	*Bombs*
A.E.A.F.	8,736	10,125 tons
R.A.F. Bomber Command	8,751	44,744 tons
U.S. Eighth Air Force	4,462	11,648 tons
	21,949	**66,517 tons**

63. In the attacks made by the United States Fifteenth Air Force on 25th May, I944, and the subsequent two days, I,600 sorties were flown against I4 targets and 3,074 tons of bombs were dropped. Of these I4 targets allocated in Southern France, at D-Day five were Category "A", one was Category "B" and eight were Category "C".

64. The first of the really heavy and damaging attacks on rail centres was that made by Royal Air Force Bomber Command on Trappes on the night of 6th-7th March, I944.

65. An immediate interpretation of photographs taken after this attack showed extremely heavy damage throughout the yards, the greatest concentration of craters being in the "Up" reception sidings. I90 direct hits were scored on tracks, as many as three tracks having, in several cases, been disrupted by one bomb. Numerous derailments and much wreckage were caused by 50 bombs which fell among the lines of rolling stock with which the yard was crowded. All the tracks of the main electrified line between Paris and Chartres which passes through this yard were cut, several of the overhead standards having been hit, and at the east end of the yard, at least five direct hits were scored on the constriction of lines. To the northeast of the target, the engine shed was two-thirds destroyed.

66. Of the other early attacks carried out in March and early April, some of the

most successful were those on Paris/La Chappelle, Charleroi/St. Martin, Paris/Juvisy, Laon and Aachen, at each of these centres the locomotive servicing and maintenance facilities were rendered almost, if not completely, useless and great havoc was wrought in the marshalling yards. At Paris/Noisy le Sec, the whole railway complex was almost annihilated. Other damaging attacks in this early period were made on Ottignies, Rouen, Namur, Lens and Tergnier. Nine of these II attacks were carried out by R.A.F. Bomber Command.

67. From the first attacks, the enemy energetically set about endeavouring to make good the damage inflicted, but Trappes, first attacked by Bomber Command on 6th-7th March, I944, was still under repair at the end of April.

68. For the effort involved, the results of the attack on Charleroi/St. Martin on I8th April, I944, are worth citing, but this attack is only typical of many of these blows at the enemy communications. A force of 82 Marauders and 37 Bostons of the United States Ninth Air Force attacked the railway centre between I835 and I905 hours, dropping a total of I76 tons of bombs on the target. Photographic interpretation after this attack showed that the locomotive repair shop and two locomotive depots were very heavily damaged. The marshalling yard was ploughed up and all through traffic stopped. A single through track was later established on the north side of the yard and was completed by 2nd May, I944, I4 days later. A double track through the marshalling yard was re-established by IIth May, I944, but at D-Day (6th June), the marshalling yard was still unserviceable and the repair facilities could not be used.

69. During the last days of April and throughout the month of May, I944, the same high degree of success achieved by the early attacks was maintained. A growing paralysis was being extended over the rail networks of the Region Nord, west of a line Paris – Amiens – Boulogne and South Belgium. In these areas, all the principal routes were, at one time or another, interrupted. Other centres to the east and south of Paris had also been attacked.

70. In the last week of April, Aulnoye, Villeneuve-St. Georges, Acheres, Montzen, St. Ghislain, Arras and Bethune were all attacked. During May, the heaviest attacks were made on Mantes/Gassicourt, Liege, Ghent, Courtrai, Lille, Hasselt, Louvain, Boulogne, Orleans, Tours, Le Mans, Metz, Mulhouse, Rheims, Troyes and Charleroi.

7I. Photographic interpretation continued to show the devastating effect on the centres attacked, and other intelligence sources confirmed this evidence, as well as supplying indications of damage to signals and ancillary services, damage which did not appear in photographs.

72. In order to extend the paralysis inflicted on the regions north and west of Paris, attacks were made in the period immediately before D-Day, on the eastern routes to Paris and the important avoiding routes round the south of that city, and on centres on the Grande Ceinture. Attacks on these centres were considerably restricted by the necessity of avoiding causing heavy civilian casualties or damage to historic buildings. A typical example of this restriction was furnished by the important junction of Le Bourget which, because of the strong probability of bombing causing heavy civilian casualties, was not attacked at all.

73. At D-Day, I believed the primary object of the rail plan had been fully realised. The events which followed confirmed my belief. After the Allied advance, enquiry from the French railway authorities indicated very clearly that pre-D-Day attacks achieved the purpose intended. The Nazi controlled transport system was very badly disorganised. It had therefore, become extremely vulnerable to the attention of the medium and fighter bombers, which, in the periods just before and after the assault, caused great destruction to immobilised rolling stock.

74. *Attacks on Locomotive Power* – Attack on repair depots and facilities was the main method of achieving the desired reduction in traction power. It was accepted that these attacks would, at the same time, damage and destroy locomotives. For example, in one such attack, about five per cent, of the locomotives in the Region Nord were put out of service. In addition, however, it was planned to attack directly trains and locomotives on open lines.

75. I first initiated special large scale fighter sweeps against trains and locomotives in Northern France and Belgium on 2Ist May, I944. On this day, concentrated efforts were made in certain areas in France, with some attention to connections from Germany and Belgium. Fighters of A.E.A.F. and the United States Eighth Air Force swept over railway tracks covering a very wide area and created havoc among locomotives, passenger trains, goods trains and oil wagons.

76. On this day, 2Ist May, 504 Thunderbolts, 233 Spitfires, I6 Typhoons and I0 Tempests of A.E.A.F. operated throughout the day, claiming 67 locomotives destroyed, 9I locomotives damaged and six locomotives stopped. Eleven other locomotives were attacked with unknown results and numerous trains were attacked and damage inflicted on trucks, carriages, oil wagons, etc.

77. On this same day, United States Eighth Air Force Fighter Command sent out I3I Lightnings, I35 Thunderbolts and 287 Mustangs against similar targets in Germany. They claimed 9I locomotives destroyed and I34 locomotives damaged. In addition, one locomotive tender, six goods wagons and three boxcars were destroyed, whilst seven goods wagons, seven trains, three rail cars, four box cars and thirteen trucks were damaged, and sixteen trains set on fire.

78. From 22nd May to D-Day, A.E.A.F. flew I,388 sorties with the primary purpose of attacking locomotives. In this period they claimed I57 locomotives destroyed and 82 damaged, as well as numerous trucks.

79. On 25th May, United States Eighth Air Force Fighter Command flew 608 sorties over France and Belgium, with the result that 4I locomotives, I troop train with approximately 300 men and I9 trucks were destroyed, and 25 locomotives and 50 trucks were damaged. Though outside the "Neptune" area, it is interesting to record that on 29th May, aircraft of Eighth Air Force Fighter Command flew 57I sorties over Eastern Germany and Poland, attacking 24 locomotives, 32 oil tank cars, I6 box cars and 3 freight trains with unobserved results. In addition to these special attacks, aircraft of Eighth Air Force Fighter Command frequently attacked locomotives and trains amongst other ground targets, when returning from escorting heavy bombers.

80. The total effort by fighters against rolling stock from I9th May to D-Day was as under:-

A.E.A.F.	2,201 sorties
U.S. Eighth Air Force	1,731 sorties
	3,932 sorties

8I. With the capacity and flexibility of the enemy rail system destroyed, the enemy armies in the field were denied the freedom of movement necessary to mount decisive counter-attacks. Further, the enemy armies and their supplies were forced on to the roads, thus not only slowing up their movement and making them more vulnerable to air attack, but also by compelling the enemy to use motor transport making him draw more heavily on his precious reserves of oil and rubber. Air attacks on these road movements eventually forced the enemy to move mainly by night.

82. During the assault and post-assault phases, this stranglehold on the enemy rail communications was effectively maintained. Details of the attacks involved and some evidence of the delay produced in the enemy build-up are given in Part III (*c*) of this Despatch.

83. *Destruction of Bridges* – As I have already explained, complementary to the plan to destroy, by air attack, the enemy's rail motive power, I planned also to endeavour to destroy all the principal rail and road bridges leading into the assault area. If these were destroyed, not only would the enemy's rate of build-up in that area be further checked and his flow of reinforcements and supplies be further impeded, but also his ability to escape rapidly from the assault area in the event of his being forced to retreat would be very seriously impaired. The implications of the attacks on bridges were, therefore, somewhat wider than those of the other attacks on his communications system. In conjunction with these other attacks, the attacks on bridges were designed to seal off the assault area and so force the enemy to stand and fight, and since he could not easily retreat, any defeat would be decisive.

84. A bridge is, by nature of its size, very difficult to hit and, by nature of its construction, even more difficult to destroy completely. Calculation suggested that approximately 600 tons of bombs per bridge would be needed if the task were entrusted to heavy bombers. In fact, it was found that an average of 640 tons of bombs per bridge was needed. What was not at first realised was how effectively, and relatively cheaply, the task could be carried out by fighter bombers. It was learnt from the attacks on bridges by the aircraft of A.E.A.F. that a bridge could be destroyed for the expenditure of approximately I00 sorties, that is between I00 and 200 tons of bombs.

85. In order not to betray a special interest in the "Neptune" area, attention was paid in the preparatory phase principally to the bridges over the Seine, with some others over the Oise, Meuse and the Albert Canal, leaving to the assault phase the task of attacking bridges south of Paris to Orleans and west along the Loire.

86. On 2Ist April, I944, the first of a series of attacks against bridges was made by Typhoons. Subsequent attacks were carried out by formations of fighter bombers

which included Thunderbolts, Typhoons and Spitfires and by the medium bombers of the United States Ninth Air Force. The early operations were of an experimental nature, the intention being to explore the possibilities of attacks by fighter bombers and medium bombers against this type of target. The success of the early operations by fighter bombers surpassed expectations. It is probable that in one or two early attacks, a lucky hit exploded the demolition charges that had been set in place by the Germans and in such cases, the destruction caused was out of all proportion to the effort expended. Nevertheless, proof was speedily available that fighter bombers could carry out the task of destroying bridges effectively and relatively cheaply.

87. As D-Day approached, so the intensity of the attacks increased, until a crescendo of effort was achieved over a period of about 10 days prior to D-Day. These attacks were carried out, in the main, by fighter bombers and medium bombers of the United States Ninth Air Force, although Royal Air Force Second Tactical Air Force and the heavy bombers and fighter bombers of the United States Eighth Air Force also provided a contribution to the success of the plan. The marked success of the low level fighter bomber attacks of the Ninth Air Force, as well as the results obtained by the medium bombers is a tribute to the high standard of bombing accuracy developed by this force during the preparatory period. These attacks were often met by heavy anti-aircraft fire, and the resultant losses were not light.

88. The outcome of these attacks was that, on D-Day, twelve railway bridges and the same number of road bridges over the River Seine were rendered impassable. In addition, three railway bridges at Liege and others at Hasselt, Herenthals, Namur, Conflans (Pointe Eifel), Valenciennes, Hirson, Konz-Karthaus and Tours, as well as the important highway bridge at Saumur, were also unserviceable.

89. After D-Day, the assault on bridges of tactical and strategical importance to the enemy was maintained and the results are confirmed in prisoner of war reports of the disruption and delay in the movement of troops and equipment which the enemy experienced. Details of these attacks are given in Part III (*d*) of this Despatch.

90. The statistical summary below is necessarily incomplete as, in many cases, road and rail bridges were attacked as targets of opportunity by fighter bombers of A.E.A.F. and the Eighth Air Force while engaged on offensive patrols against miscellaneous targets. In these instances, therefore, no separate appreciation of attacks on bridges, is possible.

91. *Attacks on Road and Rail Bridges for period 21st April-6th June.*

Force	Attacks	Sorties	Bombs
	(a) Rail		
A.E.A.F.	78	3,897	2,784 tons
			904 x 60-lb. R.Ps[5]
U.S. Eighth Air Force	11	201	227.5 tons
	(b) Road		
A.E.A.F.	28	987	1,210 tons
			495 x 60-lb. R.Ps
U.S. Eighth Air Force	1	24	24 tons

92. There can be no doubt that the enemy's transport difficulties after D-Day were the result of the cumulative and combined effects of all the attacks levelled against his communications system. The attacks on nodal points in the railway system, the complementary attacks on bridges and the line-cutting by fighter bombers, all contributed to the restriction placed upon enemy movements.

Neutralisation of Coastal Defences

93. I now come to air operations directed to the support of the landing (see paragraph 25). These operations had to be begun well in advance of D-Day. It was essential, as far as possible, to destroy the enemy's capacity to prevent Allied shipping from approaching the assault area and to blind him to that approach. I deal below, therefore, with air operations during this preparatory period directed to the neutralisation of the enemy's coastal defences and the disruption of his Radar cover.

94. There were forty-nine known coastal batteries capable of firing on shipping approaching the assault area. Included in this number were some batteries still under construction. In the conditions that would obtain at the time of the assault, it would clearly be impossible for the naval forces successfully to engage all the coastal batteries. They, therefore, had to be dealt with before the landing and the air forces undertook this task at the request of the Naval and Army Commanders. I did not consider that aerial attacks against batteries whose casemates were completed were likely to be very effective. Fortunately those batteries in the Cherbourg area were the last to be casemated, and it was possible therefore, to attack many of them while they were still incomplete.

95. To avoid showing particular interest in the assault area, it was planned to attack batteries outside the assault area ranging as far north as Ostend, in the proportion of two outside to one within the area.

96. Interpretation reports revealed that, in a great many instances, the bombing was more successful than I at first expected; by D-Day, the majority of the coastal batteries within the area had been subjected to damaging attack.

97. *Attacks on Coastal Batteries for period 10th April 5th June.*

(a) Inside Assault Area		
Force	**Sorties**	**Bombs**
A.E.A.F.	*1,755*	*2,886.5 tons*
		495 x 60-lb. R.Ps.
U.S. Eighth Air Force	*184*	*579.0 tons*
R.A.F. Bomber Command	*556*	*2,438.5 tons*
	2,495	*5,904 tons*
		495 x 60-lb. R.Ps.
(b) Outside Assault Area		
Force	**Sorties**	**Bombs**
A.E.A.F.	*3,244*	*5,846 tons*
U.S. Eighth Air Force	*1,527*	*4,559 tons*
R.A.F. Bomber Command	*1,499*	*6,785 tons*
	6,270	***17,190 tons***

Total for the period 10th April to 5th June, 1944 – 8,765 sorties, 23,094 tons of bombs and 495 x 60-lb. R.Ps.

98. Of these attacks, one of the most outstanding was that carried out by 64 Lancasters of R.A.F. Bomber Command, with 7 Mosquitoes acting as a Pathfinder Force. During this raid, on the night of 28th-29th May, 356 tons of H.E. bombs were dropped on the coastal battery at St. Martin de Varreville, with excellent results. These results, reported by A.P.I.S. Medmenham, after a photographic reconnaissance sortie made on 29th May, were confirmed by a captured German report made by the troop commander of the battery. The two reports are given below for comparison.

Photographic Reconnaissance Report.

A heavy concentration of craters is seen in the target area with excellent results.
Damage to Casemates:

No. I. Five very near misses, all within 45 feet. Casemate walls damaged.
No. 2. Damaged by at least five near misses.
No. 3. Destroyed and no longer identifiable; six near misses.
No. 4. Excavation undamaged.

Damage to Command Post:

Demolished by a direct hit and five near misses or probable hits.

Damage to Accommodation:

Personnel shelters in rear of each emplacement all indistinguishable amidst the craters.

Captured German Report.

The position is covered with craters ....

Several direct hits with very heavy bombs were made on No. 3 shelter (casemate) which apparently burst open and then collapsed.......The rest of the shelters remain undamaged.

......the iron equipment hut which contained signals apparatus, the armoury, the gas chamber and artillery instruments received a direct hit, and only a few twisted iron girders remain.

......the men's canteen received several direct hits and was completely destroyed. The messing huts, containing the battery dining room, the kitchen and clerks' office, were completely destroyed by near misses. A concrete-built hot shower bath was completely destroyed by a direct hit; as well as the nearby joiner's shop.

99. Effective attacks were also carried out by aircraft of R.A.F. Bomber Command against the six-gun battery at Morsalines, and by Marauders of the United States Ninth Air Force on the batteries at Houlgate, Ouistreham and Point de Hoe.

I00. Out of forty sites allotted to A.E.A.F., thirty-seven were attacked, sixteen out of eighteen in the assault area and twenty-one out of twenty-two outside. Of these, nine in the area and fourteen outside received hits on one or more emplacements. Forty-eight sites were allotted to R.A.F. Bomber Command, fourteen of which were outside. Hits on essential elements were secured on five batteries in the area and nine outside. Of the fifty-two targets allotted to the United States Eighth Air Force, thirty-two of which were in the assault area, only six sites in the area and sixteen outside were attacked. Some of the batteries were allotted to two commands.

I0I. In addition to the targets listed in the plan, many other coastal defence targets in and out of the area were attacked as targets of opportunity.

I02. During the hours of darkness preceding the actual assault, a tremendous air bombardment was directed on to the batteries which could not be destroyed within the assault area, aimed at neutralising them during the critical assault period. This the attacks succeeded in doing. Details of the effort employed are given in Part III (*c*) of this Despatch.

Disruption of Enemy Radar Cover and W/T Facilities.

I03. The enemy Radar cover on the Western Front was complete from Norway to the Spanish border. This cover was obtained by a chain of coastal stations, each composed of a number of installations. The density of these stations was such that there was a major site, containing an average of three pieces of equipment, every ten miles between Ostend and Cherbourg. This coastal chain was backed by a somewhat less dense inland system and by numerous mobile installations. The attached map[6] shows the location of the principal enemy Radar sites and the coverage of this Radar Chain.

I04. The scale and variety of equipment in this Radar organisation was such that completely to destroy the system by air attack alone would have been a formidable proposition. This, however, was not necessary – the destruction of certain vital Radars and the comprehensive jamming of others could so gravely interfere with the operation of the system as almost to make it useless. I therefore decided to attack Radar stations between Ostend and the Channel Islands in accordance with the following principles:-

(*a*) Radar installations which could not be jammed electronically, or were difficult to jam, should be destroyed:

(*b*) Radar installations capable of giving good readings on ships and of controlling coastal guns should be destroyed:

(*c*) Radar installations likely to assist the enemy in inflicting casualties to airborne forces should be destroyed:

(*d*) Two targets outside the assault area were to be attacked for every one attacked in the area.

The attacks had a dual purpose. They aided both current air operations and naval operations in the Channel, and they prepared for the assault by blinding the enemy.

105. On 10th May, 1944, a series of attacks was begun against the long range aircraft reporting stations, and on 18th May, on the installations used for night fighter control and the control of coastal guns. On 25th May, 42 sites were scheduled for attack. These sites included 106 installations; at D - 3, fourteen of these sites were confirmed destroyed.

106. To conserve effort, I then decided, three days before D-Day, to restrict attacks to the twelve most important sites; six were chosen by the naval authorities and six by the air authorities. These twelve sites, containing thirty-nine installations, were all attacked in the three days prior to D-Day.

107. Up to D-Day, 1,668 sorties were flown by aircraft of A.E.A.F. in attacks on Radar installations. Typhoons in low level attacks flew 694 sorties and fired 4,517 x 60-lb. R.Ps. Typhoons and Spitfires made 759 dive-bombing sorties, dropping 1,258 x 500-lb. bombs and light and medium bombers dropped 217 tons of bombs. In addition, the sites and equipment were attacked with many thousands of rounds of cannon and machine-gun fire.

108. These Radar targets were very heavily defended by flak and low level attacks upon them demanded great skill and daring. Pilots of the R.A.F. Second Tactical Air Force were mainly employed and losses among senior and more experienced pilots were heavy. There is no doubt, however, that these attacks saved the lives of countless soldiers, sailors and airmen on D-Day. The following details of some of the successful attacks made during the last three days before the assault, show the outstanding results obtained by Typhoon and Spitfire pilots in low level attacks pressed home to very close range.

(*a*) *Cap de la Hague/Jobourg.* This site was attacked by rocket firing Typhoons of 174, 175 and 245 Squadrons, Second Tactical Air Force, on 5th June, and 200 x 60-lb.R.Ps. were fired. The "Hoarding", an installation used for long range aircraft reporting, was destroyed. Three of the attacking aircraft were destroyed by flak.

(*b*) *Dieppe/Caudecote.* This site was attacked by 18 R.P. Typhoons of 198 and 609 Squadrons, Second Tactical Air Force, on 2nd June. 104 x 60-lb. R.Ps. were fired, with the result that the "Hoarding" was destroyed and the "Freya" and "Wuerzburg" installations, used for medium range aircraft reporting, night fighter control and control of coastal guns, were damaged. One of the Typhoons was destroyed by flak.

(*c*) *Cap d'Antifer.* This station was attacked several times. On 4th June, 23 Spitfires of 441, 442 and 443 Squadrons, Second Tactical Air Force, dive-bombed with 23 x 500-lb. M.C. instantaneous bombs; nine direct hits were scored. The "Chimney" and one "Giant Wuerzburg" were destroyed, and other installations damaged.

109. In addition to the attacks on the enemy Radar stations, attacks were also made on the most important of his navigational beam stations and on certain special W/T stations.

II0. *Navigational Stations.* There were two enemy radio navigational stations important to the assault area, one at Sortosville, south of Cherbourg, and the other at Lanmeur, near Morlaix. Both of these stations were attacked, the first target being destroyed and the second rendered unserviceable, at least temporarily.

III. *W/T Stations.* Four W/T stations of the highest importance were subjected to attack by R.A.F. Bomber Command. These attacks were triumphs of precision bombing and completely achieved their object. Details of these attacks are given below:-

(a) *Boulogne/Mt. Couple.* This large installation contained about 60 transmitters. The first attack was unsuccessful, but two nights later, 3Ist May/Ist June, in an attack by I05 heavy bombers dropping 530 tons of bombs, at least 70 heavy bombs were placed on the target, which is some 300 yards long and I50 yards wide. Only a negligible fraction of the transmitters on this site survived the attacks, a maximum of three being subsequently identified in operation.

(b) *Beaumont Hague/Au Feure.* This installation was attacked on the night of 3IstMay/Ist June by I2I aircraft; 498 tons of bombs were dropped and good results were obtained. The main concentration of bombs fell just outside the target area, but a number scored direct hits. The station was rendered completely unserviceable.

(c) *Dieppe/Bernaval le Grand.* The attack on this station on the night of 2nd/3rd June was completely successful. I04 aircraft dropped 607 tons of bombs. The majority of the eight or nine blast-wall protected buildings received direct hits, and the remainder suffered so many near misses that their subsequent operational value was negligible. In addition, the aerial masts were all demolished, and the two dispersed sites were also hit.

(d) *Cherbourg/Urville-Hague.* This station is now known to have been the headquarters of the German Signals Intelligence Service in North-Western France. The attack on this important W/T centre was made on 3/4th June by 99 aircraft dropping 570 tons of bombs. The results were remarkable, the centre of a very neat bomb pattern coinciding almost exactly with the centre of the target area. The photographic interpretation report may be quoted:

"The station is completely useless. The site itself is rendered unsuitable for rebuilding the installation, without much effort being expended in levelling and filling in the craters."

II2. The success of this last attack on the Headquarters of the German Air Force Signals Intelligence must have been a major catastrophe for the enemy, and it may well be that it was an important contributory factor to the lack of enemy air reaction to the assault.

II3. *Radio Counter-Measures.* On the night of 5/6th June in the opening phase of the assault, counter-measures against such installations as were still active were put into operation. These counter-measures covered five separate and distinct tasks:-

(*a*) a combined naval/air diversion against Cap d'Antifer:

(*b*) a combined naval/air diversion against Boulogne:

(*c*) a jamming barrage to cover the airborne forces:

(*d*) a V.H.F. jamming support for the first three counter-measures:

(*e*) feints for the airborne forces.

These various components of the counter-measure plan were inter-dependent and the results can, therefore, best be summarised by giving an indication of the enemy's reactions.

II4. The most important fact concerning this reaction was that the enemy appeared to mistake the diversion towards Cap d'Antifer as a genuine threat; at all events, the enemy opened up, both with searchlights and guns on the imaginary convoy. Further, the V.H.F. jamming support which was flown by a formation of aircraft operating in the Somme area apparently led the enemy to believe that these aircraft were the spearhead of a major bomber force, as he reacted with twenty-four night fighters, which were active approximately three hours, hunting the "ghost" bomber stream.

II5. The other counter-measures all fulfilled their purpose and it can be stated that the application of radio counter-measures immediately preceding the assault proved to be extraordinarily successful. Only three out of the total number of I05 aircraft employed on these operations were lost, and the crew of one of these aircraft was saved.

II6. While it is not possible to state with certainty that the enemy was completely unaware of the cross-Channel movement of the assault forces, the success of the plan to disrupt his Radar cover and W/T facilities both by attacks and by the application of counter-measures, can be judged on the results obtained. In the vital period between 0I00 and 0400 hours on 6th June, when the assault Armada was nearing the beaches, only nine enemy Radar installations were in operation, and during the whole night, the number of stations active in the "Neptune" area was only I8 out of a normal 92. No station between Le Havre and Barfleur was heard operating. Apart from the abortive reaction mentioned in paragraph II4, no enemy air attacks were made till approximately I500 hours on D-Day, and this despite the presence of more than 2,000 ships and landing craft in the assault area, and despite the fact that very large airborne forces had, of necessity, been routed down the west coast of the Cherbourg Peninsula right over the previously excellent Radar cover of the Cherbourg area and the Channel Islands.

II7. These results may be summarised as follows: the enemy did not obtain the early warning of our approach that his Radar coverage should have made possible; there is every reason to suppose that Radar controlled gunfire was interfered with; no fighter aircraft hindered our airborne operations; the enemy was confused and his troop movements were delayed.

II8. Prior to the launching of Operation "Neptune" each service had almost complete freedom to use radio counter-measures, as desired. To eliminate any clash of interests when very large forces would be employed in confined areas, an inter-Service staff was set up at my Headquarters. The primary concern being to get the Armada safely across the Channel, it was agreed that for the 30-hour period immediately prior to the moment of assault, control should be vested in the Allied Naval Commander-in-Chief; subsequently, control of radio counter-measures became my responsibility. The advisory staff with representatives of the three Services, assisted both the Allied Naval Commander-in-Chief and myself.

Attacks on Military Facilities.

II9. As well as preparing the way for the assault forces by attacking the enemy's coastal defences and Radar system, it was planned to prepare the way further for the landing by reducing the enemy military potential, both in the assault and rear areas. Certain ammunition and fuel dumps, military camps and headquarters were considered suitable targets for attack, in order to fulfil this purpose.

I20. In the period Ist May to 5th June, I944, the following effort was made on these targets.

Force	Sorties	R.Ps. Fired	Bombs dropped
A.E.A.F.	423	282 x 60-lb.	I52 tons
R.A.F. Bomber Command	I,139	–	5,218 tons
	1,562	282 x 60-lb.	5,370 tons

I2I. The following details of some of these attacks indicate the very great damage done to the enemy supply dumps, and the attacks must also have had considerable moral effect on enemy personnel in addition to the actual casualties inflicted.

I22. On the night of 3rd/4th May, R.A.F. Bomber Command attacked in force the tank depot at Mailly-le-Camp. I,924 tons of bombs were dropped and assessment photographs show the whole target to have been severely damaged. In the mechanical transport section and barracks, 34 out of 47 buildings were totally destroyed. Even more remarkable results were obtained by an attack on an ammunition dump at Chateaudun carried out on the same night. Eight Mosquitoes of R.A.F. Bomber Command attacked with approximately I3 tons of bombs. The bombs were dropped very accurately and caused sympathetic detonation throughout the dump. In the resulting explosion, the entire western wing of the depot, containing 90 buildings, was completely destroyed.

I23. The Bourg Leopold military camp in Belgium was heavily attacked on two occasions. On IIth/I2th May, aircraft of R.A.F. Bomber Command dropped 585 tons of bombs on this depot. On the night of 27th/28th May, a force of 324 aircraft, also from that Command, dropped I,348 tons of bombs, and photographic reconnaissance revealed very heavy damage throughout the whole area of the camp. Six large buildings and at least I50 personnel huts received direct hits.

I24. Smaller in scale, but very effective, were the attacks made by A.E.A.F. aircraft on other targets of this type. On 2nd June, a force of 50 Thunderbolts of the United States Ninth Air Force attacked a fuel dump at Domfront. 54 x 500-lb incendiaries and 63 x I,000-lb. G.P. bombs were dropped and severe damage was caused to this dump.

Harassing of Coastwise Shipping and Sea Mining.

I25. As a result of the successful attacks on the overland communications of the enemy, his coastal shipping became increasingly important. The task of dealing with this shipping was very largely the work of R.A.F. Coastal Command, but Typhoons of A.E.A.F. also operated on occasions in an anti-shipping role under the operational control of Coastal Command, and Spitfires of A.E.A.F. provided when needed, fighter escort to the strike aircraft of Coastal Command. The sea mining programme was carried out by R.A.F. Bomber Command in direct consultation with the British Admiralty.

I26. During the period Ist April to 5th June, I944, R.A.F. Coastal Command flew 4,340 sorties on the anti-shipping and anti-U-Boat patrols in the Bay of Biscay, along the Dutch Coast and in the Channel. During these sorties, I03 attacks were made on shipping and 22 on U-Boats.

I27. The minelaying had as its objectives not only the interruption of enemy coastal shipping, but also in the closing stages of preparation for the assault, the laying of minebelts, to afford protection to the Allied assault and naval bombardment forces from attacks by E and R boats, especially those operating from Le Havre and Cherbourg.

I28. In the period Ist April to 5th June, R.A.F. Bomber Command flew 990 sorties and laid 3,099 mines in the areas east of Texel and along the Dutch, Belgian and French coasts. Other mines were also sown in German home waters, including many in the Baltic Sea.

Attacks on Airfields.

I29. I have already dealt (see paragraphs 42 to 47) with the preliminary operations designed to wear down the G.A.F. and render it powerless seriously to interfere with the assault. As D-Day approached however, it became necessary to ensure that our measure of air superiority was fully adequate to our needs. Plans had accordingly been made for direct attacks upon the enemy air force, particularly in France and the Low Countries. The effect of these plans was to deny the German Air Force the advantage of disposition which its fighter squadrons would otherwise enjoy as compared with our own in the initial stages of the assault. It was, therefore, necessary to neutralise a considerable number of airfields within a radius of I50 miles of Caen. The primary object of these attacks was to destroy the aircraft repair, maintenance and servicing facilities and thereby cause the maximum interference with the operational ability of the German Air Force.

I30. I planned that these attacks should start at least three weeks before D-Day, and they actually began on IIth May, I944. It was necessary to bear in mind in the planning of these attacks that no indication should be given as to the selected area for the Allied landings.

I3I. *Allocation of Targets* – Forty main operational airfields were selected for attack. Twelve were assigned to R.A.F. Bomber Command and the remaining twenty-eight to A.E.A.F. and the United States Eighth Air Force.

I32. Fifty-nine other operational bomber bases with important facilities located in France, Belgium, Holland and Western Germany within range of the assault area and ports of embarkation in the United Kingdom were also selected for attack, as opportunity permitted, by aircraft of the United States Eighth and Fifteenth Air Forces, the latter based in the Mediterranean area.

I33. From IIth May, I944 to D-Day, thirty-four of the most important airfields were attacked by 3,9I5 aircraft dropping 6,7I7 tons of bombs with the result that four airfields were placed in Category "A" and fifteen in Category "B". Twelve airfields of the second list were attacked by the Eighth Air Force with very satisfactory results.

I34. The following categories of airfield damage were used:-

Category "A" – major installations completely destroyed; no further attacks needed.

Category "B" – major installations severely damaged; further attacks warranted.

Category "C" – minor damage; further attacks required.

I35. *Statistical Summary of Attacks on Airfields during the period IIth May to D-Day.*

Force	Attacks	Sorties	Bombs
A.E.A.F.			
Ninth Air Force	*56*	*2,550*	*3,197 tons*
Second T.A.F.	*12*	*312*	*487 tons*
R.A.F. Bomber Command	*6*	*119*	*395 tons*
U.S. Eighth Air Force	*17*	*934*	*2,638 tons*
	91	*3,915*	*6,717 tons*

I36. These attacks on enemy airfields accomplished the desired object of placing the enemy under the same handicap as the Allied fighters by forcing them to operate from airfields a long way from the assault area. They were also largely responsible for the lack of enemy air interference with our landings and undoubtedly contributed much to the ineffectiveness of the German Air Force at the really critical times.

Photographic Reconnaissance.

I37. The photographic reconnaissance units of the Allied air forces were the first to begin active and direct preparation for the invasion of Europe from the West. For more than a year, much vital information was accumulated which contributed very greatly to the ultimate success of the assault. The variety, complexity and moreover, the detailed accuracy of the information gathered and assiduously collated was of great importance in the preparatory phase of the operation.

I38. Each particular service had its own requirements and individual problems which only photographic reconnaissance could hope to solve. Then again, within each service, specialised sections relied to a great extent for their information on these sources, e.g. as early as possible after each major bombing attack, damage assessment sorties were flown.

139. Photographic coverage of the entire coastline from Holland to the Spanish frontier was obtained to gather full details of the coastal defences. Verticals and obliques were taken of beach gradients, beach obstacles, coastal defences and batteries. Full photographic coverage from Granville to Flushing, both in obliques and verticals, was obtained. This very large coverage also served to hide our special interest in the selected assault beaches.

140. Obliques were taken at wave top height, three to four miles out from the coast, in order to provide the assault coxswains with a landing craft view of the particular area to be assaulted or likely to be their allotted landing spots. Then obliques were flown 1,500 yards from the coast at zero feet, to provide platoon assault commanders with recognition landing points. Further obliques were taken, again at 1,500 yards from the shore, but at 2,000 feet to provide, for those who were planning the infantry assault, views of the immediate hinterland.

141. Inland strips were photographed behind the assault areas, looking southwards, so that infantry commanders could pinpoint themselves after they had advanced. Again, it was necessary to photograph hidden land behind assault areas, so that the infantry commanders would know the type of terrain behind such obstructions as hills or woods.

142. Bridges over rivers were photographed and special attention was paid to the river banks to enable the engineers to plan the type of construction necessary to supply temporary bridges in the event of the enemy blowing up the regular bridges.

143. The prospective airfield sites were selected by the engineers after they had studied the vast quantity of reconnaissance photographs available. The success of the Airfield Construction Units, some details of which are given in Part IV of this Despatch, is testimony to the value of this reconnaissance.

144. It was also necessary to cover all the likely dropping areas for the use of the airborne divisions, and to pay special attention to each area for concealed traps such as spikes, etc. These traps were observed on photographs of many sites chosen and it was necessary to make other plans accordingly.

145. Flooding areas, too, throughout Holland, Belgium and France were all photographed at different periods, thus ensuring to the Army Commander full knowledge of these defences in planning the deployment of his forces. The extent to which army commanders depended upon photographic reconnaissance may be gauged by the volume of cover they received. In the two weeks prior to D-Day, one R.A.F. Mobile Field Photographic Section alone made for Army requirements more than 120,000 prints.

146. Continued photographic reconnaissance was also flown covering enemy communication centres, petrol, oil and lubricant dumps, headquarters, inland defences and military concentrations. These reconnaissances provided invaluable information as to the enemy order of battle and his capabilities.

147. Many small scale sorties were flown for Combined Operations, enabling them to make landings at selected spots, long before the real offensive was launched and to bring back vital information.

148. Another important task undertaken was the photographing of Allied landing craft, equipment and stores in the United Kingdom, to facilitate experiments with the type of camouflage most likely to be effective.

149. The demands of all three services for photographic cover were very varied and so great in number that it was necessary to set up a controlling body to deal with them. Accordingly, the Central Reconnaissance Committee was established at your headquarters. This inter-service committee received requests for photographic cover from all services and allocated the task to the most suitable reconnaissance force. One of the most important functions of this Committee was to watch the security aspect of the reconnaissance effort and by ensuring that this effort was judiciously distributed, conceal from the enemy our special interest in the assault area.

150. The bulk of this invaluable reconnaissance effort was flown by aircraft of A.E.A.F. which, in the period Ist April to 5th June flew no less than 3,2I5 photographic reconnaissance sorties. Aircraft of other commands, however, including I06 Group, R.A.F. Coastal Command and United States Eighth Air Force, operating under the control of R.A.F. Station, Benson, also contributed notably to this work, flying a total of I,5I9 sorties during the same period. The excellent co-operation between British and American reconnaissance units in fact enabled the needs of all services to be fully met by D-Day.

15I. If we had had to rely, however, entirely on orthodox high altitude reconnaissance aircraft for this work, not more than a small proportion of these needs could have been met. The weather in Western Europe, never very suitable for high altitude photography, was particularly bad in the early part of the year. There was an urgent need for a medium/low altitude photographic reconnaissance aircraft to supplement high altitude reconnaissance. It was decided therefore, to convert some Mustang fighters into tactical and strategical medium/low altitude reconnaissance aircraft. They were equipped with oblique cameras, were armed to protect themselves and were fast enough to outpace most German fighters.

I52. Low altitude reconnaissance, however, whether visual or photographic was at all times a hazardous business in view of the risk of being jumped by higher flying enemy fighters. Nonetheless, early results achieved by Mustangs were very encouraging and eventually a number of reconnaissance squadrons were partly re-equipped with converted Mustangs to supplement their high altitude aircraft. Their work proved invaluable and the development of this aircraft for photographic reconnaissance work has been one of the outstanding lessons of the air war.

Protection of the Assembling of the Assault Forces.

I53. I stated in paragraph 25 that one of the main tasks of the air forces was to support the landing of the Allied armies in Europe. As a corollary, the air force was required to protect the assembling of the assault forces. A.E.A.F. was directly charged with this responsibility.

I54. More than 2,000 ships and landing craft were used to lift the initial assault forces and other equipment, and they were supported by task forces of over I00 warships including battleships and more than 200 escorts and other naval vessels. In all, over 6,000 ships and landing-craft were employed in the first week.

155. The assembly, preparation and loading of these ships and other special beach installations necessitated the concentration of enormous forces in the ports and harbours of the south coast of England, in the Bristol Channel and in the Thames Estuary, over long periods, with especially heavy concentrations in the final six weeks. Moreover, large scale embarkation had to be practised to ensure that speed and flexibility could be attained. To provide this practice, a series of exercises were staged in which the forces to be employed were brought into the concentration areas and in some cases, embarked and sailed to practice assault beaches on the south coast of England.

156. *Enemy Action against Assault Forces* – It was estimated by my Planning Staff that the German Air Force would have available 850 aircraft, including 450 long range bombers to use against the Allied assault operation. I anticipated that these bomber forces would be used against shipping in ports and in transit, both in bombing attacks and in sea mining. It was further estimated that this force would be capable of the following scale of effort over a period of three weeks during the assembling and loading periods:-

> Sorties.
> *Sustained per night* *25*
> *Intensive per night for 2-3 nights per week* *50-75*
> *Maximum in any one night* *100-150*

157. In fact, the enemy activity did not reach this maximum scale of effort. There were three periods of activity in the six weeks prior to 6th June, and they involved only 377 bombing sorties.

158. On 25th-26th April, approximately 40 aircraft operated against Portsmouth and Havant. On 26-27th April, approximately 80 aircraft again attacked Portsmouth and a triangular area between the Needles, Basingstoke and Worthing. On 29-30th April, approximately 35 aircraft operated over and off Plymouth.

159. The second phase of these attacks took place on the nights 14-15th and 15-16th May, when approximately 100 and 80 aircraft respectively operated against Southampton and along the coast, and against Weymouth.

160. The third phase was during 28-29th, 29-30th and 30-31st May; on the first of these nights, approximately 35 aircraft attacked from Dartmouth to Start Point and on the next two nights small forces operated indiscriminately.

161. The night fighter forces of the Air Defence of Great Britain were ready to deal with this activity. Of the total of 377 enemy sorties, night fighters claimed 22 destroyed, 6 probably destroyed and 5 damaged, while a further 2 were destroyed by anti-aircraft fire.

162. A valuable contribution to the defence of the assembly areas for the assault forces was made by balloons and anti-aircraft guns. Units were provided for this purpose by R.A.F. Balloon Command, the R.A.F. Regiment, Anti-Aircraft Command and certain Anti-Aircraft artillery formations of the United States forces. Operational

control of these units was in general exercised on my behalf by the Air Marshal Commanding, Air Defence of Great Britain.

163. The work of these units not only in protecting the assembly, but later, in defence against attacks by Flying Bombs, was of exceptional value to the launching and maintenance of the assault. I deal with certain other features of this work later in this Despatch.

164. It was also of the utmost importance to deny to the enemy, air reconnaissance of Southern England. Special precautions had to be taken to this end.

165. Mastery of the air over the Channel, wrested from the enemy in earlier years by aircraft of R.A.F. Fighter Command (later Air Defence of Great Britain), had done much to ensure this end already. Daylight operations of enemy aircraft overland were almost unheard of and it was appreciated that only dire necessity would prompt the enemy to expose his aircraft and pilots to the heavy risk they would run in attempting to spy out our preparations. None the less, the enemy had now so much at stake that a great effort on his part was to be expected. To deal with possible enemy reconnaissance efforts, therefore, I directed that standing high and low level fighter patrols should be maintained by aircraft of Air Defence of Great Britain during daylight hours over certain coastal belts.

166. In the six weeks immediately prior to D-Day, however, the enemy flew only 125 reconnaissance sorties in the Channel area and 4 sorties over the Thames Estuary and the east coast. Very few of these sorties approached land, most of them being fleeting appearances in mid-Channel. Our fighters rarely got even a glimpse of these enemy aircraft, which could have seen very little and could only have taken back, therefore, information of very small value; but as an extra deterrent, standing patrols were maintained as far out as 40-50 miles south of the Isle of Wight and intruder aircraft were directed to the enemy airfields in the Dinard area, from which it was believed such enemy reconnaissance aircraft as appeared were operating. In the result, the enemy appears to have learnt very little.

167. These defensive measures, coupled with the others to which I have already referred, achieved for the assault a complete tactical surprise on D-Day and did much to ensure the safety of the cross-Channel movement of the assault forces. The weather factor relating to this aspect of the operations is considered in paras. 405 and 406.

168. On many days Allied air forces flew more photographic reconnaissance sorties in one day than the enemy flew in the whole of the vital period of six weeks prior to D-Day. In view of the fact that the enemy was aware, in general terms, of our intention to invade the Continent the small scale of his air reconnaissance effort is, to say the least, extraordinary.

"Crossbow" Operations.

169. It became known early in 1943 that the enemy was preparing an attack on the United Kingdom with flying bombs and rockets launched from the French coast. Much experimental work on these projectiles had been done in the Baltic Sea area, and it was believed that the enemy would shortly be in a position to begin constructing sites, from which the projectiles could be launched. Construction began chiefly in the Pas de Calais and the Cherbourg areas during the autumn of 1943.

170. Considerable research into the nature of these novel weapons was carried out by Operational Research Sections and by a special Committee set up in the Air Ministry, and it was concluded that they represented a potentially serious menace, both to the United Kingdom and to the preparation and build-up of forces for the projected Operation "Neptune". Accordingly, it became necessary to divert part of the available air effort to attacks on these constructional sites in order to prevent the threat becoming a reality.

171. At this time it was not considered desirable to divert any large part of the heavy bomber effort from the commitment on "Pointblank" targets. I was, therefore, made responsible for taking the necessary countermeasures with the forces of A.E.A.F. In addition, however, a proportion of the effort of the heavy bombers of the United States Eighth Air Force was made available to me for this task on days when weather was unsuitable for deep penetration raids into Germany. The United States IXth Bomber Command was committed, up to 1st April, to assist the strategical air forces with diversionary raids, and therefore, was not always available for these operations. R.A.F. Bomber Command was also originally allotted five sites for attack, but this commitment was subsequently re-allotted to A.E.A.F.

172. As is now known, the menace was not under-estimated, and the air effort prior to D-Day did not succeed wholly in removing it.

173. The sites were classified as follows:-

(*a*) Ski-sites – (so called because of a big store room construction which from the air looked very like a ski) – designed for launching flying bombs.

(*b*) Rocket sites – larger constructions designed for the launching of heavy rocket projectiles.

(*c*) Supply sites.

174. The sites were given the code word of "Noball" and operations against them were carried out under the code word "Crossbow". These operations began on 5th December, 1943, and accordingly the summary of activity in this section of the Despatch is shown from this date to D-Day.

175. On 5th December, 1943, 63 ski sites and 5 rocket sites had been identified. It appeared that the sites in the Pas de Calais area were aligned on London and those in the Cherbourg area on Bristol. It was calculated that the enemy was completing new sites at the rate of three every two days.

176. A schedule of priorities based on the British Air Ministry recommendations was carefully worked out. It was most important to ensure that no more bombs than were absolutely necessary to neutralise one target should be dropped before an attack was made against the next target on the priority list. A system was devised of "suspending" a site from further attack, whereby a Command which considered that it had inflicted sufficient damage to a site to neutralise it temporarily, was authorised to notify any authority concerned that the site was "suspended" from further attack, pending photographic confirmation of the damage done.

177. The attacks on sites prior to D-Day are listed below. At D-Day it was estimated

that out of 97 identified flying bomb sites, 86 had been neutralised, and out of 7 identified rocket sites, 2 had been neutralised.

178. In addition, heavy attacks were launched on several special supply or storage sites which had been observed under construction.

179. The ski sites were normally well hidden, either in or at the edge of woods, well camouflaged and heavily defended by flak so that low flying attacks on them were costly. In photographs their presence was recognised not only by the shape and layout of the buildings, particularly the comprehensive water supply system, but also by the specially built roads and railways that led to them.

180. It was not appreciated before D-Day that in addition to these specially constructed ski sites, there were modified ski sites with all the facilities of the original sites except for the distinctive ski buildings and the water supply system. After D + 7, the day on which the enemy first launched flying bombs against the United Kingdom, photographic reconnaissance revealed the existence of 74 of these modified sites. They were camouflaged more completely than the original sites and made use of existing roads and buildings. Details of attacks on these modified ski sites or launching sites are included in my account of air operations in the post-assault phase.

181. The exact number of flying bombs which the known number of ski sites were capable of launching against the United Kingdom if they had not been attacked by aircraft can only be estimated, but it is thought that some 6,000 flying bombs per 24 hours is a reasonable estimate. The success of the air forces, therefore, in attacking and neutralising Germany's capacity to use this secret weapon may be judged in terms of the figures of actual flying bombs launched after D-Day. These figures are set out in the account of the post-assault phase.

182.

Summary of Attacks on Ski Sites prior to D-Day.

Force	Sorties	Bombs
A.E.A.F.	22,280	13,515 tons
U.S. Eighth Air Force	4,589	7,968 tons
	26,869	**21,483 tons**

Summary of Attacks on Rocket Sites prior to D-Day.

Force	Sorties	Bombs
A.E.A.F.	434	667 tons
U.S. Eighth Air Force	2,045	7,624 tons
	2,479	**8,291 tons**

Summary of Attacks on Supply Sites and Dumps prior to D-Day.

Force	Sorties	Bombs
A.E.A.F.	852	1,148 tons and 126 x 60-lb. R.Ps.
U.S. Eighth Air Force	166	479 tons 126 x 60-lb. R.Ps.
	1,018	**1,627 tons and**

Statistical Summary of Preparatory Operations.

183. The following statistics show the immense scale of the effort of the Allied air forces operating from the United Kingdom against both "Overlord" and "Pointblank" targets during the preparatory phase Ist April to 5th June, 1944. That the achievements referred to in the foregoing paragraphs were not accomplished without considerable cost in skilled manpower is evident from the aircraft casualty figures included. Statistics covering personnel casualties in the preparatory period are included in the schedule at paragraph 408 in Part III (d).

Preparatory Operations

Period 1st April – 5th June, 1944

Force	Aircraft despatched	Tons of bombs dropped	Aircraft lost in combat	E/A destroyed in combat
A.E.A.F. :-				
Ninth A.F.	53,784	30,657	197	189
2nd T.A.F.	28,587 }	6,981	{ 133	66
A.D.G.B.	18,639 }		{ 46	111
R.A.F. B.C.	24,621	87,238	557	77
U.S. Eighth A.F.:-				
VIIIth B.C.	37,804	69,857	763	724
VIIIth F.C.	31,820	647	291	1,488
	195,255	195,380	1,987	2,655

Total sorties as above	195,255
R.A.F. Coastal Command	5,384
	200,639

184. The sorties of Coastal Command included are only those on anti-shipping and anti-U-boat patrols in the Bay of Biscay and Channel areas and off the Dutch coast. The weight of depth charges, bombs, etc., dropped and casualties or claims arising from these sorties are not included.

(c) The Assault

Decision to make the Assault.

185. After consultations with the Commanders-in-Chief of the three services, during May, you had fixed the date of the Assault for 5th June. The decision as to date had to be taken in good time to permit of the completion of final preparations. Some of the ships in the invasion Armada, for example, had to sail a week before the time planned for the assault.

186. As the date approached, the weather forecasts pointed to very serious deterioration in conditions for D-Day. On 3rd June, you summoned a conference at your Advanced Headquarters at Portsmouth to consider the weather situation. This

conference included yourself, the Deputy Supreme Commander, Air Chief Marshal Sir A.W. Tedder, G.C.B., your Chief of Staff Lieutenant General W.B. Smith, Admiral Sir Bertram H. Ramsay, K.C.B., K.B.E., M.V.O., and his Chief of Staff, General Sir Bernard L. Montgomery, K.C.B., D.S.O., and his Chief of Staff, and the Heads of the Naval, Army and Air Meteorological Services. I attended this conference with my Senior Air Staff Officer, Air Vice-Marshal H.E.P. Wigglesworth, C.B., C.B.E., D.S.C.

187. The first meeting took place at 2100 hours on 3rd June. It lasted until after midnight, when you decided to postpone any decision until the meteorological staffs could collect later reports.

188. The second meeting took place at 0400 hours on 4th June, and in the light of weather forecasts then available, you decided to postpone the time of the assault for 24 hours, primarily on the grounds that the air forces would be unable to provide adequate support for the crossing and assault operations, and could not undertake the airborne tasks.

189. The meeting reassembled at 2100 hours on 4th June, and after considerable deliberation a decision was again deferred to enable the meteorological staffs to study later data.

190. The final meeting took place at 0430 hours in the morning of 5th June. Weather conditions forecast for the following day were still far from satisfactory and from the air point of view, below the planned acceptable minimum.

191. Nevertheless, taking into account the fact that the adverse weather conditions imposed an equal handicap on the enemy air forces, I considered, and I gave this as my opinion, that the Allied air effort possible would provide a reasonable measure of air protection and support and that airborne operations would be practicable.

192. After considering also the weather conditions as affecting the land and sea operations, you made the decision that the assault was to take place on the first high tide in the morning of the 6th of June and that the airborne forces were to be flown over and dropped in their allotted zones before dawn of that day.

The Assault is made.

193. The assault was on a five divisional front on the east side of the Cherbourg Peninsula immediately north of the Carentan Estuary and the River Orne.

194. The First United States Army landed between Varreville and Colleville-sur-Mer; I R.C.T.[7] landed between Varreville and the Carentan Estuary, 2 R.C.T. between the Carentan Estuary and Colleville-sur-Mer. The Second British Army with five brigades, landed between Asnelles and Ouistreham. These seaborne forces were supported on their flanks by two airborne forces, two United States Airborne Divisions being dropped and landed in the area of St. Mere Eglise, and a British Airborne Division in the area between the Rivers Orne and Dives. The map[8] facing shows the landing beaches and the positions gained in the first three weeks of the assault.

195. The first airborne forces landed before dawn on 6th June and the landing barges and craft coming in on the first tide, touched down at 0630 hours. Follow-up

forces were landed with the second tide, and in the evening, additional airborne forces were flown in.

196. There was no enemy opposition to the original passage of the assault or airborne forces. This fact is all the more remarkable when it is remembered that many of the ships had, of necessity, been at sea for periods of some days.

197. I have set out in Section (b) of Part II at paragraph 35, the tasks undertaken by the air forces in support of the assault. For convenience of presentation, these tasks have been dealt with under the five headings shown below:-

Protection of the Cross-Channel Movement,
Neutralisation of Coastal and Beach Defences,
Protection of the Beaches,
Dislocation of Enemy Communications and Control,
Airborne operations.

198. The Order of Battle of A.E.A.F. as at D-Day is set out at Appendix "D",8 the strength of aircraft available was as follows:-

United States

Type	Forces	Royal Air Force	Grand Total
Medium Bombers	532	88	620
Light Bombers	194	160	354
Fighter and Fighter Bombers	1,311	2,172	3,483
Transport Aircraft	1,166	462	1,628
Reconnaissance Aircraft	158	178	336
Artillery Observation Aircraft	–	102	102
A.S.R. (Miscellaneous)	–	96	96
Powered A/C Total	3,361	3,258	6,619
Gliders	1,619	972	2,591
Grand Total	4,980	4,230	9,210

Protection of the Cross-Channel movement.

199. The task of assisting the naval forces to protect the passage of the assault armies from surface and U-boat attack, was undertaken chiefly by R.A.F. Coastal Command though aircraft of A.E.A.F. assisted in this task. I deal with these operations in more detail in paragraph 387 et seq. Here I need only mention that on D-Day and D + I, aircraft of R.A.F. Coastal Command flew 353 sorties on anti-shipping and anti-U-boat patrols. A line of patrols was provided at either end of the Channel. The air protection thus afforded contributed much to the safety of the Allied shipping from both surface and underwater attack by enemy naval forces.

200. Fifteen squadrons of fighters were allotted the task of protecting the shipping lanes. These squadrons flew 2,015 sorties during the course of D-Day and D + I, the cover being maintained at six squadron strength throughout this period. Owing to the lack of enemy reaction, I was able later to reduce this cover to a two squadron force.

201. For convenience of presentation, I have set out the full plan for the

employment of fighter forces during the assault and post assault phase in the next section. (See paragraph 308 et seq.)

Neutralisation of Coastal and Beach Defences.

202. The task of neutralising as many of the coastal defence positions as possible during the crucial period of the assault was shared by naval and air bombardment. The air bombardment plan called for attacks to commence just before dawn on D-Day.

203. R.A.F. Bomber Command commenced the bombardment with attacks on the following ten selected heavy coastal batteries in the assault area:-

Coastal Batteries	Sorties	Tons of Bombs
Crisbecq	101	598
St. Martin de Varreville	100	613
Ouistreham	116	645
Maisy	116	592
Mont Fleury	124	585
La Parnelle	131	668
St. Pierre du Mont	124	698
Merville/Franceville	109	382
Houlgate	16	468
Longues	99	604
	1,136 [sic]	5,853 tons

204. As R.A.F. Bomber Command left the assault area, United States Eighth Air Force heavy bombers took over the bombardment role. In the thirty minutes immediately preceding the touch-down hour, 1,365 heavy bombers attacked selected areas in the coastal defences, dropping 2,796 tons of bombs. The result of these operations added to the previous air bombardment and combined with the naval shelling, neutralised wholly or in large part almost all of the shore batteries and the opposition to the landings was very much less than was expected.

205. Medium, light and fighter bombers then took a hand in the attacks on the enemy defensive system by attacking artillery positions further inland and other targets in the coastal defences. The immense scale of this effort maybe gauged from the statistics which appear after para. 233.

206. The heavy bombers of the United States Eighth Air Force operated again later in the day and although cloud interfered with bombing about midday, necessitating the recall of some missions, a further 1,746 tons of bombs were dropped. In all, the Eighth Air Force flew 2,627 heavy bombers and 1,347 escort and offensive fighter sorties during the day.

207. *Spotting for Naval Gunfire.* The naval bombardment took place according to plan. In this bombardment, aircraft of A.E.A.F. played an important role. The Fleet Air Arm had stated early on in the planning that it would be unable to find from its own resources enough aircraft to provide for spotting for the gunfire of all the capital ships it was planned to use. Accordingly, despite the unfortunate diversion of effort

from air resources that were far from inexhaustible, I had agreed that two squadrons of Spitfires from A.D.G.B. and two wings (each of three squadrons) of Mustangs from R.A.F. Second Tactical Air Force should be trained for this task. At various times, therefore, well before D-Day, these squadrons had been trained with No. 3 Naval Fighter Wing.

208. The result was that on D-Day and subsequently, we were just able to meet the heavy calls for spotting for naval gunfire that were made on us. On D-Day, no less than 394 sorties were flown on this task of which 236 were flown by five squadrons of A.E.A.F. Each of the two Spitfire squadrons, No. 26 Squadron and No. 33 Squadron made 76 sorties in the course of the day. In all, during the period of consolidation in the beach-head, that is from 6th June to 19th June, a total of 1,318 sorties on naval gunnery spotting were flown. Of this total, aircraft of A.E.A.F. flew 940. Five aircraft of A.E.A.F. were destroyed on these operations during this period.

209. It may be pointed out here that further calls were made on these same A.E.A.F. squadrons at later stages in the campaign. The gunfire of the capital ships bombarding the isolated German garrisons in the fortresses of Cherbourg in late June, and of St. Malo and Brest in late August, was spotted for by these squadrons. On these duties a further 124 sorties were flown apart from those flown by aircraft of Fleet Air Arm.

Protection of the Landing Beaches.

210. In addition to the cover given to the cross-Channel movement of the assault forces, I provided a continuous daylight fighter cover of the beach-head areas. Nine squadrons in two forces of six squadrons of low cover and three squadrons of high cover continuously patrolled over the British and American beaches. A reserve of six fighter squadrons on the ground were also kept at readiness to strengthen any point if the enemy came up to challenge.

211. On D-Day alone, 1,547 sorties were flown on beach-head cover. Night fighters also patrolled continuously during the hours of darkness over the beach-head and shipping lanes; six squadrons of Mosquitoes were available for these operations. Details of the organisation and control and of the scale of effort of the fighter forces are set out in the next section of this Despatch (see paragraph 308).

212. *Balloon Defence of the Beach-head* – To supplement the defences provided by fighter aircraft and anti-aircraft guns, it had been decided to provide balloon protection for all beaches and artificial ports (Mulberries). It was thought that balloons would give valuable protection against low-flying attacks and would permit economies in the number of light A.A. weapons that would be needed in the early stages of the assault.

213. Operational control of these balloons was vested in the local A.A. Defence Commander. In practice, balloons flew at 2,000 feet by night and just below cloud base by day. Suitable control funnels, within which balloons were grounded by day, were arranged so as to avoid interference with approaches to air strips.

214. In Part IV of this Despatch I give further details of some of the difficulties experienced and overcome in planning the employment of these balloons. Here I need

only comment on the results achieved. The passive nature of balloon defence and the monotonous lack of results make it difficult to compute its value. There were practically no reports of low-level bombing attacks by enemy aircraft during the periods the balloons were flying, and such bombing as did occur was scattered, doing little damage to the beach maintenance and none to the Mulberries. One enemy aircraft was destroyed by a balloon on the beaches in the U.S. sector. Apart from the positive value of balloons as a deterrent to low-flying enemy attacks, I feel that the presence of balloons has, in itself, a definite morale value for both Naval and Army personnel.

Dislocation of enemy communications and control.

2I5. Air operations to dislocate enemy control of operations in the field were begun on the day before the assault. This dislocation of the enemy control went even further than the previous attacks on his Radar chain. The latter had blinded the enemy to the movement of the Allied assault forces; the air operations now proceeded to impede and disrupt in advance any possible enemy moves to make good his initial setback. To do this I tried during the initial stage of the assault, to break up the enemy machinery of control and signals communications and by so doing to make as difficult as possible the co-ordination of enemy counterattacks. Chateaux known to house German Corps and Divisional Headquarters and also German Army telephone exchanges were attacked on the evening of 5th June and through D-Day by fighters with bombs and rocket projectiles. These operations undoubtedly seriously embarrassed the enemy, both during the assault and later, when a large number of enemy headquarters were knocked out.

2I6. The Air Forces also were quite successful in causing casualties among German Generals. Field Marshal Rommel himself was fatally wounded in an air attack and it is believed that a further six to eight Commanders were also casualties. The killing in an air attack of a Divisional Commander during a critical stage of the fighting at St. Lo is thought to have had an important effect on the course of the Battle.

Airborne Operations.

2I7. The general plan of the airborne operations called for the dropping and landing of three divisions of parachute and gliderborne troops, and for the initial reinforcement and re-supply of these formations.

2I8. Two of these divisions were the I0Ist and 82nd United States Airborne Divisions and their task was to assist in the capture of the Cotentin Peninsula by aiding the seaborne landing of the First United States Army, and by preventing enemy reinforcements from moving into the peninsula from the south. The particular tasks of these divisions were to capture the areas of St. Mere Eglise and St. Martin and the neighbouring coastal defences.

2I9. The third division was the 6th British Airborne Division and its task was to operate on the left (eastern) flank of Ist Corps of the Second British Army, in the area between the Orne and Dives Rivers. The particular tasks of this division were:-

(*a*) to secure intact, and hold, the two bridges over the River Orne-Caen canal at Bonouville and Ranville:

(*b*) to neutralise an important enemy coastal battery and capture or neutralise a key strongpoint:

(*c*) to secure a firm base, including bridgeheads east of the River Orne:

(*d*) to prevent enemy reinforcements (including Panzer units) from moving towards the British left flank from the east and southeast.

To accomplish these objects, 3 and 5 Paratroop Brigade Groups flew in with a limited number of gliders carrying details of the 6th Airborne Division Headquarters on the night of D - I/D-Day, and were followed by the 6th Air Landing Brigade on the evening of D-Day.

220. A limited number of S.A.S. troops were dropped in selected areas before and after D-Day for special missions, by aircraft of No. 38 Group.

22I. The airlift of all these forces was provided by the transport aircraft of A.E.A.F. United States, IXth Troop Carrier Command carried the American divisions and No. 38 Group and No. 46 Group of the Royal Air Force, carried the British Force.

222. *U.S. IXth Troop Carrier Command.* – The paratroops of the I0Ist Division were dropped by aircraft of the United States IXth Troop Carrier Command in the general area of St. Mere Eglise, shortly after midnight on the night of June 5th-6th (Operation Albany). The glider force of the I0Ist Division went in at dawn of D-Day into the same area, in 58 gliders (Operation Chicago). A re-supply mission was flown for the I0Ist Division on the night of D + 1(Operation Keokuk). This re-supply mission was necessary as there had been no contact between the I0Ist Division and the seaborne assaulting forces.

223. Paratroops of the 82nd Division were flown in in aircraft of IXth Troop Carrier Command and dropped in the general area of St. Sauveur le Vicomte (Operation Boston), shortly after midnight of 5th-6th June. Glider elements of this division were flown in as follows:-

52 Gliders at dawn of D-Day (Operation Detroit).
I77 Gliders at dusk of D-Day (Operation Elmira).
98 Gliders at dawn of D + I (Operation Galveston).
I0I Gliders at dusk of D + I (Operation Hackensack).

Re-supply missions for the 82nd Division were flown on the nights of D + 1 and D + 2 with I48 and II7 aircraft respectively, carrying a total of approximately 432 tons of supplies. (Operations Freeport and Memphis.)

224. *Nos. 38 and 46 Groups, Royal Air Force.* The tasks of these groups were as follows:-

(a) *Dropping of S.A.S. troops* –
  (i) *D - I/D-Day:*
    Reconnaissance parties to be dropped in each of six areas (Operation Sunflower I).

    (ii) D + 1/2:

       Dropping of task forces in Brittany (Operation Coney).

    (iii) D + 3/4:

       Dropping of base parties in the six areas mentioned above (Operation Sunflower II).

    (iv) Re-supply to base parties as required (Operation Sunflower III).

  (b) Dropping and landing of 3rd and 5th Paratroop Brigade Groups plus a proportion of Division troops on the night of D - 1/D-Day (Operation Tonga).

  (c) Landing of the 6th Air Landing Brigade on the evening of D-Day (Operation Mallard).

  (d) Re-supply of the 3rd and 5th Paratroop Brigade Groups on the night of D/D + 1 (Operation Robroy I).

  (e) Subsequent re-supply mission for the 6th British Airborne Division (Operation Robroy II, III, etc.).

225. All these operations were carried out successfully, and with a remarkably low casualty rate, as will be evident from the statistics following para. 233. Total losses amounted to 3½ per cent. and 2½ per cent. respectively of the British and American sorties flown.

226. These airborne operations constituted the greatest air lift of assault forces that had ever been attempted. Up to date, they are exceeded only by the immense operations of the First Allied Airborne Army in mid-September. The accuracy with which these forces were delivered to the allotted zones contributed greatly to the rapid success of their coups de main.

227. *Provision of Air Support.* All the airborne forces and re-supply missions which were flown in daylight were given adequate fighter cover; in addition, the fighter cover to the assault areas and reserves were held in readiness to assist in the protection of these forces. There were no losses due to attack by enemy aircraft on any formation of troop carriers.

228. In the period D-Day to D + 4, 1,839 sorties were flown by special fighter escort to airborne forces, and a further 419 sorties were flown as escort to later re-supply missions. As additional support, special forces of intruders operated against anti-aircraft positions in the vicinity of the dropping and landing zones and others preceded the main forces across the coast to silence light anti-aircraft batteries on the run-in. The lightness of the casualties, which were much fewer than might reasonably have been expected, is evidence of the effectiveness of these support operations.

Review of Additional Air Operations in Support of the Assault.

229. In addition to the specific tasks set out in the preceding paragraphs, many subsidiary ones were also undertaken by the Allied air forces during the assault period. These operations are briefly reviewed in the next paragraphs.

230. Fighter escort was given to the bombers operating by day and these fighters then went on to attack enemy movements. The fighters of A.E.A.F. flew offensive patrols against all road and rail movement within the tactical area and the fighters of the United States Eighth Air Force continued this work farther afield beyond the boundary of the tactical areas.

23I. A large effort was expended on reconnaissance sorties on both D-Day and D + I. The deep reconnaissances revealed the reactions of the enemy, as shown by his movements of reinforcements to the battle area. The short range reconnaissances were also of invaluable assistance to the Army Commanders.

232. With such large forces operating, the Air/Sea Rescue Service was fully occupied. I98 patrols were flown during the two days and, together with the surface craft, these patrols succeeded in locating and rescuing a considerable number of Allied personnel.

233. The following statistics, covering the air operations in support of the assault, show the great effort of the Allied air forces on D-Day and D + I. This effort, concentrated over a comparatively small area, surpassed in strength any air operations that had ever before been mounted.

TOTAL AIR EFFORT FOR PERIOD 2100 HOURS 5TH JUNE – 2100 HOURS 7TH JUNE

	Heavy Bomber		Medium Bomber	Light Bomber	Fighter Bomber	Tonnage Of Bombs	R.P. Fighters	No. Of R.P.'s Fired	Beachhead Cover	Shipping Cover	Offensive Patrol	Defensive Patrol	Reconnaissance			Weather	Escort		ASR
	Bomb.	Misc.											Shipping	Photo	Visual		Bombers	Transport	
D-Day																			
A.F.	-	-	693	296	665	1,517	24	192	1,547	496	73	211	20	84	384	25	484	187	87
R.A.F. B.C	1,136	199	-	-	-	5,853	-	-	-	-	-	-	-	-	-	-	-	-	-
U.S. Eighth A.F.	2,627	-	-	-	-	4,542	-	-	-	-	-	-	-	-	-	-	1,347	-	-
Fleet Air Arm	-	-	-	-	-	-	-	-	-	-	-	-	-	-	-	-	-	-	-
	3,763	199	693	296	665	11,912	24	192	1,547	496	73	211	20	84	352	25	1,831	187	87
D+1																			
A.E.A.F.	-	-	622	424	1,213	1,557	285	1,255	708	1,519	238	154	34	123		26	20	1,658	111
R.A.F. B.C	1,097	63	-	-	-	3,996	-	-	-	-	-	-	-	-	320	-	-	-	-
U.S. Eighth A.F.	1,623	-	-	-	-	2,277	-	-	-	-	-	-	-	-	150	-	1,445	-	-
Fleet Air Arm	-	-	-	-	-	-	-	-	-	-	-	-	-	-	-	-	-	-	-
	2,720	63	622	424	1,213	7,800	285	1,255	708	1,519	238	154	34	123	470	26	1,465	1,658	111

Analysis of Loads Carried

Troops	17,262	Gasoline	1,947 gallons
M/T	281	Bombs	26,652 lbs.
Artillery Weapons	333	Rations	87,373 lbs.
		Ammunition	798,683lbs.
		Other Combat equipment	1,141,217 lbs.

OPERATION "NEPTUNE"

Air Lift U.S. IXth Troop Carrier Command

Mission	Aircraft						Gliders		
	Despatched	Effecive	Abortive	Missing	Destroyed	Damaged	Despatched	Released at DZ	Lost before DZ
Albany	443	433	10	-	13	83	-	-	-
Boston	378	372	6	8	-	115	-	-	-
Chicago	52	51	1	1	1	3	52	51	1
Detroit	52	52	-	1	1	6	52	46	6
Elmira	177	177	-	5	-	92	176	176	-
Freeport	208	148	55	5	3	94	-	-	-
Galveston	100	98	2	-	-	24	100	98	2
Hackensack	101	101	-	-	-	-	100	100	-
Keokuk	32	32	-	-	-	-	32	32	-
Memphis	119	117	2	-	3	35	-	-	-
	1,662	1,581	76	20	21	452	512	503	9

Analysis of Loads Carried

Troops 17,262
Gasoline............................1,947 gallons
Ammunition 798,683lbs
M/T 281
Bombs ....26,652. lbs.

Artillery Weapons 333
Rations..................................87,373 lbs.
Other   }
Equipment }........................141,217 lbs

Air Lift Nos. 38 and 46 Groups, Royal Air Force

Mission	Aircraft						Gliders		
	Despatched	Effecive	Abortive	Missing	Destroyed	Damaged	Despatched	Released at DZ	Lost before DZ
onga	373	359	14	9	-	7	98	80	18
lallard	257	247	10	2	6	21	257	247	10
ob Roy I	50	47	3	9	-	19	-	-	-
ob Roy II	6	6	-	-	-	-	-	-	-
ob Roy III	12	5	7	-	-	-	-	-	-
ob Roy IV	15	15	-	-	-	-	-	-	-
inflower I	3	3	-	-	-	-	-	-	-
inflower II	2	1	1	-	-	-	-	-	-
inflower III	6	6	-	-	-	-	-	-	-
oney	9	9	-	-	-	-	-	-	-
	733	698	35	20	6	47	355	327	28

Analysis of Loads Carried

Troops..7,162
Tanks...18
Bombs ....2,000 lbs.
M/T 286
Bicycles..35

Artillery Weapons 29
Signals Equipment 12
Other   } ....731 panniers and
Equipment } ....622 containers

(d) Operations subsequent to D-Day.

Plan of Presentation.

234. As in the previous sections of the narrative part of this Despatch, I propose to deal with the operations in the period D-Day to 30th September, I944, under types of operations, rather than on a time basis. For this purpose the following headings have been adopted:-

Attacks on Enemy Communications.
Close Support Operations.
Attacks on Coastal Garrisons.
Fighter Cover to the Assault and the Shipping Lanes.
Enemy Air Reaction and the Allied Attacks on the G.A.F. and its bases.
Defence against Flying Bombs and Attacks on "Crossbow" targets.
Operations of First Allied Airborne Army.
Attacks on Naval Targets.
Strategical Bombing – "Pointblank."

Attacks on Enemy Communications.

235. I have dealt with the task undertaken by the air forces (see para. 5I et seq.) of dislocating, prior to D-Day, the enemy rail system. I considered that one of the most important contributions which the air could make to the ground battle, after the launching of the assault, was to continue this work of dislocation. With this view you agreed, as did the other Commanders-in-Chief.

236. In order to gain a clear picture of the state of enemy road and rail communications, as I saw it at D-Day, reference should be made to the two maps.[9] facing pages I4 and I8. The lines in Northern France and Belgium were very seriously disorganised, but the lines south of Paris/Rheims/Luxembourg were not nearly so devastated, nor were the railways south of the Seine. Of the bridges over the Seine below Paris, all except two were cut, and although the Loire bridges had not been cut, the crossings at Tours, Orleans, Angers and Saumur had all been rendered impassable by attacks on the railway junctions. In addition, there had been an enormous reduction in the capacity of the whole rail system in Northern France and Belgium.

237. The interruption of enemy communications during the post assault phase falls naturally into two separate periods:-

  (*a*) From the moment the contending armies had joined battle, it became
    of paramount importance that the enemy should be denied the freedom
    of movement necessary to prepare and mount successful
    counterattacks, and that the reinforcements he sought to bring into the
    battle zone should not only be hampered in movement, but also
    subjected to the severest casualties possible by air attack.

(*b*) After the break through of the Allied armies, the task of the air forces
against communications was to harry the fleeing enemy columns,
block the defiles and police the river crossings, thereby removing the
possibility of orderly retreat. In the following paragraphs I try to show
how these two tasks were carried out.

238. *Attacks on Rail and Road Systems – June and July.* – In the earlier part of this
period I was concerned to impose the maximum delay and to inflict the heaviest
casualties on the flow of reinforcements and supplies to the enemy armies. The attacks
were carried out according to a prepared pattern. This pattern was necessarily
developed as the situation changed, following the information I received from deep
and tactical reconnaissance.

239. The weather during June severely hampered operations. Frequently I was
denied vital information on the progress and direction of German troop movements.
Despite this handicap of weather, however, reconnaissance squadrons operated
effectively, and the information they provided proved invaluable to the Army
Commander as well as to myself.

240. Immediately the battle started, the enemy began to transfer his immediate
reserves to the battle zone over the railways between the Seine and the Loire. Action
against this movement consisted of low flying fighter bomber attacks against the
trains and of line cutting by fighter bombers. The fighter bombers of the United States
Ninth Air Force particularly had developed a very effective technique of line cutting.
I also employed medium bombers with excellent results in attacks against sidings
being used as detraining points.

24I. By D + I, those parts of the enemy close reserves which had escaped these
attacks had been committed to the battle. I therefore decided to initiate a series of
attacks against railway junctions in the tactical area and thus establish a line beyond
which enemy movements by rail to the battle zone could not proceed. R.A.F. Bomber
Command attacked Rennes, Alencon, Fougeres, Mayenne and Pontaubault and
followed up with attacks on the next two nights, on Dreux, Evreux and Acheres.
Within the boundary of the tactical area thus drawn, A.E.A.F. fighter bombers caused
such destruction that after three days, all railway and all major road movement by
day had been virtually halted.

242. The enemy was forced to travel mainly by night and along minor roads. No.
2 Group of the R.A.F. Second Tactical Air Force, whose crews had been specially
trained in night harassing, by the light of flares, operated light and medium bombers,
frequently in very difficult weather conditions, with outstanding success against this
movement.

243. Outside the tactical areas, both road and rail movements were dealt with by
fighters of the United States VIIIth Fighter Command. Their fighter bomber attacks
on line cutting and against railway centres, and also in offensive fighter sweeps
against road and rail movements were outstandingly successful.

244. On I2th June, I re-drew the boundary of the tactical area as follows – along
the Seine to Vernon, thence to Dreux, Chartres, Le Mans, Laval and St. Nazaire.

Within that area the tactical air forces policed all roads and railways. Outside that area, the United States Eighth Air Force was busy attacking the Loire bridges to prevent any reinforcement from the south; but due, no doubt, to the threat of Allied invasion on the Mediterranean coast, there were no heavy enemy movements from the south for some time.

245. The principal difficulty in maintaining a complete blockade on all movement in the tactical area was the persistent bad weather which hampered the air operations very considerably. Further, the enemy showed great energy and ingenuity in repairing rail cuts and in running shuttle services between cuts. Because of these factors, the enemy was able to move a certain amount of material by rail within the tactical area itself, though he had to move mainly by night.

246. Apart from the forces in Brittany which it was anticipated would move by road, the main source from which the enemy could draw his reinforcement at this time was the Pas de Calais area. I therefore arranged for R.A.F. Bomber Command to attack centres in that area. On the night of 12-13th June, that Command made heavy attacks on Poitiers, Arras, Cambrai and two rail centres at Amiens. On the following night Douai, St. Pol and Cambrai were the targets. These attacks, together with those of the fighter and fighter bombers harassing movements on the railway lines, effectively delayed the transfer of the enemy reserves into the battle zone.

247. Since most of the fuel and ammunition dumps in the tactical area were attacked at one time or another by aircraft of A.E.A.F., on armed reconnaissance, the enemy quickly began to run out of immediate reserves and was forced to use dumps further afield. As early as the second week of the battle, he was committed to drawing supplies of fuel and ammunition from dumps in the Marne area. These supply columns also had to run the gauntlet of our air attacks.

248. During the third week in June, I again extended the tactical area, following the attacks I have described in para. 244. At this time the enemy was using two particular routes, one through Strasbourg and the other through Saarbrucken and Metz, to transfer reinforcements and supplies from Poland and Germany proper to the Western Front. How much the movement of traffic on these lines had already been embarrassed may be gauged from the move of the 9th and 10th S.S. Panzer Divisions. These divisions, which had been hurriedly pulled out of Poland, were forced to detrain as far east as Nancy and then move approximately 300 miles by road to reach the battle zone. Others detrained as far east as Mulhouse. To complete the disorganisation on these routes, I laid on attacks, at the end of June, on Metz, Blainville, Strasbourg and Saarbrucken.

249. During July, the enemy was committed to move further formations both from the Pas de Calais and the Low Countries, and some of these he tried to bring to centres in the Paris area for detrainment. Heavy attacks were accordingly laid on these centres as well as on others in the Low Countries. I also extended the tactical area to include Northern France, so that A.E.A.F. aircraft could take in the areas north of the Seine in their operations. The fighters of the Eighth Air Force continued to sweep over the routes east, and south-east of Paris.

250. The following statistics show the weight of the air attacks on rail centres in the period I have been reviewing:-

Attacks on Rail Centres, Tunnels and Embankments from 6th June – 31st July, 1944

Force	Sorties	Tons of Bombs
A.E.A.F.	7,736	7,147
R.A.F. Bomber Command	5,738	23,440
U.S. Eighth Air Force	1,615	3,842
	15,089	34,429

25I. The above figures, however, do not cover the attacks by the fighters and fighter bombers against the enemy rail movements. Their work was made easier in that the general disorganisation resulted in the enemy having at best only one or two circuitous routes open at any one time. This canalisation of traffic presented some excellent fighter bomber targets, and the pilots of A.E.A.F. and the United States Eighth Fighter Command took full advantage of them.

252. As the period of static fighting ended and the Allied armies broke out from their bridgehead, I called off the attacks on rail targets, as they were then more likely to hamper than help the Allied advance.

253. *Attacks on Bridges – June and July.*

The destruction of the bridges leading into the battle zone was also continued after the assault was launched. These attacks, as I have already explained, formed part of the general plan of attack on the enemy's transport system. At D-Day, all the Seine bridges below Paris except two were cut. During June, these two were destroyed as well as the principal bridges, both road and rail, across the Loire. Several important bridges on the lines through the gap between Paris and Orleans were also rendered impassable. The map[10] facing page 18 indicates the ring thus drawn about the battle area.

254. Briefly, this ring ran along the Seine and Loire. A second line of interdiction further afield had been planned, and to this end a large number of the more important bridges in the rail systems of North-Western France and Belgium were also cut; in addition, a number of minor bridges within the tactical area were rendered impassable.

255. In fact, however, this second line of interdiction was never completed. There were several reasons. Chief amongst them was the weather which curtailed operations. Next were the priority claims on the fighter bombers of the United States Eighth Fighter Command. Finally, there came a time when, because of the speed of our advance, further destruction of bridges was no longer necessary and indeed, would have been to our disadvantage. At this time I sought and secured your agreement, and that of the two Army Group Commanders-in-Chief, to stop these attacks.

256. The attacks on bridges had been mainly the work of A.E.A.F. and the United

States Eighth Air Force and in the period D-Day to 31st July, the following effort was expended on these targets:-

Force	Sorties	Tons of Bombs
A.E.A.F.	12,823	14,27I
U.S. Eighth A.F.	3,225	9,397
R.A.F. B.C.	260	975
	16,308	24,643

257. *Effect of Attacks on Communications.*

The enemy endeavoured to overcome the restrictions the air attacks placed on him by moving his stores and equipment both by road and by barges down the Seine from the unloading points near Paris to the ferries he had established at Elbeuf and in the neighbourhood of Rouen, as well as along the water-ways of Northern France. Both of these channels were dealt with by air attack, and there is a large amount of intelligence material to testify to the effectiveness of these fighter bomber attacks. Prisoners of war have confirmed pilots' stories of losses and have told of divisions moving very long distances by bicycle and being committed to the land battle piecemeal, without heavy equipment, as a result of Allied air attacks.

258. The following accounts of the difficulties encountered by German divisions moving to the battle zones in July are of interest in this connection:-

(a) Air reconnaissance indicated, and prisoner of war reports confirmed, that the 363rd Infantry Division began to move from Ghent in mid-July. A number of the entraining stations, the junctions along the route and the trains themselves were attacked. The movement became so disorganised that approximately half the trains were cancelled and the troops moved by road. The division did not reach the front until the beginning of August.

(b) The 33Ist Infantry Division attempted to move from the Pas de Calais by rail. The route originally chosen was the main line Lille-Arras-Amiens, but as a result of line cutting by fighter bombers, a diversion had to be arranged via Lille-Cambrai-Chaulnes, and later through Eastern France via Valenciennes-Aulnoye-Mezieres. This movement eventually became so involved that the attempt to travel by rail was abandoned altogether. Air reconnaissances revealed that loaded trains which had stood by at entraining stations for 48 hours were finally unloaded without having moved at all.

(c) The 326th Infantry Division was also moved from the Pas de Calais at this time. In this move the Germans were evidently not prepared to risk a full-scale rail movement. Less than half the division travelled by rail, and the remainder moved on bicycles by a very circuitous route.

(d) It has been estimated that, in favourable circumstances, the move of the Ist S.S. Panzer Division from Louvain to the Caen area would have taken about three days. In fact, although detraining took place in the vicinity of Paris, and the move was completed by road, the rail journey alone took as long as a week for some elements, presumably because their trains were committed to a "Pilgrim's Progress" as a result of incidents on almost every route attempted. Stories of delays of from two to seventeen hours as a result of bomb damage to railway tracks, were a feature of the majority of interrogation reports of prisoners from this Division. One unit was delayed for two days at a badly damaged railway junction east of Paris.

(*e*) As had been anticipated, the move of the 346th Infantry Division from the area of Le Havre was conducted entirely by road. Bicycles were the means of transport and, although there is no evidence of any serious delay caused directly by bombing or strafing of columns, it should be borne in mind that the slow and laborious crossing of the Seine in ferries and motor boats was forced on the division by the previous destruction from the air of road and rail bridges over the river. Prisoners of war report that they were exhausted on their arrival and went into action without rest, food or even halts en route.

(*f*) The 27Ist Infantry Division which began to move from Montpellier on Ist July took approximately I9 days to reach the Rouen area. Some of the trains were attacked at Arenes just outside Montpellier before they started and casualties totalling I,500 were reported; other trains were delayed for several days by air attack in the Lyons-St. Etienne area. The troops which did reach the battle area marched into the Caen area under heavy air attack. The original schedules for the 49 trains in this move are interesting in that they allowed I8 hours 25 minutes for the 285 mile journey from Montpellier to Chalon sur Saone. In fact, several trains took II days to pass Lyons and 20 trains were blocked in the Lyons area and finally diverted via St. Etienne and Mouling.

259. *Effect of Weather on Operations* – It is clear, I believe, from the foregoing paragraphs that the Allied air forces succeeded in crippling one of the most dense and complex networks of railways and roads in the world, and in practically denying its use to the enemy. I must emphasise, however, the influence which bad weather had on these operations. Both heavy and medium bombers, because of this bad weather, were prevented time and again from taking part in planned attacks on railways and bridges. We needed weather consistently good enough to permit precision visual bombing in density and co-ordinated attacks of a type most appropriate, as regards aircraft and weapons, to the targets involved throughout the whole of this period. I am convinced that if we had had this weather the enemy would have been prevented from moving by rail at all, and his retreat, disastrous as it was for him, would have been virtually impossible and far more costly in casualties to personnel and equipment than it was.

260. *Attacks on Communications – August and September* – The second phase of

attacks on communications began when the enemy tried to get away, and this became almost entirely a fighter and fighter bomber war. Forced to move by day as well as by night to escape the encircling ground forces, the enemy was constantly harried and destroyed. The roads leading to the Seine, then the Seine crossings, pontoons and barges and finally the roads of Northern France were in turn successfully attacked and became littered with the skeletons of the German Army's transport and equipment.

26I. The mounting total of this destruction is evident in the following statistics of pilots' claims of mechanical transport and A.F.V's destroyed. These figures do not include those claimed as probably destroyed or damaged:-

6th-30th June	2,400
Ist-3Ist July	3,364
Ist-3Ist August	4,09I
Ist-30th September	6,238
	16,093

262. *Value of Reconnaissance* – I cannot stress too strongly the importance of reconnaissance in planning attacks on communications. Although inclement weather interfered with the programmes for both photographic and visual reconnaissances, I was generally well informed of the moves of enemy supplies and reinforcements and was able to deal with them before they reached the battle zone. The valuable information brought back also enabled the Army Commanders to make accurate forecasts of the enemy strength and intentions. This position became completely reversed when the Allied armies moved forward. There is evidence to show that, because the Allied fighters kept the G.A.F. reconnaissance down to a negligible effort, the German High Command was fighting completely in the dark, unaware of the Allied intentions or of the strength and direction of each thrust.

263. In the period D-Day to 30th September, I944, the reconnaissance units of A.E.A.F. flew 4,808 sorties on photographic and I4,I40 sorties on visual reconnaissances, a total of I8,948 sorties.

Close Support Operations.

264. In addition to the contribution made to the success of the land battle by attacks on the enemy's communications, the air forces gave direct support to the Allied armies. These operations were laid on in three ways:-

(*a*) armed reconnaissance

(*b*) pre-arranged support

(*c*) immediate tactical support.

265. The armed reconnaissances were made by fighter bomber aircraft, which with bombs, R.P. and cannon fire, attacked a variety of targets, particularly movement seen on roads or railways. The pre-arranged support was of two kinds – attacks made

according to plans prepared some time in advance and which included heavy and medium bombers; and secondly, the more normal form of attacks laid on as a result of conferences between Army and Air staff in the field, when tactical targets for the ensuing day were decided upon. For these attacks, the Army usually undertook to assist the bombers by marking the target by means of smoke signals. Immediate support was provided in the usual way by strike aircraft held in readiness to attack targets requested direct by Army forward positions, or reported by reconnaissance aircraft.

266. Much of the work of the squadrons engaged on armed reconnaissance I have described in the preceding paragraphs dealing with attacks on communications. In addition to the pre-arranged support by medium and fighter bombers (dealt with later in paragraph 284 et seq.), there were six large scale attacks by heavy bombers during the period D-Day to 30th September, apart from certain other attacks on the enemy garrisons left in the Channel ports.

267. *Pre-arranged support using heavy bombers* – The use of heavy bombers in close support to ground forces was an important development in air warfare. A word on the situation prior to the employment of heavy bombers in such a role will not, therefore, be out of place.

268. The initial impetus of the Allied assault had secured a bridgehead extending from the Cotentin Peninsula to Caen, but the enemy had been able to concentrate against this relatively short front. He held strong, well sited defence positions in depth. By stealth, ingenuity and taking advantage of frequent periods of bad weather which made air policing of road and rail in the tactical area impossible, he managed to muster just sufficient reinforcements and warlike supplies to maintain his position.

269. Concentrations of artillery had not succeeded in cracking his defences sufficiently to enable a successful breakthrough to be made without, it was considered, a prohibitive cost in both men and material. A stalemate appeared to have arisen.

270. Neither could an air bombardment sufficiently heavy and concentrated to produce a situation ripe for a successful ground attack be provided by medium, light and fighter bombers.

271. I had already submitted to you a study of the situation in which I had made suggestions as to how the air forces could help the land forces to break out of the Normandy bridgehead. After consideration of this study by the various Commands (both land and air) concerned, it was decided to use heavy bombers in the virtually novel role of army co-operation.

272. The detailed plans for these attacks were worked out at an inter-service level, being finally co-ordinated at your headquarters. The co-ordination of the actual operations of the Air Forces involved in the attacks, however, was exercised by me.

273. The first of the large scale attacks, using heavy bombers in close support took place at 0430 hours on 8th July. R.A.F. Bomber Command employed 467 bombers to drop 2,562 tons of bombs on positions North of Caen. The British and Canadian troops, held up to the North of the town for so long by the enemy, followed up the bombing with a frontal attack. By nightfall they had entered the streets of Caen. The

bombing had therefore succeeded in its object and had opened a way for a breakthrough by the ground forces.

274. The second, and largest, of these operations (Operation Goodwood) took place on 18th July, when the combined weight of the United States Eighth Air Force, Royal Air Force Bomber Command and the Allied Expeditionary Air Force supported an advance by elements of the Second British Army in the Caen area.

275. This attack was the heaviest and most concentrated air attack in support of ground forces ever attempted. No less than 1,676 heavy bombers and 343 medium and light bombers were committed to the attack and the total tonnage of bombs dropped reached 7,700 U.S. tons.

276. In view of its interest I set out the plan for this large attack in some detail. The plan provided for the destruction of enemy installations and forces to allow the ground troops to advance along the axis Escoville-Cagny. The ground forces prior to the jump-off, were generally along an east/west line through Herouvillette. R.A.F. Bomber Command were employed to destroy the installations and forces in the areas marked A, H and M on the map[11] facing. Cratering was acceptable in these areas to prevent the possibility of the enemy making flanking attacks over this ground. Heavy bombers of the United States Eighth Air Force were concentrated on the installations and forces in the areas marked I, P and Q. Cratering was acceptable in the first of these areas, but not in the other two, as our own forces were to pass over this ground. The medium and light bombers of the tactical air forces were detailed to neutralise the enemy forces in the areas marked C, D, E, F and G. Pinpoint targets were given in areas, C, F and G, while the whole areas marked D and E were to be swept with an even pattern of fragmentation bombs. The laying-on of this attack, involving more than 2,000 bombers, meant very careful timing.

277. The other four attacks by heavy bombers were generally based on the same principle of destroying the enemy strongpoints, and cratering given areas to prevent the enemy from attacking the flanks of our forces while they were advancing through the swept but relatively undamaged centre of the assault area.

278. The third of the large scale attacks involving heavy bombers was launched on 25th July, when 1,495 heavy bombers and 388 fighter bombers of the United States Eighth and Ninth Air Forces dropped 4,790 tons of bombs in a bombardment preliminary to an advance by elements of the First United States Army across the Periers – St. Lo highway. Unfortunately some of the bombs in this attack fell short and caused some casualties to our own ground forces in the area.

279. The fourth attack was in support of the Second British Army south of Caumont. The preliminary heavy air bombardment was launched early on 30th July and 693 heavy bombers of R.A.F. Bomber Command and over 500 light and medium bombers of A.E.A.F. dropped 2,227 tons of bombs.

280. The fifth attack assisted the advance of the First Canadian Army along the Caen – Falaise road on the night of 7-8th August and during the succeeding day. 1,450 heavy bombers of the United States Eighth Air Force and of R.A.F. Bomber Command, and fighter bombers of the Second Tactical Air Force dropped 5,210 tons of bombs on enemy installations, strong points and forces in the area of the advance.

281. The sixth attack, also by R.A.F. Bomber Command, took place on the morning of 14th August and assisted the Canadian forces to advance into Falaise. 811 bombers were employed and 3,723 tons of bombs were dropped in the attack. Again, in this operation, some of the bombs fell short of the targets causing casualties to our own ground forces.

282. In each case, the ground forces were able to move into the bombarded positions practically without opposition. That they failed to exploit fully the break-through is known, but there are doubtless many reasons for this failure. In the second attack, the principal cause of delay was the bottleneck across the Caen bridges which delayed the moving of armoured formations sufficiently long to enable the enemy to remount his screen of guns outside the area which had been bombed. In the third attack, the Army Commander agreed that the "carpet" bombing did put his troops through the enemy positions; difficulties which arose in moving the army forces forward as rapidly as was necessary again prevented a complete exploitation. Nevertheless, these heavy attacks did finally succeed in starting off the break-through of the ground forces across the Periers – St. Lo highway, and it was this break-through which eventually determined the battle of Normandy, which liberated France.

283. I have referred to the lessons learned from this series of attacks in close support in Part V of this Despatch. From an air point of view, the attacks definitely proved that saturation bombing by heavy bombers on a narrow front can enable an army to break through, but they also showed the need for the army to exploit, without delay, the favourable situation created. Further, the heartening moral effect of these large scale air support formations on our own forces and the corresponding shattering of the will to resist among the enemy has been stated by Army Commanders to have been of vital consequence. Air and land action must be closely co-ordinated. The land forces must be ready to step off at least immediately the bombing is over, if not just before, accepting some slight risk of casualties from our bombing, and the artillery programme must be directly related to the bombing plan to ensure economy of effort by both arms.

284. *Pre-arranged Close Support by Medium and Fighter Bombers* – The operation of medium and fighter bombers on pre-arranged support was often in small formations against targets such as gun positions, tank laagers, chateaux suspected of housing headquarters formations, and defended positions. The effectiveness of the support may be judged from the following extract from a captured document:-

> "C.-in-C. West (Von Kluge) in a report to General Warlimont, Hitler's representative, on the position at Avranches says – 'Whether the enemy can be stopped at this point is still questionable. The enemy air superiority is terrific, and smothers almost all of our movements. Every movement of the enemy, however, is prepared and protected by its air forces. Losses in men and equipment are extraordinary. The morale of the troops has suffered very heavily under constant murderous enemy fire'."

285. *Immediate Support* – The immediate support of the armies was provided by the fighter bombers of the tactical air forces and in this role the fighter bombers have

shown their greatest effectiveness. Never before have they been used in such strength and with such decisive results. I have divided my review of their operations in the following paragraphs into four phases of the land battle, as follows:-

(i) The period of static fighting.

(ii) The break-through of the Allied armies.

(iii) The period of encirclement.

(iv) The retreat across Northern France and Belgium.

286. In the early period of the operations of offensive fighter and fighter bomber forces, the co-operation between the Commander of the United States IXth Tactical Air Command, General Quesada, and the Air Officer Commanding No. 83 Group, Royal Air Force, Air Vice-Marshal Broadhurst, C.B., D.S.O., D.F.C., A.F.C., was close and effective. Each gave the other assistance as the occasion arose and whenever a good target presented itself, neither hesitated to call on the other to take advantage of it. The development of common methods of control and target indication and reference greatly assisted this British and United States mutual support.

287. *Period of Static Fighting* – During this phase of the land battle, the tactical air forces concentrated upon the close support of the armies within the tactical boundary. The technique of this form of support was considerably developed. A system of Visual Control Points was perfected by which an experienced fighter controller rode in one of the leading tanks, equipped with the necessary V.H.F. radio-telephony equipment for the control of fighter aircraft. By these means an extraordinary flexibility of control of the fighter bombers on army co-operation was maintained. Another interesting development in technique was provided by the use of the American M.E.W. mobile Radar station, which, because of its ability to locate low-flying aircraft and of its range of detection, proved of great assistance to the fighter forces covering the battle areas. However, I feel that the chief value of the tactical air forces during this first period lay in their ability to smash up the enemy's attempted concentrations of tanks and vehicles before a counter-attack could be launched.

288. *The Break-through of the Allied Armies* – When the United States armies achieved their break-through which carried them to the Brittany Peninsula and on into the country north of the Loire, the close support work of the air forces took on a new aspect. Continuous fighter cover was provided to the advancing armoured spearheads. This cover, not only protected them from enemy air attack, but also reached out, destroying enemy tanks, M/T and gun positions that lay in the path and along the flanks of the advancing armies. In this respect the work of the United States Ninth Air Force, particularly of the IXth and XIXth Tactical Air Commands, deserves special mention. Fighter pilots of this force destroyed hundreds of enemy tanks and vehicles. They had developed a technique of attacking tanks from the rear, which experience had shown was most vulnerable to their .50 calibre machine gun bullets.

289. It was to hold up this break-through that the enemy, under personal orders from Hitler, attempted, on 7th August, his really large scale armoured counter-attack,

launched against Mortain in an effort to reach the sea at Avranches and split the advancing American armies from their main bases. This concentration of armour gave the tactical squadrons of A.E.A.F. a great chance to inflict a crushing blow on the enemy and prove the superiority of their weapons and training. The opportunity was fully accepted, particularly by the Typhoon squadrons of R.A.F. Second Tactical Air Force.

290. On 7th August there were nineteen squadrons of Typhoons operating from French airfields. These squadrons carried out 59 missions, flying 458 sorties in all during that day. 294 of these sorties were in the Mortain area. No less than 2,088 rocket projectiles were fired, and 80 tons of bombs were dropped; and the pilots claimed very large numbers of tanks, A.F.V., and M.T. destroyed and damaged.

291. This tremendous blow at the Nazi armour was achieved at the cost of 5 aircraft lost and 10 damaged, and was one of the most vital factors in defeating the enemy attacks.

292. The scale of effort of these Typhoon squadrons is indicative of the sustained activity of the tactical air forces. The number of missions flown by Typhoons in the five-day period, 7th-11th August, rose to 298, involving 2,193 sorties. 9,850 rocket projectiles and 398 tons of bombs were aimed at enemy targets, and many more enemy tanks and vehicles were destroyed. These results were achieved at the cost of 13 Typhoons destroyed and 16 damaged.

293. After the Typhoon attacks on the first day, the fighter-bombers of the United States Ninth Air Force took over the responsibility for the Mortain area, and in many attacks accounted for many more of the enemy armoured vehicles. By this effort, the air forces broke up and partly destroyed the enemy concentrations of armour, and although a number of spearheads did penetrate our forward positions, they were effectively dealt with by the ground forces. In this counter-attack Hitler threw away the one force of armour which could have enabled him to extricate his army. As a result, the disaster to the Army was complete. Between 8th and 14th August, the IXth Tactical Air Command flew a total of 4,012 sorties; virtually all of them in co-operation with ground action in the Mortain region. On 12th August 673 sorties were flown and 310.8 tons of bombs dropped.

294. To the outstanding success of these attacks on the enemy armour, the weather effectively contributed, not only because it cleared and remained fine during the critical days from 7th to 11th August, but also because it had been so bad earlier. This bad weather had drastically restricted air operations and, there seems reason to suppose, had lulled the enemy into a sense of false security.

295. It is difficult to find any other reason why he should have abandoned first principles and moved his armour head to tail in long convoys over roads in daylight. These convoys, once the weather cleared, gave the tactical air forces their unique chance of scoring an outstanding success.

296. *The Encirclement* – During the period in which the German 7th Army was rapidly becoming encircled by the sweep of the American ground forces to Alencon and Argentan and by the pressure of the British and Canadian forces towards Falaise, the German Commander had to decide whether to withdraw before the gap was closed

or to stay and fight it out. I feel certain that any such withdrawal in the face of the overwhelming air superiority of the Allied air forces would have been disastrous, and it would appear that the German Commander also had serious misgivings as to the practicability of such a withdrawal. In large part, the enemy army stood to fight. While the front was more or less clearly defined, the air forces were able to inflict destruction on the concentrations of enemy troops. However, when the encirclement became complete, the ground position naturally became confused. In these conditions it was inevitable that our air forces should have once or twice attacked our own troops in error. Such misfortune could not be avoided. As a result, however, the Army Commanders eventually fixed bomb lines which automatically severely restricted attacks in close support of the land forces and thus denied to the fighter bombers many excellent targets. I pressed for revision of these bomb lines to allow more freedom to operate closer to the fighting, but the Army Commanders maintained their caution. I am convinced that, as a result of this action, the reasons for which I fully appreciate, the air forces let through a great deal of enemy material and troops that would otherwise not have escaped.

297. *The Retreat across Northern France and Belgium* – Once the enemy had begun his retreat to the Seine, the fighter and fighter-bomber forces of A.E.A.F. were presented with some first-class targets. Low flying attacks inflicted enormous personnel casualties, while skeletons of burnt-out transport littered every road and track and were ample evidence of the effectiveness of these attacks.

298. During this retreat it was reported more and more frequently that very large columns of ambulances were moving to the German rear. I was almost certain that these ambulances were faked and did, in fact, contain fighting soldiers and equipment. It was a critical decision to take as to whether or not these ambulances should be attacked. You finally decided against attacking them. Although we were thereby likely to miss some targets, it was preferable to win the battle without laying ourselves open to criticism, however unjustified. In a number of cases, however, it was found that ordinary vehicles were intermingled with the ambulances and these were attacked. It was significant that whenever this happened, the doors of the ambulances opened and German soldiers poured out in every direction and made for cover with a speed and agility quite remarkable for wounded men. Occasionally too, fire was opened on our aircraft from these ambulances.

299. At this time, reconnaissances began to show what was in the circumstances, a relatively considerable enemy movement on the railways north-east of the Seine, particularly through Rheims. This rail movement was apparently to carry up reserves to stabilise a line, probably on the Seine or the Marne. I therefore directed a proportion of the fighter bomber effort against these movements. The United States Ninth Air Force fighters, and further east, the United States Eighth Air Force fighters, did extremely well against these targets, and this effort, I believe, virtually broke up the enemy's last chance of bringing up sufficient forces to re-form a line in France.

300. Once the remnants of the enemy divisions had crossed the Seine (and in the crossing they had to run the gauntlet of continuous air attacks on their ferries) they dispersed rapidly into a widening area. In consequence there were fewer and fewer

large targets offering themselves for attack. In the main, therefore, fighters and fighter bombers reverted to direct support of the Allied columns and attacked the enemy rearguards just ahead of them.

301. In general, I would like to emphasise again the terrific havoc that was created by the air forces during the enemy's withdrawal to and across the Seine. Thousands of vehicles were destroyed and from this onslaught the enemy succeeded in getting away only small sections of his previously very powerful army.

302. The two outstanding days for the tactical air forces in this period were 18th and 25th August. The R.P. fighters and the fighter bombers of R.A.F. Second Tactical Air Force particularly claimed many victims, and the fighter bombers of the United States Ninth Air Force added their quota. The densest congestion of these enemy concentrations was in the Trun-Vimoutieres area, and the wreckage later found in this area is ample testimony to the effectiveness of these air attacks.

303. On 25th August, the G.A.F. attempted in force to protect the efforts of the German Seventh Army to use the river crossing in the Rouen area. They were met by the fighters of the United States Ninth Air Force. 77 enemy aircraft were destroyed in combat and a further 49 were destroyed on the ground. On this and the subsequent three days, approximately 3,000 vehicles were destroyed and several thousand dead German soldiers were found among the wreckage in the area of the Seine crossings.

Attacks on Coastal Garrisons.

304. During the last week in August and through September, strong bombing forces were used to reduce the enemy garrisons holding onto the Atlantic and Channel ports. The attacks on Brest between 24th August and 6th September were shared by the United States Eighth and Ninth Air Forces and R.A.F. Bomber Command. More than 6,000 tons of bombs were dropped on the garrisons of this city. The attacks on Le Havre, Boulogne and Calais were R.A.F. Bomber Command operations, and provided excellent examples of reduction of a town by air bombing. This was especially so in the case of Le Havre. The Allied casualties in the subsequent assault against a strongly fortified garrison of II,000 defenders totalled only 400. Between Ist and I2th September, 2,042 sorties were flown against Le Havre alone and II,000 tons of bombs were dropped, 5,000 tons of this total being aimed in one massive daylight attack on an extremely small area.

305. This bombing was undertaken at the express wish of the Army Commanders and undoubtedly it succeeded in paving the way for and in saving the lives of thousands of our soldiers in the final assault. It must be recorded however, that casualties to French civilians shut up with the German garrisons in these ports were inevitably high, particularly so at Le Havre. I feel, that in the broad view, this bombing effort would have been more profitably directed against targets inside Germany, particularly as the disorganisation of her retreating army was most acute at this time. I should have been happier to see it used against focal points in the communications system behind the enemy frontier, in an effort to delay the movement of reinforcements with which the enemy succeeded, in mid-September, in stabilising a line along the Rhine and the Moselle.

306. It must also be remembered that the bombing had to be laid on to suit the Army plan, and in consequence it was sometimes delayed or postponed because the Army could not always be ready to attack at the agreed time or because of unfavourable weather conditions over the target. Bad weather over the target areas coincided sometimes with good weather over Germany. Because the heavy bombers had been committed to, and were standing by for, attacks on the garrison towns, opportunities for using them in good conditions against vital industrial targets in Germany were lost.

307. The following statistics give the weight of effort against coastal defences and gun positions during the month of September. This effort was very largely made up of the attacks laid on for the reduction of besieged garrisons.

Attacks on Coastal Garrisons during September, 1944.

Force	Sorties.	Tons of Bombs.
A.E.A.F.	5,567	4,406
U.S. Eighth A.F.	1,327	4,50I
R.A.F. Bomber Command	4,5I0	25,8II
	11,404	34,7I8

Fighter Cover to the Assault and the Shipping areas.

308. In the foregoing paragraphs I have tried to describe the support both direct and indirect which the air forces gave to ground forces after the assault was launched. I come now to the equally important task undertaken by the air forces, the task, namely of protecting the beach-head area and our shipping from attacks by the G.A.F. I have already explained (see para. 32) my reasons for retaining a large fighter force to ensure that the air superiority we had won was maintained on D-Day and afterwards, and in addition, in para. 20I have briefly mentioned the fighter protection given to the cross channel movement of assault forces. There were, in fact, I7I squadrons of day fighters and fighter bombers available for all the tasks that they were called upon to undertake in support of the invasion. These forces were made up as follows:

Day Fighters	U.S. Ninth A.F.	U.S. Eighth A.F.	2nd T.A.F.	85 Group	A.D.G.B.	Total
Mustang III	6	12	6	–	–	24
Thunderbolt	39	21	–	–	–	60
Lightning	9	12	–	–	–	21
Spitfire	–	–	27	4	15	46
Tempest	–	–	–	–	2	2
						153
Fighter Bombers						
Typhoon	–	–	18	–	–	18
						171

Burnt out tanks and landing craft lie strewn across the beach at Dieppe after the Allied withdrawal. (Courtesy of the War and Peace Archive)

In all, twenty-nine Churchill tanks, comprising of assorted Mark I, II and III examples, were disembarked during the Dieppe Raid. Of these, twenty-seven would eventually get ashore – two "drowned in deep water". Fifteen would make it to the esplanade – though not much further. (Courtesy of the War and Peace Archive)

A number of Allied prisoners under guard at Dieppe before being marched away to captivity. (Courtesy of the War and Peace Archive)

The Royal Navy's landing craft LCA-1377 transporting American troops across Weymouth Bay during preparations for the Normandy invasion, circa May–June 1944. (Courtesy of the Conseil Régional de Basse-Normandie/US National Archives)

At exactly 08.32 hours on 6 June 1944, Sergeant Jim Mapham of No.5 Army Film and Photographic Unit photographed this scene on "Queen Red" Beach, a sector in the centre-left of Sword Beach (the precise location is near La Brèche, Hermanville-sur-Mer). The shutter clicked just as the beach came under heavy artillery and mortar fire from German positions inland. One US newspaper which published this image in the aftermath of the landings described it as "the greatest picture of the war". (HMP)

US troops hit the shore on the morning of 6 June 1944. Titled "Into the Jaws of Death", this image was taken by Chief Photographer's Mate Robert F. Sargent. The landing craft seen here was crewed by US Coastguard personnel, and had set off for the Normandy beaches from the U.S. Coast Guard-manned USS *Samuel Chase*. (US National Archives)

A cameraman peers between men crowded in a landing craft to obtain this shot of the first wave going ashore as his own LCA nears the smoke-shrouded Omaha Beach. (Conseil Régional de Basse-Normandie/US National Archives)

Taken by one of the seven Canadian Army Film and Photographic Unit personnel to go ashore on Juno Beach on D-Day, this image shows second-wave troops of the 9th Canadian Infantry Brigade, probably Highland Light Infantry of Canada, disembarking with bicycles from LCI(L)s – Landing Craft Infantry Large – on to "Nan White" Beach at Bernières-sur-Mer shortly before midday on 6 June 1944. (HMP)

Some of the images taken on D-Day were in colour – though this is more unusual amongst the pictures taken by the British and Canadian photographers. One of the exceptions was this snapshot taken by one of the CAFPU personnel and shows troops making their way towards Bernières-sur-Mer on Juno Beach. (Conseil Régional de Basse-Normandie/Canadian National Archives)

US troops wade through the surf on to French soil – more specifically Utah Beach. (US National Archives)

Canadian soldiers guard German prisoners on Juno Beach, a scene captured by Lieutenant Frank L. Dubervill of the Canadian Army Film and Photographic Unit. (Conseil Régional de Basse-Normandie/Canadian National Archives)

A photograph of the battle-scarred church in Bernières-sur-Mer taken in the weeks after the D-Day landings, with the effects of the shell fire visible on the tower. (Regional Council of Basse-Normandie/National Archives of Canada)

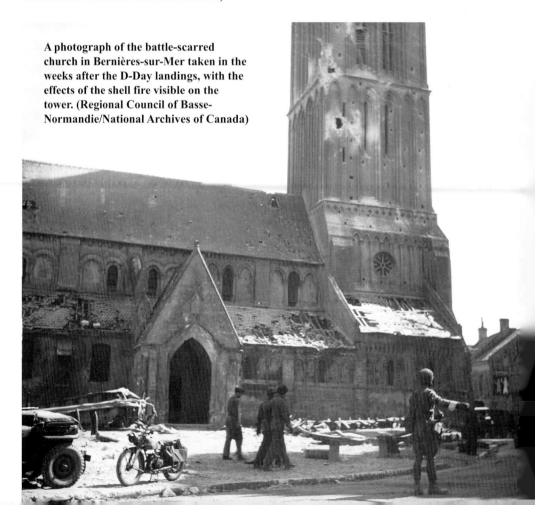

Scenes of jubilation as British troops liberate the Belgian capital on 4 September 1944. Major General A.H.S. Adair, GOC Guards Armoured Division, acknowledges the ecstatic crowd from his mobbed Cromwell command tank. (Courtesy of Richard Doherty)

An RAF officer poses beside his Jeep on the German border as the Allied advance eastwards continues. (HMP)

British armour pictured during the entry of Allied forces into Hamburg, which surrendered with little fighting, on 3 May 1945. Note the distinctive Elbe bridge in the background. (HMP)

The German surrender underway – captured soldiers hand in their weapons at Soest, in North Rhine-Westphalia, on 10 May 1945. (Dutch National Archives)

309. In addition, A.D.G.B. retained 9 Spitfire, I Mustang and 2 Typhoon squadrons for the air defence, by day, of the United Kingdom.

3I0. The night fighter forces available for the protection by night of the assault area and shipping lanes consisted of 6 Mosquito squadrons.(The defence of the United Kingdom by night was undertaken by A.D.G.B. which had 8 Mosquito and I Beaufighter squadrons and a further 2 Mosquito Intruder squadrons.) This force allowed me to operate 30 to 40 night fighters over the assault area and shipping lanes during the night.

3II. In order to achieve the most economical and effective use of resources these fighter forces were pooled and placed under the control of a Combined Control Centre. This Control Centre was situated at Uxbridge, where it was able to make full use of the tried and proven static control organisation built-up by No. II Group, Royal Air Force, which had previously handled the very large air cover given to the Dieppe operation, in August, I942. This unified control ensured the necessary flexibility to cover the principal tasks allotted to these day fighter forces. The principal tasks were:-

(*a*) continuous cover of the beach-head areas.

(*b*) continuous cover of the main naval approach.

(*c*) direct air support of the ground forces, including close support.

(*d*) escort to day bomber and troop carrier formations.

(*e*) withdrawal cover for night bombers leaving the assault area after first light.

(*f*) to provide a striking force for employment as the air situation required.

3I2. Initially, the following allocation of squadrons was made for employment in these specific tasks.

Beach Cover	54 squadrons
Shipping Cover	15 squadrons
Direct Air Support	36 squadrons
Offensive Fighter and Bomber Support	33 squadrons
Strike Force and Escort to Airborne operations	33 squadrons
	171 squadrons

3I3. These squadrons were prepared to operate up to a maximum of 4 sorties per day on D-Day, 3 sorties per day on D + I, and thereafter 2 sorties per day. In fact, because of the lack of G.A.F. reaction, this scale of effort was not necessary. On D-Day, A.E.A.F. fighter and fighter bomber squadrons, including night fighter squadrons, flew I.44 sorties per aircraft available and on D + I, 2.28 sorties per aircraft available. Owing to the lack of enemy activity and the serious deterioration of the weather, the average sorties per fighter aircraft available during June fell to I.00 per day. However, in the first three weeks of the operation, more than 30,000 sorties were flown on beach-head and shipping cover. Detailed figures are set out below.

3I4. *Scale of Effort of A.E.A.F. Fighters and Fighter Bombers.*

	No. of operational Aircraft available	No. of sorties flown	Average No. of sorties per available a/c per day
2nd T.A.F.:-			
D-Day	883	1,266	1.43
D + 1	843	2,467	2.93
June (average)	840	988	1.18
Ninth A.F.:-			
D-Day	1,158	2,139	1.84
D + 1	1,049	2,804	2.80
June (average)	1,005	1,022	1.02
A.D.G.B. (including 85 Group):-			
D-Day	885	811	0.92
D + I	852	984	1.15
June (average)	838	678	0.81
Total:-			
D-Day	2,926	4,216	1.44
D + 1	2,744	6,255	2.28
June (average)	2,683	2,688	1.00

315. Commencing at 0430 hours on D-Day and continued throughout the daylight hours during the assault period, a continuous fighter cover was maintained at nine squadrons strength over the whole assault area. Of this force of nine squadrons, six Spitfire squadrons provided low cover and three Thunderbolt squadrons, high cover. Of the six Spitfire squadrons, one squadron patrolled over each of the two American beaches with a third squadron on the western flank; two more covered the length of the three British beaches with one squadron on the eastern flank. Of the three Thunderbolt squadrons maintaining high cover, one was disposed centrally over the western area, a second over the eastern area, and the third was positioned between the two areas, but some eight to ten miles inland from the beach area itself. In this position it was readily available to reinforce any particular area or to engage enemy aircraft approaching the beach from the south, south-east or south-west.

316. The high and low cover fighters operating over the eastern area were under the control of F.D.T. 217; the fighters over the western area, under the control of F.D.T. 216. The "free" high flying Thunderbolt squadron operating inland, was also controlled by F.D.T. 217 (see para. 322).

317. The scale of the effort described above was maintained, whenever weather permitted, until 13th June, when the force involved was reduced to three low cover and two high cover squadrons. All these squadrons operated from England. In addition, a reserve of two squadrons from those by then operating on the Continent was maintained at readiness for extra low cover if required. This arrangement continued, again whenever weather permitted, until sufficient fighter squadrons had been moved to the Continent to take over the commitment (see para. 329).

318. Four squadrons of Lightnings (each of 16 aircraft strength) maintained throughout the daylight hours a continuous patrol over the assault forces and the shipping lanes leading to the beaches. They operated normally at between three

thousand and five thousand feet or just below cloud base, in four distinct areas, and all were under the control of. F.D.T. I3 (see para. 322). This cover was maintained for the first three days, but because of the lack of enemy reaction it was then reduced to three squadrons, and finally to two squadrons on IIth June. Additionally, a reserve of not less than six squadrons was also available for reinforcement of any sector requiring it.

3I9. It was essential to provide adequate fighter cover over the beach-head and shipping lanes during the critical periods of first light and last light. To ensure that sufficient aircraft could be in the area at these times, twelve British and twelve American fighter squadrons were trained to take off and land in darkness. Thus, with the night fighter operations, fighter cover was maintained, whenever weather permitted, continuously throughout the twenty-four hours.

320. *Control of Fighter Forces.* – I have already dealt with the activities of fighter aircraft on offensive patrols and in direct support, and those of the strike force. The arrangement for meeting the calls for air support during the assault were as follows. A Headquarters ship accompanied each Naval Assault Force: this ship carried an Air Staff Officer who was the representative or the Commander, Advanced A.E.A.F. This officer kept the Commander, Advanced A.E.A.F., informed of the Military and Naval Commanders' intentions and requirements, through naval channels to Portsmouth and thence to Uxbridge. These Headquarters ships were equipped for the control of direct support aircraft and also to act as stand-by to the Fighter Direction Tenders (referred to below) for the control of fighter cover forces. In neither case did the need for them to exercise direct control of fighters arise. In addition, each Headquarters ship received reports in the clear from reconnaissance aircraft and relayed this information on targets to Uxbridge. They also provided liaison when needed (and it was frequently needed) between the bombarding warships and their spotting aircraft (see paragraph 207).

32I. As stated in paragraph 3II, the central control of both the night and day fighter squadrons was exercised by the Combined Control Centre, Uxbridge, using the static organisation of A.D.G.B. Three Fighter Direction Tenders operated as forward controls. One of these Fighter Direction Tenders was placed in each of the United States and British sectors and one in the main shipping lane. This ship later moved to a position off Barfleur, to counter enemy night operations. Detailed arrangements were also made to ensure that the loss of one or all of these ships should not leave us without control of our fighter forces. These arrangements, briefly, provided for a reciprocal stand-by between these F.D.Ts., certain naval vessels, the Headquarters ships, the G.C.I. Stations landed in France, and the control centres in the United Kingdom.

322. *Fighter Direction Tenders.* – Some details of the operations of the Fighter Direction Tenders follow:-

   (i) F.D.T. 2I6 was at first located five to fifteen miles off shore opposite
      the "Omaha" section of the beach; later it moved closer in to a position
      off St. Laurent. The tasks allotted to this F.D.T. were to control the day
      and night fighter cover over the western assault area. Control was

effective on the only occasion the enemy attacked beaches in the United States sector in any strength.

(ii) F.D.T. 217 sailed with the Eastern Assault Forces. It was also placed five to fifteen miles off "Sword" beach, but later moved closer in shore. It controlled the day and night cover to the Eastern Assault Area and co-ordinated the cover over the whole area. The control of the night fighter pool was handed over to the far shore G.C.C. on D + 6 and the day fighter cover on D + 8. The ship then moved to a position off St. Laurent to act as stand-by control and continued to control night fighters until D +17.

(iii) F.D.T. 13 was located forty to fifty miles off the beach-head to control both day and night fighters protecting the shipping lanes. On 12th June, the control of day fighters in these areas was handed back to a fixed station in the United Kingdom and the ship sailed to a position twenty miles east north-east of Barfleur, where from 15th to 27th June it controlled night fighters protecting shipping.

323. The figures below indicate only partially the excellent work of these Fighter Direction Tenders, and when the low scale of enemy effort and the steady and prolonged deterioration of the weather are considered, the number of enemy aircraft claimed destroyed and damaged by the Allied aircraft controlled by these ships, is high. The figures show the number of aircraft controlled by Fighter Direction Tenders at night, and the number of casualties inflicted by day and night by aircraft actually under the control of a Fighter Direction Tender at the time of the combat:-

Operations of Fighter Direction Tenders Day

Day (6th-13th June inclusive):-

F.D.T. 216	13 enemy aircraft destroyed.
F.D.T. 217	35 enemy aircraft destroyed, others probably destroyed and damaged.
F.D.T. 13	Nil.

Night (6th-13th June inclusive):-

	N/F controlled	Contacts	Friendly	E/A destroyed
F.D.T. 216	62	49	33	3
F.D.T. 217	275	123	67	10
				1 damaged
F.D.T. 13	18	13	10	–

Night (15th-27th June inclusive)

	N/F controlled	Contacts	Friendly	E/A destroyed
F.D.T. 13	64	195	144	12
				1 damaged

324. The story of the setting up of Fighter Control units on the Continent is dealt with in Part IV. Here it may be recorded that at 2230 hours on D-Day, the first G.C.I, station on the far shore began controlling night fighters and on D + 6 took over the co-ordination of all night fighters from the F.D.T. previously responsible. On D + 8, this G.C.I, station had expanded into No. 483 Group Control Centre, and control of

both day and night fighters over the battle zones passed to this centre.

325. *Allied A.A. Gunfire.* – The operation of our fighter aircraft was at times rendered difficult by the actions of our own anti-aircraft guns. In fact, I regret to say that engagements of friendly aircraft did occur with some frequency in the initital stages of the operation. I made representations to the Allied Naval Commander about certain instances of promiscuous and uncontrolled fire and both Naval Task Force Commanders decided to prohibit any A.A. gunfire from merchant vessels unless these ships were being directly and individually attacked. From many reports of observers, it would appear however, that the merchant ships were not alone to blame. This gunfire occurred despite the fact that it had been agreed, during the planning stages, that no A.A. gunners should be permitted to engage aircraft unless they were qualified to recognise by their appearance all aircraft, both friendly and hostile, which were likely to operate in the area concerned. Furthermore, the Naval and Army Commanders were charged with the responsibility of nominating the type of personnel or unit which should be allowed to engage aircraft under this rather general classification.

326. It must, however, be admitted that the weather conditions generally were so indifferent that the aircraft providing fighter cover and close support was often forced to operate below the height which had previously been agreed as a minimum, except in pursuit of the enemy. This factor must have caused complications for the A.A. gunners, especially when there was enemy activity at the same time.

327. A complete solution to the problem of using A.A. guns and defensive aircraft together in any amphibious operation has clearly not yet been found, and I am of the opinion that the whole question should be given considerably more scientific and practical study on an inter-service and inter-Allied basis than has been done in the past. I refer again to this problem in Part V.

328. On a limited number of merchant vessels, Royal Observer Corps personnel were provided, and this arrangement has drawn very favourable comments from all concerned. I have already recommended elsewhere that an extension of this use of specialised aircraft recognition personnel deserves further examination with a view to more general adoption by both the Army and the Navy.

329. *Transfer of Fighter forces to the Continent.* – It was appreciated that the effort of the fighters and fighter bombers over the beachhead would inevitably be seriously reduced after three or four days if they had to operate at such distances from their bases in the U.K. In the early planning therefore, a high priority had been arranged for naval lift of the stores and equipment which would be needed to operate the fighters and fighter bomber squadrons planned to be flown into bases on the Continent as soon as possible after D-Day. This precaution was fully warranted. The weather throughout June frequently prevented the operations of squadrons based in the south of England. Had the scheduled squadrons not arrived on the Continent as planned, fighter cover over the beach-head and shipping lanes would at times have been impossible, at times, moreover, when weather would have permitted the G.A.F. to operate against us. Nor would fighter bombers have been available to answer calls by the ground forces for urgent support. Actually, the beach-head and shipping lanes

were left without fighter cover only when the weather both in England and the Continent made all operations by Allied Air Forces and the G.A.F. impossible.

330. The operations of these fighter squadrons from bases on the Continent were made possible only by the work of the Airfield Construction engineers, of the maintenance personnel, and of the supply organisation which ensured the provision of the necessary stores and equipment. I refer to the work of these sections in more detail in Part IV.

331. The first British squadrons to land in France since 1940 were Nos. 130 and 303 which put down at 1200 hours on D + 4 on a strip on the "Gold" area. They were quickly followed by No. 144 (R.C.A.F.) Fighter Wing, consisting of Nos. 441, 442 and 443 squadrons, which at 1637 hours that same day, were airborne for a sweep. These were the first Allied squadrons to operate from French soil since the evacuation from Dunkirk.

332. The strength of squadrons based on the Continent was gradually built up in the first fourteen days of the operation; eight Spitfire, three Typhoon and three Auster squadrons moved in to, and were operating from, beachhead airfields by the end of this period.

333. During the following week, United States forces began moving in and nine Thunderbolt and three Mustang squadrons arrived. A further British contingent of one Spitfire, three Typhoon and one Auster squadrons arrived to make a total of thirty-one Allied squadrons operating from beach-head airfields three weeks after D-Day.

Enemy Reaction and Allied Counter-action.

334. I have dealt in para. 156 *et seq.* with the activities of the G.A.F. directed against our preparations for the assault. I now turn to the G.A.F.'s operations after the assault was launched.

335. The strength of that part of the German Air Force likely to be committed against the invasion was estimated at 1,750 front line aircraft. This figure included such aircraft of Reserve Training Units as were expected to be operationally used. The total was made up as follows:

Long Range Bombers	385
Ground Attack	50
Single-engine Fighters	745
Twin-engine Fighters – Day	55
– Night	395
Long Range Recce.	85
Tactical Recce.	25
Coastal Recce.	10
	1,750

336. The disposition of these forces is shown in the map[12] facing page 70. The Units based in Southern France (Mediterranean area) and in Denmark and Norway are also shown on this map, although I have not included them in the total given above.

337. The enemy air strength on D-Day was considerably greater than its strength

in this area six weeks before. Bomber strength had increased by approximately 200, single-engine fighters by 500 and twin-engine fighters by 125.

338. It was estimated that the service ability of these forces would be 55 per cent. for long-range bomber types and 60 per cent. for all others. The destruction of facilities at airfields in the rear of the assault area and the continued pounding of the fields themselves had forced the Luftwaffe to make extensive use of satellite landing fields, with the inevitable attendant difficulties of maintaining serviceability.

339. After D-Day, there was some reinforcement of units on the Western Front, though not as great as might have been expected. The reasons probably included the following:-

(i) a decision not to denude the Reich proper of its air protection, even at the expense of leaving the German armies in the field relatively uncovered.

(ii) the destruction of airfield facilities, making it difficult to service and operate from the fields at the enemy's disposal forces any larger than those already there.

(iii) the lack of fuel and lubricant supplies in the area and the difficulty of replacement of consumed stocks, owing to the dislocation of transport facilities.

340. The enemy scale of effort throughout the whole period D-Day to 30th September was considerably lower than was expected. As I have already stated, I had expected at the outset a week of fairly heavy air attacks, after which I felt confident that the enemy air effort would dwindle and require much less attention from our own air forces. In fact no serious air battle took place during this period.

341. *Enemy Air Opposition – June.* – Throughout June, the squadrons which showed the most aggressiveness were bomber units which operated by night, principally on sea mining in the shipping lanes but also on bombing operations against shipping in the approach lanes and against the beaches. The fighter units operated mainly in a defensive role against Allied bomber attacks and principally in the Paris area and south of the Seine, where they tried to provide cover to the reinforcement assembly areas and to the main airfields.

342. The scale of effort by a few enemy units was, however, relatively high. On days when flying conditions were good, many aircraft flew more than one sortie and three and four sorties per aircraft were not unusual. The frequent periods of bad weather gave respite from Allied air attack, rested the pilots and allowed ground staffs to keep up serviceability.

343. Except on isolated occasions during this month, the enemy fighter and fighter bomber formations showed a marked disinclination to engage Allied fighters, and they were often deterred, with relative ease, from carrying out their primary tasks. However, the night fighter activity against Allied bombers continued to be fairly heavy and vigorous.

344. On D-Day, the first enemy air reaction to the assault was a reconnaissance of

the Channel areas. At approximately 1500 hours, the first enemy fighters and fighter bombers appeared. This was nine hours after the assault began and fifteen hours after the first of very large formations of airborne transports and of the air bombardment squadrons had arrived over enemy territory. The enemy formations consisted of some FW 190s and one formation of 12 Ju 88s; four of this latter force were destroyed.

345. On the night of D/D + 1, approximately 85 enemy aircraft were active over the beach and shipping lanes. Some of the units operating were known to be specialised anti-shipping units. Activity on this scale was maintained on most nights during June.

346. During the morning of D + 1, a total of 59 enemy aircraft were sighted in the battle area. Ju 88s and Ju 188s were routed by low cover patrols and a formation of 16 FW 190s attempting to dive bomb the area north of Caen was forced by a Spitfire Wing to jettison their bombs. In all, fifteen enemy aircraft were claimed as destroyed by Allied fighters over the battle area during that morning.

347. In the afternoon of D + 1, the main enemy effort was defensive patrolling over assembly and rearward areas. Offensive fighter sweeps of Allied aircraft accounted for sixteen aircraft destroyed and five probably destroyed.

348. The principal enemy gains by air action during June were against shipping, and these were mainly as the result of night attacks. On D + 2, however, attacks against shipping off "Sword" beach resulted in a destroyer being sunk. Another destroyer was sunk by day by an aircraft torpedo attack off Portland Bill on 13th June. Sea mines laid in the shipping lanes and approach waters during the month also caused damage and loss to some ships and involved continuous employment of naval minesweepers. Considering the number of ships employed in narrow waters, these enemy gains were remarkably low.

349. *Enemy Air Opposition – July.* – Throughout July, the enemy air effort continued to be sporadic; in the first few days, a scale of effort of up to 450 day sorties was observed, but this quickly fell away and was not again reached until 27th July. Most of the day sorties were directed against Allied positions in the battle area, particularly at the western end of the Allied line.

350. The aggressiveness of the enemy also fluctuated. On some days, attacks were pressed home, on others a marked disinclination to fight was evident. The reaction to our bomber forces also varied; on some days, there was almost no opposition, while on others, determined defensive efforts were put up. The reaction to R.A.F. Bomber Command's night attacks was, however, sustained and on some occasions produced violent activity. Night offensive operations by the G.A.F., principally against shipping targets, were also maintained.

351. *Enemy Air Opposition – August.* – At the beginning of this month, with the break-out of the Allied armies accomplished, the G.A.F. day forces became even more committed to ground support. It was also evident that the enemy could no longer support his ground forces on both the British and American sectors and for a time he left the British sector alone to concentrate on what he considered the more dangerous threat. At about this time, too, the enemy began to use his long-range bombers by night against land targets, with only occasional attacks on shipping. Another feature

of his night activity was the use of single-engine day fighters to support twin-engine night fighters.

352. During the second week of August, when the enemy launched his strongest counter-attack in the Mortain area, the German Air Force again rose to an effort of approximately 400 sorties a day. To counter this activity I laid on heavy attacks on the airfields in use by the G.A.F. I refer to these attacks later. The enemy activity declined steeply after the first two days. The decline was due partly to our attacks and partly to the fact that the G.A.F. was compelled to move most of its units to airfields further east with the consequent need of reorganisation; the enemy shortage of fuel and his need of reinforcements for operationally tired units were additional causes.

353. This shortage of fuel was the result, not only of the air attacks on the various oil installations in Germany, but also of the attacks on the enemy's transport system. The G.A.F.'s problem of distribution of supplies to frequently changing bases had become one of extreme complexity.

354. By mid-August, new G.A.F. units began to appear on the Western Front, but although these units pushed up the average daily effort to nearly 300 sorties, the fighting value continued to deteriorate. An effort was, however, made by the G.A.F. throughout the fourth week in August, to assist the land forces trying to scramble back to the Seine by providing cover and relief from air attack at the Seine crossings, but on very few occasions were the attacks pressed home. The enemy losses mounted steadily all the time. On 25th August, United States Ninth Air Force fighters destroyed 77 aircraft in combat and a further 44 on the ground. On 29th August, there was evidence that the enemy units were in flight back to Germany.

355. *Enemy Air Opposition – September.* – Activity in the first ten days of September was not very heavy, the close support units of the G.A.F. being still very disorganised owing to their moves back to Germany. Later in the month, however, fighter units staged a very spirited revival of effort against strategical bomber attacks. United States Eighth Air Force suffered fairly heavy losses on two days. About this time also, jet-propelled aircraft began to appear in operations.

356. The landing of airborne troops in the Eindhoven – Nijmegen – Arnhem area in mid-September produced a more violent reaction from the G.A.F. than had been encountered for some time in the battle areas although a tactical surprise was gained and the original landings were made without opposition. During the first three days of the operation, many sightings were made and signals intelligence reported many more enemy aircraft airborne, but in spite of favourable weather on the fourth day, this offensive was not sustained. It can only be deduced that the scale of effort of the three previous days had imposed too great a strain upon the G.A.F. organisation and possibly its crews.

357. From the 20th September to the end of the month, close support of the enemy ground forces in the area of the Allied airborne landings was the chief object of the G.A.F. in the battle areas. The scale of effort was fairly low, probably owing to weather, except on 26th September, when a total of over 200 sorties was put up, chiefly ground attacks, by fighter bombers; the pilots showed little inclination to

engage in air fighting. Our claims for this day's fighting were I6 enemy aircraft destroyed.

358. The stiffening of German resistance in the air during September, mainly in the Nijmegen area in Holland was, however, accomplished at high cost. There is reliable evidence that the G.A.F. had to scrape up from its training organisation its older and more experienced pilots, a policy not calculated to produce a long term improvement in its condition. However, the G.A.F. is by no means a spent force yet, and recent technical developments, in jet-propelled aircraft, for example, are likely to make it more formidable. It would be folly to regard the G.A.F. as "down and out". In addition, it is certain that it is working on a policy of conserving effort and building up reserves for the defence of the Reich proper. A reduction in heavy bomber attacks on G.A.F. centres of production after D-Day is a factor to be remembered in this connection. (See para. 40I.)

359. *Enemy use of Jet-propelled Aircraft.* – The most important feature of G.A.F. activity during the second half of September was the appearance of jet-propelled aircraft, at first in ones and twos, later in fours and fives. In view of the fact that within the period covered by this Despatch (namely until 30th September) we have had insufficient experience of them to form reliable estimates of their activities or capabilities, I do not propose to comment on them at length. That they are a momentous landmark in the history of the air will not be denied, but final judgment on their value must be reserved for the moment.

360. Within the limits of our present experience, they appear to have been employed chiefly as fighter bombers for ground attack in a close support role, and for tactical reconnaissance. In both these roles their very high speed makes them formidable weapons and presents problems of defence not yet solved. As fighters, they have so far played a less decisive part, though their speed and particularly their rate of climb, would seem to equip them admirably for these duties. From aerial combats that have occurred up to the date of writing between orthodox Allied fighters and these jet-propelled aircraft, it would appear that their lack of manoeuvrability puts them under some disadvantage in a "dog fight", but their qualities of speed and rate of climb make them deadly if they are given the chance to "jump" the opposition.

361. When it is remembered that the G.A.F. so often refused to fight and had to be diligently sought out before it could be attacked, the losses inflicted on it are remarkable. The following figures give the victories gained by Allied pilots in air fighting alone, but do not include the destruction of aircraft on the ground or by the anti-aircraft forces of the British and American armies:-

Enemy Losses on the Western Front – 6th June-30th September, 1944

	Destroyed	Probably Destroyed	Damaged
A.E.A.F.	1,368	187	18
U.S. Eighth A.F.:			6
VIIIth F.C.	1,325	50	372
VIIIth B.C.	193	108	208
R.A.F. B.C.	240	33	121
	3,126	378	1,319

362. The losses inflicted on the G.A.F. in the heavy and damaging attacks made on its airfields subsequent to D-Day cannot be estimated with sufficient accuracy to warrant the statement of a figure. It is known they were very heavy. The chief difficulty is that photographic reconnaissance never revealed all aircraft destroyed by the Allied air forces' attacks. There is considerable evidence from the airfields now in Allied hands that the G.A.F. continued to use hangars, even after heavy raiding, for the parking and servicing of aircraft, and it was frequently found that even more wrecks of aircraft were under cover than were at dispersal points. This G.A.F. habit made impossible the exact evaluation of the success of our attacks on its airfields.

363. *Attacks on Enemy Airfields.* – Attacks on airfields after D-Day were not made to any set plan, as they had been before the invasion. They were made as a security measure when it was found that enemy air activity was interfering with the success of our land and air operations. Even so, they were laid on only when intelligence indicated concentrations of enemy aircraft in sufficient strength to justify attacks or revealed that certain airfields were being used for maintenance and servicing purposes. During July and early August, it proved unnecessary to maintain any serious effort against enemy airfields, but from 13th to 16th August, strong forces of heavy bombers operated against several night fighter airfields in Holland and Belgium, from which night fighters, maintaining a high operational effort, were hampering our heavy bombers on night operations. In these attacks, 1,004 aircraft of R.A.F. Bomber Command and 1,743 aircraft of the United States Eighth Air Force dropped over 10,000 tons of bombs in three days. There was an immediate cessation of enemy activity from these airfields.

364. During the enemy withdrawal from France and the Low Countries, an excellent chance was afforded of making profitable attacks on aircraft on a number of airfields. These aircraft were grounded through lack of fuel. Hitherto the heavy concentrations of flak on G.A.F. airfields had make attacks on them costly and had frequently compelled us to use heavy bombers in high level attacks when medium and fighter bombers could have been better spared for this task. During this period of hasty withdrawal however, the enemy flak defences were weakened. In consequence, our losses were reduced and we were allowed much greater freedom in the selection of method of attack.

365. The following statistics show the weight of bombing attacks on airfields in the period D-Day to 30th September. The chief contribution of the aircraft of A.E.A.F. was, however, in low level strafing and destruction of aircraft on the ground.

Total Sorties against Airfields during the period
6th June to 30th September, 1944

Force	*Sorties*	*Tons of Bombs*
A.E.A.F.	310	156.7
U.S. Eighth Air Force	11,118	24,747.0
R.A.F. B.C.	2,433	12,283.7
	13,861	37,187.4

Defence against Flying Bombs and Counter-Action against Flying Bomb Installations.

366. In paragraph 169 et seq. I have briefly described air operations prior to D-Day, against the sites the enemy was preparing for the launching of flying bombs and rocket projectiles against the United Kingdom. It was not fully appreciated at the time, that the enemy was also preparing modified and less conspicuous sites. Air operations against "Noball" targets had been suspended before D-Day in order to release the air forces for the major tasks of "Overlord". It was thought that the operations by then carried out had virtually eliminated the menace; in fact, it is known that these operations, coupled with our attacks on his transport system, oil and manufacturing centres had reduced the enemy's potential capacity to launch flying bombs from a probable 6,000 per day to a relatively very small fraction of this number. Nonetheless, his power to hit us with these weapons had not been entirely destroyed.

367. On the night of 12/13th June, the enemy launched his first jet-propelled flying bomb against England and aimed at London. In the first phase between 0405 hours and 0430 hours on 13th June, seven of these flying bombs were observed, one of which reached London. Later, three more operated over Kent.

368. No further flying bombs were reported until the evening of 15th June, when activity began afresh on a fairly large scale. Long-prepared defence plans were immediately put into operation. Direct responsibility for this defence was allotted to Air Marshal Sir Roderic Hill, K.C.B., M.C., A.F.C., the Air Marshal Commanding Air Defence of Great Britain. Additional guns and balloons were deployed to counter these weapons, whilst airborne and fighter patrols were put up both over the Channel and south of London. The United States forces contributed wholeheartedly to this defence with A.A. guns and fighter patrols. Large scale bombing operations were also undertaken against the launching sites and their ancillary installations. The diversion of effort from "Overlord" tasks now assumed larger proportions.

369. From the commencement of flying bomb activity until 30th September, fighter aircraft flew 24,572 sorties on interception patrols. This commitment was almost exclusively met by the aircraft of A.D.G.B. These patrols accounted for 1,915 flying bombs out of a total of 7,503 launched. The following figures give the results of all types of defence against these weapons:-

Period 12/13th June to 2100 hours 30th September, 1944

Despatched	Made Landfall	Reached Greater London
7,503	5,431	2,421

Flying Bombs Destroyed – period 12/13th June to 30th September, 1944

(*a*) By Fighter Patrols :-

	Day	Night	Total
Overland	287	388½	675½
Oversea	1,034½	205	1,239½
Total	1,321½	593½	1,915

(*b*) By all causes :-

Fighter Patrol	A.A.	Balloons	Other Causes	Total
1,915	1,547	278	33	3,773

370. Our rapid advance through France forced the enemy to abandon his launching sites in the Pas de Calais; in consequence there was no flying bomb activity over the United Kingdom after the 9th September for a period of ten days. When it recommenced, the launching was from carrier aircraft, chiefly Heinkel III, operating over the North Sea. The scale of activity of these air-launched flying bombs was never heavy; nevertheless a fully organised defence scheme, involving nine squadrons of fighters, had to be maintained to combat the menace.

37I. The scale of the bombing attacks on the launching and ancillary sites and also on large constructional sites believed to be associated with preparations for launching large rocket projectiles is shown in the figures given below:-

"Crossbow" Operations
Period 14th June to 31st August, 1944

Force	Aircraft attacking	Tons of Bombs
A.E.A.F.:-		
14th-30th June	1,005	1,335
1st-31st July	246	419
1st-31st August	–	–
	1,251	1,754
R.A.F. B.C.:-		
14th-30th June	4,050	17,773
1st-31st July	5,833	26,487
1st-31st August	4,384	21,385
	14,267	65,645
U.S. Eighth Air Force:-		
14th-30th June	1,835	4,709
1st-31st July	1,401	3,639
1st-31st August	869	2,329
	4,105	10,677

372. It is very difficult to estimate the success of these counter attacks; the number of flying bombs launched per day varied considerably, as also did the number and location of the sites used. It can, however, be stated that these attacks hampered and kept in check the launching rate; the average number launched per day over the period I3th June to 3Ist August was 95 against the estimated possible number of 6,000 per day, had the German plan not been upset by Allied bombing. It has already been noted that the air bombing in the preparatory period was so successful in countering the enemy's preparations for the use of the flying bomb, that it was no longer a direct threat to the preparations for, or the carrying out of the Allied assault and subsequent land operations. In the event, the flying bomb was launched mainly as a "terror" weapon against the civilian population of Southern England and not as a counter to the plans for the invasion of the Continent. I do not propose, therefore, to make any

wider comment beyond emphasising the cost to the invasion operations by virtue of the diversion of available air effort that had to be made in order to secure this degree of immunity. An indication of the scale of this diversion is given by the statistics in the paragraphs above. Another less calculable cost was the fact that a number of Tempest and Mustang fighters – which had been allocated to re-arm squadrons in Second British Tactical Air Force – had to be transferred to A.D.G.B. for duties on flying bomb interception patrols. We thus lost the use of these very valuable and latest type of fighters over the battlefront.

Operation "Market" – First Allied Airborne Army.

373. On 17th September, airborne forces of the First Allied Airborne Army, comprising United States 82nd and 101st Airborne Divisions, 1st British Airborne Division and a Polish Parachute Brigade were dropped and landed in the Eindhoven – Nijmegen – Arnhem areas of Holland. The lift of these airborne forces exceeded that made during the initial landings on the Continent. The operation was designed to facilitate an advance by the northern group of armies up to and over the rivers Waal and Lower Rhine. With this end in view, the chief objectives of the airborne troops were the bridges at Arnhem and Nijmegen.

374. The initial drops were successful, being carried out accurately and with very few casualties. During the subsequent nine days, as weather permitted, reinforcements and supplies were flown in to the airborne troops and to the supporting ground troops which had linked up with them. Despite an heroic struggle by the troops of the 1st British Airborne Division the bridge at Arnhem, although secured initially, could not be retained. The bridge at Nijmegen, however, was secured and the operation paved the way for a subsequent advance up to the river Waal and beyond. It provided many lessons for the future and marked a definite step in the evolution of airborne operations.

375. The planning for and execution of these operations, which were carried out under the code name "Market", was the work of the First Allied Airborne Army, to which the operational control of the United States and Royal Air Force troop carrier forces, previously under my command, had been transferred in accordance with your direction, in August, 1944. A full report on these operations is being issued by the Commanding General of the First Allied Airborne Army, Lieutenant General Louis Brereton, who had relinquished the command of the United States Ninth Air Force to take over this new appointment.

376. Besides the aircraft of the troop carrier air forces, the aircraft of A.E.A.F., United States Eighth Air Force, R.A.F. Bomber Command and R.A.F. Coastal Command were engaged in support of these operations. The co-ordination of the activities of all the air forces concerned in a supporting role was carried out at my headquarters at meetings with representatives of the interested commands.

377. The chief meeting took place on 12th September, and at this meeting the principal tasks of the air forces were assigned. These tasks were:-

(i) The attacking of airfields and known flak positions by heavy bombers.

(ii) The dive bombing of flak positions which might be developed by the enemy during the operation.

(iii) The provision of top cover along the route to be followed by the airborne trains, and a fighter screen east and north of the dropping and landing areas.

(iv) The provision of night fighter patrols.

(v) The arrangements for dummy drops.

(vi) The arrangements for diversions by R.A.F. Coastal Command.

(vii) The arrangements for re-supply of airborne forces by heavy bombers on D + I.

378. All these operations as planned at this meeting were actually carried out, and in addition, the air forces continued to lend support to the ground operations during the whole period that the intense phase of the operation lasted. I have referred to some of these activities by the air forces at other points in this Despatch, but below is summarised briefly what was actually done.

379. On the night of I6/I7th September, R.A.F. Bomber Command attacked with 200 Lancasters and 23 Mosquitoes, four airfields at Leeuwarden, Steewijk-Havelte, Hopsten and Salzbergen. These enemy airfields were those from which fighters could attack the transports and gliders carrying the airborne forces. Nearly 900 tons of bombs were dropped with good to excellent results on these airfields. On the same night, 54 Lancasters and 5 Mosquitoes dropped 294 tons of bombs on flak positions at Moerdijk, also with good results. On the following morning, 85 Lancasters and I5 Mosquitoes dropped 535 tons of bombs on coastal defence batteries in the Walcheren area. For these daylight operations Spitfires of A.D.G.B. provided escort.

380. These operations by R.A.F. Bomber Command were followed up on the morning of D + I by heavy bombers of the United States Eighth Air Force which attacked II7 flak positions along the routes to be followed and near the dropping and landing zones, just prior to the arrival of the troop carriers. In these attacks, 8I6 heavy bombers dropped 3,I39 tons of bombs with fair to good results in most cases. A further six bombers also attacked the airfield at Eindhoven.

38I. During the afternoon of D +I, I8th September, 252 heavy bombers of the United States Eighth Air Force dropped 782 tons of supplies to the ground forces with good to excellent results.

382. The airborne forces were carried in two great trains of troop carrier aircraft and gliders, one following a northerly, the other a southerly route. The plan for the protection of these two trains of troop carriers provided for a high cover of fighters and a force of fighter bombers at low level, ready to dive bomb any flak positions that opened fire. On the northern route, aircraft of A.D.G.B. carried out these two tasks, as far as the turning point near 'sHertogenbosch, employing 37I fighters for this purpose. Fighter aircraft of the United States Eighth Air Force then took over covering the train of troop carriers to the dropping and landing zones. Fighters of this

air force also provided top cover to the train approaching over the southern route, and in addition, provided a fighter screen to the east and north of the dropping and landing zones. In these tasks, 548 fighters were employed. In addition, 212 fighters of the United States Ninth Air Force dive bombed flak positions along the southern route between the turning point and the dropping and landing zones.

383. The attacks on the enemy flak positions along the routes were very successful. The great bulk of the land batteries were silenced and in addition, several flak ships and barges off the Dutch Islands were destroyed.

384. The G.A.F. reaction to these very large scale operations was small on D-Day, approximately 30 enemy fighters only being seen, seven of which were shot down. On the second, third and sixth days, however, the German Air Force reacted much more strongly, and up to the end of the operation a total of 159 enemy aircraft were destroyed over the area.

385. Throughout the operations, the Allied air forces continued to cover the airborne forces, to lend direct support to the ground forces and particularly to attack flak positions. In all, the supporting air forces flew over 7,800 sorties in support of Operation "Market". A total of 114 aircraft were lost, in addition to the casualties incurred by the troop carrier forces.

386. The Air/Sea Rescue Service functioned most efficiently during these airborne operations. A string of 17 launches was placed across the North Sea on the northern route and a further string of 10 launches along the southern route. In addition, special reconnaissances were flown, spotting for ditched planes and gliders. Most of the ditching occurred on D + 2, when the weather was bad and the towlines of many gliders parted. On this day, one launch picked up all the personnel from five ditched gliders. In all 205 personnel were saved by the Air/Sea Rescue Service during these operations.

Attacks against Enemy Naval Targets.

387. I now turn to the duties of the Air Force in assisting the Allied Navies in dealing with enemy naval units trying to interfere with the landing and the subsequent ferrying of reinforcements and supplies by our ships across the Channel. The following brief review covers these operations from the time of the assault to the end of September, 1944. The main burden was shouldered by R.A.F. Coastal Command, but R.A.F. Bomber Command continued to implement its extensive sea mining programme (which now embraced "Overlord" requirements) and made heavy attacks, referred to below, on shipping in harbours. Aircraft of A.E.A.F. also made attacks on coastal shipping and on E and R boats. After D-Day, Second British Tactical Air Force took over the commitment previously shouldered by A.D.G.B. to provide "Channel Stop" squadrons. The function of these squadrons was to attack enemy surface vessels attempting to enter the Channel from either end. A.E.A.F. fighters also provided escort for the strike aircraft of R.A.F. Coastal Command. Apart from the sea mining of R.A.F. Bomber Command, all these operations were co-ordinated through my headquarters.

388. *Anti-U-Boat Operations.* – In anticipation of an enemy attempt to move U-

boats into the invasion waters, R.A.F. Coastal Command flew anti-submarine patrols from the Scillies to Ushant and from St. Albans Head to Cap de la Hague. Through these barriers the enemy had to try to infiltrate. The first U-boats sighted were approaching from the western entrance to the assault area on the night of D-Day. Six of these U-boats were attacked. During the next day and night, a further ten sightings were made and seven were attacked. Some of these attacks resulted in kills.

389. Because of these continuous patrols, U-boat commanders were forced to remain submerged for very long periods; these tactics restricted their freedom of manoeuvre and from P.O.W. statements, it is obvious they had a most distressing physical effect on the crews. During June, 80 U-boat sightings were made in the approaches to the assault area; 46 were attacked, 3 of these jointly with the Navy, and 18 of the attacks appeared promising. During July, the enemy was forced to continue maximum diving tactics. This made detection and attacks by aircraft more difficult, but at least two U-boats on or near the surface were destroyed. A further 20 conning tower or periscope sightings were made and 13 attacks delivered.

390. With the Allied advance in August, the enemy began to move his U-boats away from the ports of North-Western France to the southern portion of the Bay of Biscay. This movement gave the aircraft of R.A.F Coastal Command a splendid chance to strike. 24 sightings were made in the Bay during August, and 14 attacks resulted; six U-boats were probably sunk, three of these shared with Naval forces, and two more damaged. From D-Day to 30th September, R.A.F. Coastal Command sunk or probably sunk 12 U-boats in the Channel or the Bay of Biscay, shared the destruction of five more with surface forces and damaged a further 12.

391. *Anti-Shipping Operations.* – Attacks against enemy surface vessels, including naval vessels, were made by aircraft of A.E.A.F. and by R.A.F. Coastal Command. The first of these actions took place on the 6th June, when the enemy endeavoured to bring into action three heavy destroyers from the west coast of France. These ships were attacked, west of Brest by R.A.F. Coastal Command. Some damage was caused, one was set on fire and the ships were delayed. On 8th June, they again attempted to move into the invasion waters, but were met by Allied destroyers. One was sunk, one driven ashore and the third forced back to Brest.

392. Other attacks were made against smaller enemy naval vessels and merchant shipping and some of these attacks were very successful; details of two are given below. However, not only these missions which saw and attacked enemy vessels should be reckoned as successful. Continuous patrols by fighters of A.E.A.F. and R.A.F. Coastal Command in the Western Approaches and down into the area of the Channel Islands ensured that no enemy surface vessels were able to support the garrisons holding out in coastal areas. These offensive fighter patrols were co-ordinated with the sorties of the reconnaissance aircraft of R.A.F. Coastal Command.

393. On the night of 7th June, Beaufighters and Albacores attacked a formation of E-boats in the Channel; two E-boats were sunk and a further three damaged. In the early morning of 15th June, a force of 42 Beaufighters, escorted by 10 Mustangs of A.D.G.B. attacked a north-bound convoy consisting of a merchant vessel of 8,000 tons, a naval auxiliary of 4,000 tons and seventeen escort ships off the Frisian Islands.

The large merchant vessel and the auxiliary were torpedoed and sank, one minesweeper blew up and sank, another was hit by a torpedo and probably sank, while five more minesweepers were seen on fire and four other escorts were damaged by cannon fire.

394.[13] A brief summary of the work of R.A.F. Coastal Command shows that over 200 sorties were flown in attacks on surface craft during the month of June in the invasion area and its approaches. In July more than 500 aircraft made anti-shipping attacks in the Channel area, off the Dutch and Belgian Coasts, in the Bay of Biscay and off the Coast of Norway. In July, six merchant ships, I0 escort vessels and five E/R boats were sunk, one merchant ship, II escort vessels and two E/R boats were seriously damaged, and a further seven merchant ships, nineteen escort vessels and 6 E/R boats were damaged. August saw an even higher scale of shipping effort. Nightly attacks on E/R boats operating in the Channel, five large scale attacks off the Dutch and Norwegian coasts and numerous attacks on the enemy in the Bay of Biscay produced excellent results. Nine merchant ships plus one shared, seventeen escort vessels, 2 destroyers, and I E/R boat were sunk. Eleven escort vessels and I E/R boat seriously damaged and a further four merchant ships, I destroyer, 4 E/R boats and twenty-eight escort vessels were damaged.

395. These air operations directed against enemy surface forces, including the protective mine-laying by R.A.F. Bomber Command, not only assisted the safe-guarding of the Allied merchant fleets from surface attacks, but also prevented any German attempt to evacuate by sea his beleaguered coastal garrisons.

396. *Attacks on Shipping in Ports.* – The majority of the E and R boats operating against the Allied cross-channel shipping in the early days of the assault were using the ports of Le Havre and Boulogne. The boats were well protected by large shelter pens. However, R.A.F. Bomber Command, in two attacks, inflicted great damage on the enemy's fleet of small ships.

397. On the evening of I4th June, a force of 335 Lancasters and I8 Mosquitoes attacked the port area of Le Havre, dropping I,026 tons of bombs. This tonnage included 22 x I2,000lb. special bombs, On the next evening, the same tactics were used in an attack on the port of Boulogne when 285 heavy bombers and I2 Mosquitoes dropped I,463 tons of bombs in a concentrated attack.

398. Very great damage was caused to the ports and the pens in these attacks, and in addition, the heavy bombs, bursting in the water, created huge waves which flung the small craft against the quays and the concrete sides of the pens. Photographs revealed twenty-five of these enemy naval vessels destroyed in Boulogne, and this number was exceeded at Le Havre.

399. Other air operations which were of direct assistance to Allied naval activity were the attacks on coastal defences (reviewed in Part III (b) dealing with preparatory operations), and also the co-ordination of fighter bomber attacks on Radar stations to upset the enemy warning system when Allied light surface forces operated against E and R boats.

Strategical Bombing – "Pointblank".

400. In addition to their priority operations, already described, against targets in the tactical area and against flying bomb installations, the United States and British strategical air forces maintained a considerable effort against targets within Germany after D-Day. As these operations were not directed by me, I mention them very briefly and in order simply, to round off the story of the Allied air effort.

401. The chief limitation on their effort was the weather which frequently made it necessary to cancel projected attacks. The main weight of this offensive from June to September was directed against the enemy's oil supplies and oil production centres. These targets were given priority over aircraft production and assembly plants (although attacks on these latter were not entirely suspended) and other industrial objectives as being, at this time, of more critical importance to the enemy. The G.A.F. had, by D-Day, been very seriously weakened by the efforts already directed against it, although the deep penetration daylight raids of the United States Eighth Air Force still provoked violent enemy air reaction on most occasions. In consequence, there was a steady attrition of the G.A.F. in aerial combat as well as a depletion of Germany's oil resources. Heavy and concentrated attacks on these targets have produced an oil situation which, taken with the loss of Roumanian supplies, must be seriously worrying the German High Command. The influence of this situation is already being, and will be increasingly, felt on the battlefield.

402. Other operations against "Pointblank" targets included attacks on aircraft and motor transport manufacturing centres, on several important communication centres and on German cities.

Brief Summary of Air Effort for the period D-Day to 30th September, 1944.

403. At 30th September, the Allied armies stood on and in some places, over the borders of the Reich proper. In 117 days since the assault began, France, Belgium, Luxembourg and a large part of Holland had been liberated. These 117 days had also been unprecedented in the scale of air effort employed. The aircraft of A.E.A.F. alone had flown 316,248 sorties, an average of 2,703 per day. The effort of the strategical air forces based in the United Kingdom raised this total to 552,197 sorties, an average of 4,719 per day.

404. The remarkable achievement of such a high rate of effort is due, in no small measure, both to the detailed administrative plans which facilitated the transfer of forces to Continental airfields without interruption to the current operations, and to the work of the ground staffs who supplied, serviced and armed the aircraft and provided the ancillary services.

405. *Weather.* – The weather throughout the whole period was frequently unfavourable for air operations, and on many occasions interfered greatly with my plans. This was especially so in the first days of the assault. Before D-Day it was known that unsettled weather was approaching and there was a distinct possibility that the unsettled period might be prolonged and severe. I was, however, confident of the ability of the air forces to carry out their allotted tasks, and in particular to deal

with the German Air Force, despite the weather handicap. In the event, just after D-Day, the weather was nearly as bad as it possibly could be.

406. In making the Assault, despite the bad weather, there is no doubt that the invasion forces won an increased chance of tactical surprise. There is the evidence of a captured senior German meteorological officer that the Germans were in fact off their guard; he has stated that he advised the German Command that owing to the approach of unsettled conditions, no assault would be attempted.

407. The following figures show the effect of the weather on air operations during the period. The A.E.A.F. total of aircraft sorties on D-Day was 7,672, on D + I 8,283 and D + 2, when the weather began to deteriorate, 5,073 and on D + 3 the total reached 662 only. On one other day in June the total was less than 1,000 and on two further days it was under 2,000 sorties; however, despite this handicap, the average number of sorties per day for A.E.A.F. aircraft throughout the month of June was almost 4,000. Weather also affected the planning and carrying out of bomber operations between D-Day and September 30th. In fact, the lack of weather good enough to permit of high altitude precision and, above all, visual, bombing was one of the chief reasons why the start of the attacks on the enemy's transportation and communications system was planned so early.

408. *Personnel Casualties.* – The following statistics of personnel casualties cover the period from Ist April to 30th September, 1944.These figures reveal a grievous loss of highly trained men. Reference, however, to the statistics in paragraph 183, dealing with the preparatory period and paragraph 403, covering the period from D-Day to 30th September, will show that the overall losses per sorties flown are reasonably low.

Personnel Casualties of Allied Air Forces Operating in Western Europe

Period 1st April–30th September, 1944

	Killed in Action Or Died of Wounds	Missing and P.O.W.	Wounded
A.E.A.F.:-			
U.S. Personnel	216	1,839	660
British Personnel	694	1,361	864
R.A.F. Bomber Command	2,318	9,265	1,109
U.S. Eighth Air Force:-			
Bomber	931	15,057	1,716
Fighter	49	959	77
R.A.F. Coastal Command	352	597	239
	4,560	29,078	4,665

PART IV – SPECIAL FEATURES

409. The mounting of air operations of the complexity and scale recorded in this Despatch was only made possible by an adequate ground organisation. I wish, therefore, in this Section to pay some tribute to the background work against which these operations were carried out, and upon which they depended for success.

4I0. For convenience, comments on some of the special features have been arranged under the following headings:-

(i) Administration.

(ii) Airfield Construction.

(iii) Air/Sea Rescue.

(iv) Air Transport and Evacuation of Casualties.

(v) Employment of Balloons.

(vi) Provision of Maps.

(vii) Signal Communications and Radar Cover.

Administration.

4II. Although I did not have administrative control of the United States Ninth Air Force, there were many and varied administrative matters affecting all forces in the Allied Expeditionary Air Force which set difficult problems to be solved. Administration, maintenance and the provision of equipment, fuel and ammunition to keep modern air forces fighting all had their peculiar complications.

4I2. An idea of some of the special problems met and overcome by the administrative and other ground staffs is given in the following paragraphs.

4I3. On I6th November, I943, the British forces, Second Tactical Air Force and Nos. 38 and 85 Groups had been built up to about 35 per cent. only of their final strength. The United States Ninth Air Force at this time was only approximately 25 per cent. of its final strength. To develop these forces in the winter and following spring, and to have them suitably deployed in readiness for the opening of the campaign was a race against time which involved, inter alia:-

(i) A comprehensive plan whereby aerodromes and landing grounds in the south of England were progressively evacuated by units not participating directly in "Overlord", and occupied by "Overlord" forces as the U.S.A.A.F. arrived from overseas and by the British forces as they were augmented.

(ii) Providing Second Tactical Air Force with a fully mobile organisation for repair, and for the supply of Royal Air Force equipment, in substitution for the service normally provided by the Royal Air Force Maintenance Command in the United Kingdom.

(iii) Integrating the U.S.A.A.F. and R.A.F. administrative services where necessary.

(iv) Re-equipping II0 Royal Air Force squadrons with the most up-to-date types of aircraft.

(v) Changing Second Tactical Air Force from the home system of personnel administration and accounting, to the overseas systems, including the establishment of a Base Personnel Staff Office and a Base Accounts Office.

(vi) On D-Day the British totalled approximately 232,000 personnel and the American I8I,000. The organisation of the British part of the force alone involved the formulation and issue of some 250 new type establishments.

4I4. After D-Day, the principal administrative tasks to be executed, and for which full preparations had been made were:-

(i) By means of the inter-Allied and inter-Service machinery known as BUCO and MOVCO to control the transfer of Air Forces to the Continent, together with the stores for immediate use, and to build up reserves.

(ii) Special arrangements to ensure that squadrons could operate at full effort, whether from the United Kingdom or the Continent, even though their normal maintenance organisation was in process of transfer.

(iii) Arrangements by which United States air forces could re-arm and re-fuel at British air strips and vice versa.

(iv) Rapid replacement of personnel casualties, aircraft and equipment.

(v) The institution, quite early in the operations, of arrangements for salvaging aircraft carcasses and certain other equipment, and for returning this material quickly to the United Kingdom by L.C.T. for use by the production organisation there.

(vi) Finally, maintaining a high state of mobility for the Tactical Air Forces which were taxed to the limit to keep up with the advance.

4I5. There were over 6,600 operational aircraft in A.E.A.F. at D-Day. These aircraft were composed of ten basic types with a large number of varying marks, each with its own problems in servicing. That the maintenance personnel managed to keep the operational serviceability to the high levels stated below is a remarkable achievement. When it is remembered that throughout June and July most of the squadrons operated from new-made landing strips only a few miles from the front line, and that the dust on these Normandy airfields was, in the opinion of many experienced campaigners, worse than that in the North African desert campaigns, then the efforts of the maintenance personnel become even more outstanding.

4I6. *Average Strength and Serviceability of Aircraft in A.E.A.F.*

	Fighers			Bombers		
	Average Strength	Average Serviceability	Percentage	Average Strength	Average Serviceability	Percentage
Ninth Air Force :						
June	1,239	1,010	81·7	717	626	87·4
July	1,341	1,063	79·4	721	631	87·5
August	1,344	1,058	78·7	737	658	89·3
September	1,393	1,120	80·3	753	663	88·0
Second T.A.F. :-						
June	1,156	954	82·5	272	231	85·0
July	1,058	946	89·5	265	232	87·5
August	1,077	930	86·4	277	240	86·7
September	1,250	1,093	87·5	253	214	84·6
A .D.G.B. :-						
June	1,207	957	79·3	-	-	-
July	1,281	1,007	78·5	-	-	-
August	1,335	1,060	79·4	-	-	-
September	1,131	926	82·0	-	-	-

4I7. The maintenance of operational strength was also the result of a carefully prepared plan for replacement of aircraft. In this connection, it is interesting to note that the forecasting of wastage and casualties by the planning staff was sound, and since the losses were somewhat below those planned, there were never any serious difficulties of supply. The replacement pool and recovery organisation both worked extremely well.

4I8. The statistics of the average daily consumption and wastage of P.O.L. and ammunition also reveal something of the achievement of the supply organisation. During July, A.E.A.F. expended daily 750 tons of bombs and more than 200,000 rounds of ammunition. The fuel consumption of A.E.A.F. in July reached approximately 30,000,000 gallons of petrol, almost I,000,000 gallons per day. A large part of this fuel and ammunition had to be transported into the beach-head and up to forward airfields. In this connection the work of Air Force beach squadrons deserves special mention. These parties went in with the follow-up troops on D-Day and due in no small measure to their efforts, the first airfields were stocked ready for operations in the beach-head on D + 3.

4I9. The following story reveals some of the difficulties encountered and overcome in supplying an air force of the magnitude of A.E.A.F. Supreme Headquarters Allied Expeditionary Force Operational Memoranda called for special markings on aircraft in order that they might be clearly distinguished on D-Day. To achieve success the markings had to be applied on D - I so that all aircraft should have broad black and white bands painted on them on D-Day, but not before. The total requirements of distemper for this purpose to mark approximately I0,000 aircraft and gliders was

I00,000 gallons or I,500 tons. There was no such amount immediately available in the United Kingdom. Supply action on a high priority was necessary. Supply to civilians was stopped, overtime was worked in pits and factories, Whitsun week-end holidays were forgotten and by Y-Day all was ready; the distemper and 20,000 brushes to apply it were on hand.

Airfield Construction.

420. In combined operations it is obviously advantageous that fighters, fighter bombers and reconnaissance aircraft of the Tactical Air Forces should be able to work from bases in the operational theatre as early as possible, and therefore airfield accommodation is of paramount importance.

42I. The extent to which airfield requirements could be met in this operation depended, in the main, on the ability of the field engineers to locate and develop suitable sites. These sites had been previously chosen by experts after a detailed study of the coverage provided by photographic reconnaissance aircraft and available maps. It also depended upon having a sufficiently high priority within the available shipping space for the movement of equipment and material. Naturally these claims must be balanced with others of operational urgency.

422. In the initial stages, the terrain in the British sector was generally more favourable than that in the American. However, the airfield engineers achieved very fine results in both sectors. The position in the British sector deteriorated because the good area to the east and south-east around Caen was not secured as rapidly as had been planned. Neither did the situation in the American sector greatly improve until the advance had progressed to Le Mans and beyond.

423. The minimum programme for airfields to accommodate the forces allocated was as follows:-

3 E.L.S. (2 American and I British) by D-Day.

4 R. and Rs. (2 American and 2 British) by the evening of D + 3 and not later than D + 4.

I0 A.L.Gs. (5 American and 5 British) by D + 8 (these A.L.Gs. included 4 of the R. and Rs.).

I8 Airfields (8 American and I0 British) by D + I4.

27 Airfields (I2 American and I5 British) by D + 24.

43 Airfields (I8 American and 25 British) by D + 40.

93 Airfields (48 American and 45 British) by D + 90.

424. Definitions of the terms used above and descriptions of the different types of airfields are given below:-

E.L.S. – Emergency Landing Strip. – A strip having sufficient length of level surface to enable pilots in distress to make a landing. These strips have a minimum length of 600 yards and are not fit for the operation of aircraft, but are of inestimable value when operations are conducted a long way from bases especially when a long sea crossing on the way home is involved.

R. & R. – Refuelling and Re-arming Strip. – A strip possessing sufficient length of level compact surface for landing and taking off, adequate marshalling areas for the rapid turn-round of aircraft and adequate tracking to ensure operation under all normal summer and autumn conditions. These strips have a minimum length of 1,200 yards with the marshalling areas of 100 x 50 yards at each end.

A.L.G. – Advanced Landing Ground. – A landing ground possessing the same facilities as an R. and R. to be brought up to A.L.G. standard by the addition of dispersal facilities and capable of use to capacity by adopting the "Roulement" system.

Airfield. – A field with the same facilities as an A.L.G. but with improved dispersal facilities and on which squadrons are established and not operated on the "Roulement" system, as on an A.L.G.

The minimum lengths for both A.L.Gs. and airfields are 1,200 yards for fighters, with dispersal facilities for 54 aircraft, and 1,650 yards for fighter bombers, with the same dispersal facilities.

All-Weather Airfield. – The same requirements as for an airfield but possessing hard surfaced runways and fit for operation throughout all seasons and all conditions of weather for the appropriate type of aircraft. Within the limits of operational requirements, it was planned that all enemy airfields with hard-surfaced runways would be reinstated, as and when they were captured, if in the opinion of the airfield engineers, reinstatement could be effected without excessive labour and/or material.

"Roulement" System. – A means of using landing ground facilities to the maximum capacity by flying in squadrons to replace others as they complete their scale of effort appropriate to the period.

425. The priorities fixed for the construction of these airfields were as follows:-

Priority I – E.L.Ss. for emergency landing of aircraft.

Priority II – R. and R. strips for re-fuelling and re-arming fighter aircraft.

Priority III – A.L.Gs. to become airfields later.

426. The following construction units were available for allocation as required in the beachhead:-

American – 16 Aviation Engineering Battalions.
2 Airborne Aviation Engineering Battalions.

British – 5 Airfield Construction Groups.
I Field Force Basis Construction Wing.

427. Because we failed in the initial phases to gain the ground agreed in the optimum plan which was needed in the vicinity of Caen, the development of all of the pre-selected sites could not be started. This naturally caused some delay and made necessary a re-allotment of sites in the beach-head area. As a very high proportion of potential sites selected from air photographs proved to be suitable for rapid construction, the intensive preparation of the beach-head area permitted the leeway to be made up and the Air Staff requirements to be met.

428. Later, when the Allied advance became rapid, the problem of finding space to prepare airfields was eased. It became more a problem of getting the airfields constructed rapidly in the now adequate space available. The system adopted for constructing airfields near the frontline was to prepare dirt strips I5-20 miles to the rear of the ground forces. These strips were then visited by transport aircraft, which dumped stores and tools there. As a general rule, fighter strips were 50-70 miles behind the front line, and bomber strips I00-I20 miles behind. As the ground forces moved forward, so the dirt strips previously prepared were constructed as airfields and became bases for fighters and later for bombers.

429. The position at the end of June (D + 24) was as follows:-

(i) *In the British Sector.* – I0 airfields completed at Bazenville, St. Croix sur Mer, Beny sur Mer, Camilly, Coulombs, Martragny, Sommervieu, Lantheuil, Plumetot, Longues. I airfield was under construction at Ellon.

(ii) *In the American Sector.* – 7 airfields completed at St. Pierre du Mont, Criqueville, Cordonville, Deux Jamaux, Benzeville, Axeville and Carentan. 4 under construction and 75 per cent. completed at Chippelle, Picauville, Le Moly and Creteville.

430. The position at D + 90 (the end of the planned period) was:-

	American Sector		U.S.	British Sector		British	Grand
Type of Field	Operational	Under Construction	Total	Operational	Under Construction	Total	Total
Fighter ALG	24	8	32	23	5	28	60
Medium Bomber	5	1	6	1	-	1	7
Transport	9	1	10	2	-	2	12
Tactical Aerodrome	1	-	1	-	-	-	1
Liaison Strip	1	-	1	-	-	-	1
	40	10	50	26	5	31	81

43I. In addition to these airfields, which were in use at D + 90, five fields in the American sector and three in the British sector had been abandoned, as being too far from the scene of ground operations. These make the number of airfields actually completed by D + 90, 55 in the American sector and 34 in the British sector, a total of 89, as against the planned total of 93. The IX Engineer Command proved very effective and I feel that the Royal Air Force could well consider the adoption of a comparable organisation to ensure immediate operational facilities in overseas theatres. In particular, I feel that more heavy earth-moving equipment should be provided for British units and that the organisation should be reviewed to allow smaller and more flexible companies than the present Wings. These companies should be under the direct control of the air commander in the theatre and not under a ground commander.

432. The fact that airfield construction was still a little behind schedule at the end of the planned period, was due mainly to tactical reasons in the assault phase and to the consequent lack of adequate and suitable ground area, and to some delay in shipping sufficient material. The men of the American Aviation Engineer Battalions of the IX Engineer Command and of the British Airfield Construction units worked exceptionally well, as was proved by the setting-up of the first three Emergency Landing Strips at Pouppeville, St. Laurent sur Mer and Asnelles by D + I. These men worked right in the battle area, through shelling and bombing, and as well as constructing the airfields often had to lay down their tools to deal with stray snipers in the area around the airfield strip.

Air/Sea Rescue.

433. Air Defence of Great Britain and Royal Air Force Coastal Command provided the aircraft for searches in the battle area and for the forces engaged in Operation "Neptune".

434. These Air/Sea Rescue forces had been working hard prior to D-Day and had effected many fine rescues of bomber and fighter crews. Their effort was, naturally, intensified from D-Day onwards especially during the early phases before landing fields were available on the French side of the Channel. Constant standing patrols were flown so that immediately a "Mayday" call was received, rescue aircraft could be vectored onto the position. Both Warwick and Spitfire aircraft were used for these standing patrols.

435. The weather was unfortunately extremely difficult for Air/Sea Rescue operations during almost the whole of June and when Walruses were employed on searches, it was frequently impracticable for them to make landings on the water. This laid a greater burden on the high speed launches and other surface craft which, operating in all conditions, did very effective work. Two high speed launches were attached to each of the Fighter Direction Tenders located off the beach-head and achieved a number of rescues which would have been extremely difficult and lengthy for home-based craft.

436. During the first forty-eight hours of the invasion, airborne operations led to many incidents and during this period, Air-Sea Rescues squadrons were either directly or indirectly responsible for rescuing II7 paratroopers, all of whom had been previously trained in the essentials of Air-Sea Rescue. Details of the total numbers of aircrew, paratroopers and others rescued are set out in the statistics at the end of this account. These rescues were, however, not effected without some of the inevitable

hazards of war. The following three incidents are typical and illustrate the nature of the work.

437. Two Walruses of No. 275 Squadron were ordered to search for a pilot known to have gone into the sea just north of Cherbourg. On arrival at the scene, they found the pilot, who had not been able to get into his dinghy, floating alive in his Mae West. He was, however, not more than two miles from the Cherbourg coast. In spite of the fire from coastal batteries, the two Walruses landed and the pilot was picked up. When they came to takeoff, they found they had been hit and therefore set out to taxi back across the Channel; both aircraft subsequently sank when taken in tow, but the rescue was made and no one was hurt.

438. On another occasion, two high speed launches from Portsmouth were ordered to search in the same area for an American pilot. These launches faced concentrated fire from the shore batteries and came away unscathed.

439. The third rescue displays the resource and efficiency of the personnel engaged in Air/Sea Rescue work. Two high speed launches were returning after making a successful rescue of an American crew over 70 miles out to sea. A message was sent by one of the launches that some of the rescued aircrew and some of the boat's crew were seriously injured as a result of an attack by FW 190s further out. It was decided that medical aid should be flown to these injured personnel. A Walrus of No. 289 Squadron took off with two American Medical Officers, made rendezvous with the high speed launches out at sea and in this way, medical aid was brought to the wounded men three hours earlier than would otherwise have been possible. As a result, at least two lives were saved.

440. *Statistics of Personnel Rescued.* – The following figures show the totals of personnel rescued by the Air/Sea Rescue Services of A.D.G.B. and R.A.F. Coastal Command for the period 6th June to 30th September, 1944:-

Month	Personnel Rescued.
June	*685*
July	*313*
August	*247*
September	*600*
	1,845

441. It will be seen from the above data that the Air/Sea Rescue services succeeded in rescuing many hundreds of valuable personnel, including aircrew and airborne troops. Without this organisation, the great majority, if not all of these airmen and soldiers, would have perished. Even more important, perhaps, than this direct saving of life has been the moral effect which the existence and known successes of the Air/Sea Rescue Service has had, particularly on aircrews. The value of such effect in air operations is obviously incalculable, but that it is of the greatest significance there can be no doubt.

Air Transport and Evacuation of Casualties.

442. In addition to the operational flying to carry airborne troops and supplies to their

dropping and landing zones, the aircraft of the transport forces have flown many thousands of sorties on supply and evacuation missions.

443. The control of all scheduled and emergency airlift by Allied troop carrier and transport aircraft, other than those for airborne forces, was vested in CATOR (Combined Air Transport Operations Room), which was setup at my Headquarters at Stanmore. The operations section of CATOR allocated aircraft between operational tasks, scheduled and emergency demands, in conformity with the policy laid down on your behalf. The supply section of this formation arranged for the supply and movement to the loading base airfields of the loads which were demanded.

444. The variety of equipment carried in these operations was extremely wide. It included jeeps, trailers, Radar equipment, picks and shovels, propellers and shafts, explosives, mines, petrol, containers, barbed wire, magazines, books, comforts and medical stores including blood plasma and penicillin.

445. Transport aircraft returning from the Continent were utilised to the fullest extent for the evacuation of the sick and wounded. This was in accordance with my policy that although no additional special ambulance squadrons should be formed, or aircraft specially tied up for air ambulance work, the maximum use should be made of all aircraft returning to the United Kingdom after delivering supplies. This policy was naturally not always popular with the medical authorities, but no relaxation of it was found to be necessary save in conditions of extreme urgency. This policy was fully supported by you. In all, during the period from D-Day to 30th September, 107,115 medical cases were evacuated by air from forward positions.

446. The evacuation of sick and wounded in the aforementioned manner has been a great boon to the medical services and of inestimable value in securing adequate and early treatment for the seriously injured. The following is a good example – a tank trooper who was suffering from severe burns was evacuated from a landing strip on the Continent to R.A.F. Station, Broadwell, at 1815 hours, landing at base at 1945 hours. From Broadwell he was flown to R.A.F. Station, Odiham, and was admitted to the Special Burns Centre, Basingstoke, at 2100 hours, less than three hours after he had left Normandy.

447. The success of this work reflects great credit on all concerned – the doctors, nurses, nursing orderlies, stretcher bearers, aircrew and ambulance drivers. In view of the fact that the aircraft often operated from airfields within range of enemy shell fire, it is a remarkable fact that every evacuation from the Continent by air during the period covered by this Despatch, was carried out without mishap either to aircraft, aircrew or wounded.

448. When the advance of the Allied armies began to outrun the normal supply arrangements, special air supply services had to be instituted. In the critical 25-day period from 9th August to 3rd September, no less than 13,000 tons of supplies were flown to forward positions. Furthermore, during the full month of September, more than 10,000 sorties were flown and a total of nearly 30,000 tons of supplies carried. These supplies comprised principally petrol, ammunition and rations and occupied all and more than all of the available lift of the transport groups.

449. It was decided, therefore, to allocate special forces of heavy bombers, both

of the United States Eighth Air Force and R.A.F. Bomber Command, to provide additional lift. This increased lift enabled enough fuel to be taken forward to keep the Armies moving.

450. I feel that in certain cases, air supply is an overriding consideration. This was an appropriate instance. However, the diversion of valuable specialised aircraft and crews from their proper operational tasks needs very grave justification and only vital emergencies such as had occurred at this time can warrant this action.

451. The principal lesson so far learnt from the campaign is that the tactical use of air transport to supply a rapidly advancing army can be of decisive importance, and that the limiting factor in its employment is not so much the availability of suitable aircraft as the availability of sufficient landing strips in the forward area and adequate loading and re-loading arrangements at the terminus. These forward strips are primarily constructed and earmarked for the fighter squadrons operating in support of the ground forces, and their use by transport aircraft is inevitably detrimental to these operations. I therefore consider that in any future campaign the airfield construction programme should envisage the immediate provision of at least one air transport landing strip per army and that these landing strips should be constructed so as to be capable of handling a minimum of 50-60 aircraft per hour.

452. In order to minimise the influence of the weather factor, consideration should also be given to the launching of air supply missions from forward airfields in close liaison with and, where necessary, under the local tactical air command.

Employment of Balloons in the Assault Phase.

453. I have already referred to the reasons for using balloons for protection of the beaches during the assault phase and to the results achieved by their use. Here I think it proper to mention the reasons for the final choice of the Mk. VI (V.L.A.) balloon and also some of the difficulties experienced during the planning stages.

454. Mk. VI (V.L.A.) balloons flying normally at an operational height of 2,000 feet, were chosen for this work for the following reasons:-

   (i) The extreme lightness of the ancillary equipment and the practicability of using a light hand winch which could be carried ashore by crews.

   (ii) The economy in operating personnel – only two airmen were required for each balloon.

   (iii) No extra initial lift was required as the balloons were transported flying.

   (iv) The possibility of transporting replacement balloons unmanned flying from L.C.T. and L.S.T.

   (v) The comparatively small hydrogen requirements for maintenance and re-inflation.

455. During the planning stage it was realised there would be some difficulty in the employment of the balloons during the passage of the original assault forces. It was

essential that balloons should not be brought in so early or at such a height as to give any premature warning on the enemy's Radar system. Inter-Service agreement was made, permitting balloons to go into the beach-head flying at 100 feet, not less than seven miles behind the assault. This height is the worst possible at which to fly a balloon owing to its inclination to dive on encountering erratic air currents near the ground. It was decided, however, after experiments on exercises that this restriction was acceptable, and in the event, no undue casualties resulted.

456. A further problem solved in the preparatory phase was the manner of transportation of the planned number of 240 balloons for the British area and 145 for the American area. As the Navy proposed to carry balloons for their own protection on one-third of the L.C.T. and all of the L.S.T. it was necessary to devise a method of flying two balloons from each L.S.T. in order to have available the planned number in the beach-heads. After several experiments, this was accomplished.

457. To provide the necessary number of inflated balloons for each craft, to maintain them during the marshalling period and during any possible period of postponement, and to replace casualties during that time, required a large number of small vessels and extensive shore servicing and hydrogen organisations at all appropriate ports. These were comparatively easily provided in England from the resources of R.A.F. Balloon Command and the Admiralty Shore Servicing Section, but it should be remembered that such facilities, if not fortuitously available as in this case, have to be arranged.

Provision of Maps.

458. The design, production and supply of maps for use by the air forces under my Command was the responsibility jointly of the War Department, Washington, and the War Office, London. Shortly after the outbreak of hostilities, the Geographical Section, General Staff, (later the Directorate of Military Survey) War Office, attached an officer to each of the principal Royal Air Force Commands, to study their requirements and to ensure adequate production and distribution of air maps. This practice was adopted for the Allied Expeditionary Air Force, a Deputy Assistant Director of Survey (British) being appointed as Chief Map Officer. Later, an officer of the Corps of Engineers, United States Army was also assigned to the Map Section.

459. Upwards of 120,000,000 maps were prepared for Operation "Neptune", of which a large proportion was used by the air forces. They embraced small and medium scale "Air" maps, maps for use in co-operation with ground forces, and an astonishing number of special maps for planning purposes, which were widely distributed to Staff Officers, mainly of the Operations and Intelligence Branches. Equally important for successful planning was the knowledge that special maps would be available for particular operations, e.g., topographical lattice maps for use in craft fitted with special Radar navigational devices and dropping zone maps for use by pilots towing gliders.

460. Headquarters, A.E.A.F. had its own drafting section and reproduction facilities were readily accorded to it by both United States and British armies. Thus, special

maps required to illustrate plans, Operation Orders and Staff Memoranda could be made available, often in a matter of hours.

461. When all the Allied Air Forces were based in the United Kingdom, the normal British channels of supply were used, but once overseas, other methods had necessarily to be devised, and the supply of maps to Commands and sub-formations differed slightly as between United States and British forces.

462. Arrangements were made whereby Royal Air Force Commands should draw maps from the British armies to which they were affiliated, and in accordance with normal United States practice, formations of the Ninth U.S.A.A.F. obtained their maps under arrangements made by the Office of the Chief Engineer, ETOUSA. This provided for the establishment of a Ninth U.S.A.A.F. Map Depot, with an Assistant Deputy Engineer in charge, whose duty it was to supply all elements of that force. Events were to prove that although both systems worked well, modifications to improve the service were necessary from time to time, and on this matter I have made comments in later paragraphs.

463. During the initial phase of operations on the Continent, the Director of Survey, 2I Army Group, established his Base Map Depot close to Bayeux, and the Chief Engineer, Communications Zone, a depot not far from the two landing beaches "Utah" and "Omaha". The Assistant Deputy Engineer, Ninth U.S.A.A.F. placed his depot first at Carentan and later at Rennes, in order to be close to the main American Base Map Depot. These depots formed the normal source of supply for the allied air formations then gathering on the Continent. Some loss of maps by enemy action occurred during the stocking of depots, but this loss was made good from reserves held in the United Kingdom.

464. Squadrons of both air forces had carried with them overseas sufficient maps to cover any operations they might undertake during the fortnight after their landing, and ground personnel were similarly equipped. It was expected that the depots would, by that time, be able to meet any demands made upon them. Both British and American systems of map supply had been well practised in the United Kingdom and there was no reason to suppose that they would not work successfully overseas; yet late in August, Headquarters, British Second Tactical Air Force complained of delays in filling their demands, and the map depot of the Ninth U.S.A.A.F. was also unable to obtain all it required from Communications Zone base depots. In both cases the difficulty had to be overcome by flying supplies from the United Kingdom.

465. The rapid advance of the Allied armies through France and Belgium during August and the beginning of September created an embarrassing situation in regard to the supply of maps. In the planning stage, it was not expected that by D + 90, the Allied Armies would have passed beyond the River Seine. By that date they were, in fact, virtually along the line of the River Scheldt. Thus there arose, long before the forecast planning date, an immediate demand for maps of all kinds and scales covering Belgium, Holland and Germany, most of which were then either concentrated in the base depots, in the United Kingdom or in transit from America.

466. The problem was acute. To move stocks already in the base depots would have taken too long. To print in the field the full quantity required was not practicable

except for certain large-scale topographic maps produced on mobile presses. There was, therefore, no alternative but to draw upon reserve stocks in the United Kingdom and fly them as rapidly as possible to where they were most urgently needed.

467. Moreover, the rapidity of the advance had deprived the printing agencies of three valuable months. Reserve stocks of certain sheets, notably those of Germany on a scale of I/I00,000 were extremely low and since they were being demanded in quantity by armies no less than by air force, new stocks of these sheets most urgently required had to be printed as rapidly as possible in the United Kingdom by as many reproduction agencies as could be pressed into service.

468. The air lift for these maps was arranged by CATOR and the maps were flown to airfields close to Paris and Brussels where they were distributed direct to air formations, often within a few hours of their having been printed, and almost before the ink was dry upon them.

469. Although the crisis was surmounted satisfactorily, I have little doubt that a serious hitch might have occurred, and I feel that very careful consideration should be given to the question of whether some modifications in the map supply organisation should not be made (see paragraph 473 et seq.).

470. By an arrangement between the United States and British forces, the "lion's share" of the design, production and supply of general and special maps for use by the air forces under my command fell to the Directorate of Military Survey, War Office and the various Survey Directorates working in conjunction with that office. Their indefatigable co-operation, and also that of the reproduction agencies of both countries was of the utmost assistance. British resources were augmented in the United Kingdom by those of the 660th Engineer Topo (Avn) Battalion, United States Army and the 942nd Engineer Topo (Avn) Battalion, forming part of the Eighth United States Army Air Force, which produced special maps for all commands within the Allied Expeditionary Air Force.

47I. The Map and Survey Section of the G-3 Division of your Headquarters also extended their help to me, and on one occasion supplied additional staff from No. I3 Map Reproduction Section of the packing and distribution of "Top Secret" maps.

472. The theatre policy for the supply of maps to a United States Army Air Force is described in Appendix VIII of the Survey Staff Manual, issued by the Chief of Engineers, United States Army, Washington, dated Ist June, I944. It stipulates as a requirement, in amplification of United States Army regulations, 300-I5, a map depot for an air force, such as the Ninth United States Army Air Force, which would draw its maps in bulk from the Engineer, Communications Zone.

473. In the light of experience it is clear that this depot should have been stocked, before leaving the United Kingdom, with sufficient maps to last for a much longer period of the campaign than its initial phases. It would then have been less dependent upon the ability of the Engineer, Communications Zone, to meet immediately such demands as were made upon him. Alternatively, had some of the bulk stocks held by the Engineer, Communications Zone, been marked before shipment for immediate delivery to the Ninth United States Army Air Force Base Depot, the storage would not have been so great.

474. The British Second Tactical Air Force was dependent for its map supply on the Map Depots controlled by the Director of Survey, 2I Army Group. In particular, Nos. 83 and 84 Groups, Royal Air Force, drew their map stocks from the map depots of the British and Canadian Armies to which they were respectively affiliated. By the middle of August, the Air Officer Commanding British Second Tactical Air Force had decided to form a map depot at his headquarters from which these groups, in an emergency, drew those maps they required, which could not be supplied by the armies. In October, the Director of Survey, 2I Army Group, in conference with all concerned, supported this change of policy, and recommended also that the Groups, too, should materially improve until my Headquarters set up again at Versailles, by which time an almost static situation had again developed.

Establishment of Signals Communications and Radar Cover.

475. The extent to which efficient signals communications enter into the successful launching and controlling of an air operation is never fully realised until by some chance these facilities fail. That the channels of signals communications satisfied the bulk of our complex needs during the course of the operation was due to the careful preliminary planning, as well as to the training of operating and maintenance personnel. Few difficulties arose   until the break-out from the beach-head and the rapid moves forward of the air forces.

476. The planning of the W/T and R/T organisation for point-to-point communications was necessarily undertaken many months in advance of the actual assault, and was on a carefully co-ordinated United States and British inter-service basis.

477. The communications required were divided broadly into two categories:-

(*a*) tactical communications, and
(*b*) strategical communications.

478. The tactical communications were essentially operational channels required for use mainly during the assault phase, to be operated from the Combined Control Centre and Executive Control Centre to the Assault forces, the Headquarters ships and the Fighter Direction Tenders. The strategical communications were those to be used between Air Force Headquarters on the Continent and in the United Kingdom. These communications included a number of administrative channels.

479. It was decided to plan and to provide sufficient W/T communications to enable all traffic to be handled irrespective of such landline or cable circuits as might be provided. In order to handle rapidly large volumes of signals traffic, a number of high speed auto W/T mobile signals units were formed for operation on the main operational and administrative links between the Continent and the United Kingdom.

480. The British Second Tactical Air Force and the United States Ninth Air Force planned their own communications forward of their Headquarters. The communications rearward from these Air Forces were planned by A.E.A.F. and were the main operational and administrative links to the United Kingdom. As a result of a survey of traffic passed over the main W/T links in the North African theatre, it was

decided that operational signals traffic should be handled separately from administrative traffic.

48I. The implementation of the signal plan necessitated the building of a number of new W/T stations in the United Kingdom and the development of others. No less than two transmitting and four receiving stations were constructed, while a further five mobile transmitting stations were introduced. In addition, three transmitting and three receiving stations were enlarged and developed.

482. For W/T communications, five static and two mobile R/T transmitting and receiving sites were set up and put into operation at points along the South Coast. On the Continent, the R/T channels were provided by Mobile Signals Units, which worked on both Simplex and Duplex circuits; also Radio/Teleprinter facilities were provided for operation in addition to, and simultaneously with R/T.

483. During the assault, all the forward units, in Headquarters Ships and Fighter Direction Tenders, as well as terminal units on the far shore such as G.C.I, stations and even smaller units, including Beach Squadrons, successfully opened communications as planned. There was some slight interference experienced on some channels early in the operation, but this was quickly overcome and a remarkably high standard of operation was maintained.

484. In addition to the limited Radar cover given by the Fighter Direction Tenders, a plan to provide complete Radar cover over the beach-head was set in motion on D-Day. Two complete G.C.I. stations were among the first equipment to follow the original assault forces ashore.

485. One of these G.C.I. stations was landed at mid-day on D-Day and proceeded to a prearranged site. By nightfall, two of its pieces of equipment were working, together with its

V.H.F., R/T, Air to Ground and D/F channels, and from 2230 hours on D-Day, night fighters were controlled from this station.

486. The second G.C.I. station suffered severe losses, due to being landed on a beach not cleared of the enemy. There were about 40 casualties, some of which were fatal and most of the unit's communication and Radar equipment was lost. Despite these setbacks, the one Radar equipment salvaged was set up and moved to its correct site, where it commenced operating with borrowed R/T equipment on D + 4. The aircraft controlled during this first night made a number of contacts, most of them friendly, but one enemy aircraft was destroyed and one damaged.

487. By 20th June (D + I4), no less than four G.C.I. type stations, one C.O.L. station, five F.D.P's and five Light Warning sets were in operation in the beach-head area. The Radars had all been set up at pre-selected sites that had been chosen by the Operational Research Section from maps and photographic cover. That these stations were sited so well is not only a tribute to the research workers, but also to the air reconnaissance that supplied the detailed material for their work.

488. One unsatisfactory feature of signals communications arose in relation to the major operational and administrative headquarters after operational units began to move forward behind our advancing troops. On a number of occasions, both Headquarters, Second Tactical Air Force and United States Ninth Air Force lost touch temporarily with some of their units as also did Advanced Headquarters, A.E.A.F.,

with Stanmore. Moreover, after the move of my main headquarters to Julouville in September, where it set up alongside your Advanced Headquarters, I did not have adequate telephone or signals communications with my Advanced Headquarters or the Headquarters of the two Tactical Air Forces. I was much in the dark about what was going on and the co-ordination of the air effort became extremely difficult.

489. Signals facilities just adequate to service a static headquarters and provide links with its more stationary units cannot be adequate when that headquarters and its units begin to move. Because these moves must be carried out by splitting into two parties, the facilities required will be almost double those needed before. In other words, equipment and operators will be needed at two places instead of at one only.

490. This factor, which raises difficult problems of supply, training and administration for the signals service, has none the less to be reckoned with, and the problem it represents solved, if proper direction of operations is to be maintained in conditions of highly mobile warfare.

491. Some mitigation of the task of signals personnel in tackling these problems would result if the moves of main headquarters particularly were delayed longer than has been the practice in these operations, and certainly not made until the communications are suitable for operational needs. While it is important to keep operational headquarters close to the forward units, this factor must be more carefully related to the practicability of providing adequate signals facilities at the new location of the headquarters. Continuity of service is of overriding importance in air and combined operations.

PART V.
SOME BRIEF REFLECTIONS ON THE CAMPAIGN

492. The extensive air operations which are the subject of this Despatch cannot be summed up in a few paragraphs, nor, without entering fields of controversy, is it possible to discuss all the air lessons which have emerged during the campaign. What can be done, however, is to state, and where useful, to discuss briefly, certain of the more prominent issues which can be discerned in the pattern of air operations seen as a whole. Experience gained in subsequent operations in this and in other theatres may confirm these impressions, or, on the other hand, make their revision necessary.

Preparatory Air Operations.

493. Events thoroughly justified our strategic bombing policy and your insistence upon an adequate preparatory period of air operations for Operation "Neptune." As it turned out, weather conditions allowed only a partial use of our air forces in the weeks following the assault, and had these preliminary operations not been started before D-Day the task of the air forces of interfering effectively with the enemy's movement within and to the battle area could not have been achieved in time to have directly influenced the land operations in the initial phases. As it was, and in accordance with the plan, the air had, by the day of the assault, completely

disorganised the enemy's dense and complex network of rail lines of communications within France and Belgium. This having virtually been accomplished by D-Day, it was soon possible to seal off the battle area through air action, and in this way the area was prepared for the employment of ground forces, with the enemy at a critical disadvantage.

494. During the initial planning and preliminary operations some doubt – based on experience in other theatres – was expressed as to the efficacy of air action on bridges. Results of the initial attacks in France soon proved that given suitable technique, types of aircraft, and weapons, bridges can successfully be destroyed or rendered impassable, although the cost maybe a heavy one in aircraft and personnel due to flak, and also in bombs expended. Weather may, however, frequently preclude attacks as and when planned. To have relied entirely upon the destruction of bridges as the main method of achieving the disorganisation of the enemy's communications system at the appropriate moment in Operation "Overlord," would again have proved unsound in the given conditions. The attacks on bridges formed but an integral part, albeit an important one, of the whole plan of action against the movement organisation of the enemy.

Diversionary Operations.

495. Our efforts to mislead the enemy proved most effective, but their implementation, though they provided excellent operational training for crews, placed a great strain upon our air resources. In general, for every target attacked in the assault area, two had to be taken on outside that zone. Although "Crossbow" operations were taken into account in the framing of the programme, the diversion of effort from "Pointblank," communication targets, and other objectives of strategic importance, was very considerable. On the other hand, despite the fact that this great effort was directed against targets having little direct material effect on the achievement of the military object of securing the initial bridgehead, it is reasonable to deduce that these operations must at least have been a factor influencing the German High Command to dispose their reserves in the Pas de Calais area as a central position against possible landings in that area and/or any part of the long coastline from Denmark to Brest. This was obviously most advantageous to ourselves especially as our air offensive against his communications rendered movement of these reserves a lengthy and hazardous operation, particularly over considerable distances.

496. A high cost may have to be paid for diversionary activities of this kind, if they are to be realistic, and this fact must always be borne in mind when estimating the strength of the air forces required for combined operations.

Inter-Service Fire Plan.

497. The drawing up of the fire plan for the assault phase was rightly regarded as an inter-Service and inter-Allied responsibility. Throughout such planning care must he taken to ensure flexibility, and it must be accepted by the Air Forces that it may not be possible finally to fix the air tasks until a very short time before D-Day – owing to such factors as changes in information, changes in weather conditions (including

likely height of cloud bases), the development of enemy beach defences and gun positions and changes in conditions of light for air and naval bombardment and for fire by assault craft of various types. Moreover, an alternative Fire Plan is essential. There is a tendency on the part of the other Services to expect too much of the air forces from the point of view of the destruction of prepared gun emplacements, especially when completely concreted; their neutralisation for a critical and limited time is, of course, another matter. At the same time there is a strong inclination among air men to look more upon the material rather than the morale side of such bombing. The demoralisation of the gun crews through the psychological reaction to bombing contributes as much towards the neutralisation of gun defences as does damage by actual hits or by shock effects.

Spotting for Naval Bombardment.

498. The Fleet Air Arm was unable to accept the full responsibility of spotting for naval bombardment either for the assault or for subsidiary operations and in the main, this task fell to Royal Air Force fighter reconnaissance squadrons. The pilots of these squadrons had necessarily to undergo a special course of training in naval procedure. The conversion presented no real difficulty but the prolonged diversion of these units from their normal tasks caused some anxiety as our total resources were limited. In the end, all our reconnaissance commitments were fairly adequately met.

499. There are obvious advantages in training some Royal Air Force reconnaissance units for the dual role of co-operation with both ground and naval forces.

Anti-Aircraft Defences.

500. On a number of occasions, our own anti-aircraft guns, both naval and military, shot down friendly aircraft. The claims of fighter aircraft and A.A. guns in air defence have always conflicted because the ideal for the fighter is a field clear of any restrictions, and for A.A. gunfire a sky free of friendly aircraft.

50I. In comparatively static conditions, such as the Battle of Britain, it has generally been accepted that the merits of these two claims could best be resolved by an Air Defence Commander (who in the case of the United Kingdom was the Senior Defensive Air Force Commander). It is relevant to note that after much experience the same principle was adopted in the Mediterranean.

502. For Operation "Neptune", however, no one officer was made specifically responsible for Air Defence as such, primarily because in the initial stages it was held that the Army Group Commanders themselves should decide the precise allocation of their resources to the limited number of landing craft allowed them. Also, it was considered that in forward areas the only effective control which could be exercised over A.A. weapons would be by the imposition of standing instructions.

503. From the Air Force point of view, it became clear shortly after the operation had been satisfactorily launched that this policy should be revised in favour of unified control. My request on these lines was not accepted by your Headquarters in August on the grounds that the time was not opportune for a change in this particular policy.

504. I cannot help feeling, however, that if the scale of enemy air attack had in fact been heavier such a change would have been essential in order to bring about a satisfactory degree of security when and where it was really needed. Moreover, I am of the opinion that the knowledge that a well co-ordinated air defence system exists will of itself produce a deterrent effect upon the enemy.

505.[14] In the absence of serious air attack, the claims of A.A. guns were at times pressed, to my mind, without full regard to the air situation of the moment. Army Commanders declared a considerable area around the majority of river crossings or similar places of importance a "prohibited" area for the operation of friendly aircraft by night. The Tactical Air Force Commanders concerned were approached by the appropriate Army Commander for acceptance of these I.A.Z's and, although they could speak for their own night operations, which were primarily of a local nature, they were in no position to answer for the requirements of the Commanders of the Strategic Bomber Forces or for the needs of S.O.E. operations.

506. The patchwork of these restricted flying areas thereby created imposed upon both Royal Air Force Bomber Command and No. 38 Group tremendous operational difficulties and handicaps which were surmounted mainly by the navigational ability of the crews concerned. These I.A.Z's constituted an unnecessary complication of an air situation already made difficult by the restrictions which had to be imposed on the use of I.F.F.

507. I feel most strongly that the establishment of restricted areas for flying, when part of the Air Defence arrangements, is primarily an air problem and should be solved by the Air Commander, naturally after the necessary consultations with the ground and naval commanders. The issues which are involved have never been faced up to because the scale of enemy air attack has been of such a low order, but it has been our own air forces which have had to suffer unnecessary inconveniences, and at times danger, and the A.A. guns have enjoyed a freedom of action which has been out of proportion to the real defensive requirements.

Aircraft Identification.

508. It was realised for some time before Operation "Neptune" was launched that our mechanical means of identifying aircraft, namely I.F.F., was not a satisfactory type of equipment for aircraft which operate in any numbers. In fact, owing to mutual interference and the probability that no value at all could be gained by the general application of this equipment, it was decided, after consultation with all United States and British services and technical authorities concerned, to limit the use of I.F.F. to a few special types of aircraft in order that these aircraft at least could be adequately tracked.

509. This decision meant that the only remaining means of identifying aircraft was the careful passing of aircraft movements and by relating aircraft tracks to notifications of flights previously given. This was clearly an unsatisfactory situation but one which had to be accepted in the circumstances. There is no doubt that every step should be taken to hasten the production of a really effective mechanical method of indicating friendly aircraft, and I consider that a great deal more scientific study should be devoted to this subject in the future.

Balloon Defence.

5I0. In any future amphibious operation similar to Operation "Neptune" which is mounted from a country in which exists a balloon defence with all its attendant facilities, the cheapness and comparative ease of providing balloon protection unquestionably makes Balloon Defence profitable if there be any likelihood of low-level attacks by enemy aircraft. For an operation despatched from an area in which no such facilities exist, the necessary lift in hydrogen, packed balloons, and ancillary equipment to provide for initial inflation and to meet a high casualty rate would, I consider, be justified only if the enemy air effort was expected to be unusually strong and determined.

Operational Items.

5II. The enemy air effort, taken as a whole, was mediocre throughout. The lack of efficiency and the low operational effort of the G.A.F., especially during the critical assault stage, were largely the result of previous attention paid to the G.A.F., his loss of Radar coverage, and of attacks on its bases and installations, which constantly compelled him to change his operational aerodromes and A.L.G.'s and to operate his fighters outside effective range of the assault area and shipping lanes.

5I2. As was forecasted in our early planning, marked Allied air superiority made it possible to use heavy night bombers by day with outstanding success, and relatively slight losses, since, if necessary, they could be escorted by our fighters.

5I3. The fighter bomber proved to be a battle-winning weapon. It showed tremendous power in breaking up and destroying enemy concentrations, especially of armour, and contributed greatly to the paralysis of enemy road and rail movement.

5I4. Heavy bombers can be employed to decisive effect in a tactical role. A special treatise on the principles of their employment in support of the land operations has been issued jointly by 2I Army Group and A.E.A.F., with the blessing of Supreme Headquarters, Allied Expeditionary Force, and is now being considered by the U.S. Army and Air Force Commanders.

5I5. The enemy's Radar cover was effectively disrupted and neutralised by air attacks, and in consequence the enemy was virtually "blinded" at the time of the assault.

5I6. Because of the possible risk of bombing our own land forces, Army Commanders in some instances insisted on the bomb line being pushed too far ahead of the line of our forward troops. This often proved a handicap to the effective use of tactical support aircraft. The land forces should accept a bomb line as close as possible to our front line, and be prepared to run some small risk of casualties in order to enable the air to give them the maximum close support. The fixing of the bomb line for predetermined direct support when heavy bombers are participating in a co-ordinated land/air operation is, of course, a separate issue.

5I7. Armed reconnaissance of roads, rail lines and the Seine crossing by Mosquitoes of British Second Tactical Air Force during the hours of darkness proved extremely effective and disconcerting to the enemy. Intruder action of this kind could have been most effectively extended had more forces been available.

518. The value of good photographic reconnaissance cannot be overstated. Our resources in normal high altitude photographic reconnaissance were on the whole adequate, but here too the weather adversely affected the fulfilment of the reconnaissance programme after D-Day. There were long periods of inactivity when lack of strategic intelligence relating in particular to movements in rearward areas and to damage inflicted by our bombing, had serious consequences and sometimes even frustrated our plans.

519. The absence of an intermediate and low altitude photographic reconnaissance aircraft became apparent very early on, and a few armed Mustang III had to be converted at R.A.F. Station Benson for this special type of photography. There should be one medium altitude and one high flying flight in each photographic reconnaissance unit.

520. It also clearly emerged that the control of photographic reconnaissance of all types for commitments outside the allotted tactical area must be centralised in one authority. The formation of the Combined Reconnaissance Committee at Uxbridge, which filtered and took action on demands for reconnaissance from all quarters satisfied this requirement.

521. The need for a highly efficient mapping and target section which could turn out the necessary material at the shortest notice was fully appreciated before "Neptune" was launched. Experience proved that the personnel and the facilities at the disposal of the Section were not adequate for the multiple tasks by which it was faced. It is impossible to prepare in advance dossiers of every possible target which the air forces may have to hit. The only solution is to have available as large an organisation as may possibly be necessary for the task of turning out with a minimum of delay the material that might be demanded of it.

522. Modifications to the system of supply of maps were found to be necessary during the campaign. The changes made, as described earlier in this Despatch, indicate the lines along which I feel future plans for map supply should be made.

523. Unless signal facilities are much increased and well planned in advance, and staffs given ample time to develop them, major operational and administrative headquarters, when they move, are likely to get out of touch with each other and with forward headquarters and sources of intelligence. The direction of air operations would at times have been more easily and effectively achieved if the moving of headquarters had been postponed until adequate communications between the Continent and the United Kingdom had been established.

524. Signals security is also all-important. It is of little use having scramblers or other devices unless they work efficiently over considerable distances.

525. The value of scientific research into current operations may also be mentioned here since quite apart from its application to day-to-day technical problems, the information which it provides is of great use in the field of planning. An up-to-date check of bombing accuracy and the effectiveness of the weapons used makes it possible to predict within reasonably accurate limits the amount of effort which is required for particular tasks, and thus one aspect of economies of alternative operations can be assessed in advance. In this way, the cost of the major air operations in "Neptune" was assessed with a relatively high degree of accuracy. At the same

time, such studies, once again, demonstrated that too great a value cannot be placed on training, and on the improvement of bombing accuracy. As the latter improves, the potential power of a bomber force also increases, but at a far greater rate.

Relationship of Strategical to Tactical Bomber Operations.

526. The concept of strategical and tactical air forces as separate entities frequently breaks down in operations in which the activities of the air are interwoven with those of the ground forces. Phased operations by strategical and tactical air forces are sometimes different and at other times the same points within the same target system and within the same general time limits means that there is an inter-relation of effects throughout the whole period the target system is under fire.

527. The inter-relation of effects becomes evident when one considers the premier part played by the strategical air forces in setting the state for "Neptune", not only for subsequent operations of a tactical nature by the tactical air forces, but also for the ground battle. As we have already seen, this preparatory phase occupied the three months preceding D-Day by which time heavy bomber, and to a lesser extent, medium bomber attacks on rail centres achieved their full purpose of causing a catastrophic decline in the potential of the railways. The ensuing chaos, which is difficult to describe, was accentuated by the subsequent fighter and medium bomber attacks on bridges, on trains, and on open lines. If they had not been aided by the heavy blows which had already been delivered by heavy bombers on the key points of the railway systems, the tactical air forces could hardly have played the successful part they did in bringing organised rail movement to a virtual standstill; nor could the isolation of the battlefield have been subsequently achieved as rapidly as it was. Further, the preparatory bombing of the railway system by the strategical forces at the same time drove the enemy increasingly to the roads in spite of his precarious M.T. and fuel situation, and so fighter bombers and fighters were presented with road targets, which, as the record shows, they were able to exploit to the full. In fact, as we now know, road and rail movement became so hazardous an undertaking that the enemy's forward troops were as frequently as not starved of the means with which to continue the fight. These integrated and phased operations against the enemy's lines of communication were a decisive factor both in the success of our initial landings, in that they slowed down considerably the enemy's build-up and concentration of reinforcement, and in the successful outcome of the whole battle in France.

528. Again, in the sphere of direct Army support, whilst it was the fighter bomber which in general had the last word so far as the Air Forces were concerned in the tactical defeat of the enemy in France and Belgium, it was the heavy bomber and medium bomber which, two months before D-Day, began the attack on the enemy's defences. Thus, although the pre D-Day attacks on coastal batteries were unsuccessful in destroying guns under thick concrete cover, they not only stopped constructional work in half finished batteries, but critically by D-Day the efficiency of those which had been completed. In fact, opposition offered by, the coastal defences was relatively so slight that there was virtually little opportunity for the employment of the fighter bomber against enemy forces in the landing areas.

529. Moreover, the operations in Normandy again made it clear that heavy bombers when used in support of a land battle can, in addition to their direct assistance to the land forces in the attack, open up to the tactical air forces a wealth of targets normally otherwise denied them when the static battle in consequence of the bombing became a war of movement. Major retreats, or the marshalling of forces for a counter-attack, could be carried out only in the open, and once the enemy was exposed the result of the fighter bomber attacks was a foregone conclusion.

530. In a sense, this fusing of the operation of different components of the air forces is merely an extension of a principle which has already been recognised in attacks on the G.A.F. The destruction by our strategical air forces of the enemy's aircraft factories and of his fuel industry represents only one part of a single comprehensive plan. Apart from the attrition as a result of air fighting, there was also the complementary action – the exploitation in "Neptune" of the bombing of airfields. The latter operations achieved their purpose, in particular by still further reducing the resources the enemy enjoyed in France, both in aircraft and crews, in airfields, and in aircraft maintenance factories.

Unified Control of Air Effort.

531. Because of the foregoing considerations, and if the best results are to be achieved in the most economic manner, it is essential that the direction of air operations which call for the employment of air forces from various countries and commands should be placed in unity of command and planning. The need for this is equally apparent when one views the inter-relation of the ground and air forces in operations in which heavy bombers are used in a tactical role.

532. The latter operations are in every sense of the term "Inter-Service Operations". The danger of treating the bomber as merely a component part of a Corps artillery, thrown in merely to add some fire support, can at present be obviated only by co-ordinated planning between the air and land forces. If this principle were lost sight of, there would be a serious risk of the misuse of heavy bombers in a tactical role, and bombing on a large scale might be expended in profitless destruction which would add little, if anything, to the progress of a land battle. From the operational point of view, the need for unified planning stands out all the more prominently when it is realised that the strategical forces which contributed so much and so directly to the land battle in France were in themselves equivalent in fire power to vast ground forces. It is only through integrated ground and air planning that the air forces can serve usefully in a tactical role.

533. Although the tactical operations in which heavy bombers were used in Normandy were initiated by the ground force commander, there may also be times when the air force commander with his better appreciation of the effects which air effort can achieve, might in future suggest to the Army rich opportunities for a combined air and land operation.

Command and Control.

534. The relationship of Air Forces to the Army and Naval Forces and to the Supreme

Command from the point of view of Command and Control is well worth touching upon in view of the great importance of this question in future Combined Operations of the scope of "Overlord". It raises interesting though naturally somewhat controversial problems.

535. In the early days of planning and preparation for Operation "Overlord" there was a Commander-in-Chief of all Air Forces and a Commander-in-Chief of all Naval Forces each having the necessary integrated operational staffs and Headquarters but separate from those of the allied operational forces. The Commanders-in-Chief and their staffs were also service advisers to COSSAC and later to yourself as Supreme Commander. The organisation was, however, different in respect of the land forces, the direction and control of these operations in the field being undertaken by the Army staff of COSSAC itself.

536. In February, 1944, you appointed the Commander-in-Chief, 21st Army Group to co-ordinate the planning and execution for the assault for both the United States and British Army Groups and thereby raised the Commander-in-Chief, 21st Army Group to the level of Commander-in-Chief of the Land Forces. He naturally used his own staff for both these functions but the Army staff of Supreme Headquarters Allied Expeditionary Force still continued to exercise direction of the land operations from the point of view of general policy and to co-ordinate the activities of all three Services on the high level.

537. The Air Commander-in-Chief and the staff of Allied Expeditionary Air Force were, in consequence, required to work on two levels with two large Army staffs. On the one hand, they had, as your Air advisers, to contribute to the directives and numerous operational and administrative memoranda produced by Supreme Headquarters Allied Expeditionary Force and on the other, and this time on the Commanders-in-Chief operational level to plan, prepare for and execute the assault in co-ordination with 21st Army Group. Further, it was inevitable in these circumstances that the closest contact had also to be maintained with the Commanding General of the American land forces.

538. This arrangement severely taxed the staffs of Allied Expeditionary Air Force and inevitably led to overlapping and complications and at times interference with the planning of the tactical air forces and their opposite Army and Navy formations. The two staffs were, in fact, the same as those with which Allied Expeditionary Air Force itself was, at the same time, planning on a high level.

539. In the post assault period when 21st Army Group reverted to its normal position the situation was greatly eased but certain difficulties still remained in that the Army staff at Supreme Headquarters Allied Expeditionary Force retained a dual function in certain respects.

540. In spite of its inherent difficulties the organisation of Command and Control as developed through the various phases, undoubtedly worked, but I suggest that the creation of a separate Commander-in-Chief of all Allied Land Forces on the level with, and having similar functions to, the Air and Naval Commanders-in-Chief would have facilitated the execution of the responsibilities of the Air Commander-in-Chief and the Allied Air Force commanders, and no doubt also of the other service Commanders-in-Chief and staffs.

541. The geographical relationship of the Commanders-in-Chief and staffs of the Air, Army and Naval forces and the Supreme Commander and his Headquarters also has a direct bearing on the question of Command and Control.

542. In the first period of planning the Commanders-in-Chief and appropriate portions of their staffs, were housed mainly in one building in London and this arrangement naturally worked excellently.

543. Shortly after the formation of Supreme Headquarters Allied Expeditionary Force itself, part of its general staff moved out of London to Bushy Park. This inevitably led to a splitting and to some extent further duplication of my staff, part of which had to move to Bushy Park, part had to remain at Norfolk House to plan with ANCXF and the remainder of SHAEF, and part had to remain at Stanmore for the planning and control of preliminary air operations for "Neptune" – the latter being a function and responsibility which the Army and Naval Commanders-in-Chief had not to undertake prior to the assault. I was forced to keep my main staff at Stanmore if only because of communication facilities which were adequate for the control of air operations at no other Headquarters or centre.

544. A further dispersal of the Combined and Joint Planners of the operational staff resulted from the necessity to work with the Headquarters staff of 21st Army Group, whose location was at St. Pauls School, for the detailed planning of the assault.

545. The situation became even more complicated from the air point of view when, for the execution of the initial stages of the invasion, 21st Army Group and ANCXF, with a SHAEF Command Post, moved to the Portsmouth area. The operations staff at AEAF had still perforce, to remain at Stanmore and Supreme Headquarters Allied Expeditionary Force Main together with AEAF planners, who formed part of the combined planning staff of Supreme Headquarters, continued to work at Bushy Park. Later, a further echelon of Supreme Headquarters Allied Expeditionary Force Main, i.e., Forward SHAEF, which included the operations staff and planners of Supreme Headquarters with its AEAF complement moved also to the Portsmouth area. This arrangement obviously simplified the co-ordination of Army and Naval operations and plans at the Commanders-in-Chief level, but my own difficulties were proportionally aggravated as a result of these moves of Main Headquarters.

546. Only when the various Headquarters were set up at Julouville in Normandy, did the co-ordination of operations and planning become smooth and easy, although the value derived from all the principals being so closely related geographically was unfortunately to some extent negatived by lack of adequate communications between Main Headquarters and Operational Commands.

547. In my view one of the major lessons learned from "Overlord" is that the staffs of the Supreme Commander and of the Air, Naval and Land Commanders-in-Chief if created, should be located very close together during both the planning and the execution stages, and this principle should be held to be inviolate; in order to achieve this the Services must be prepared to make sacrifices.

548. The communication aspect is all important and particularly must communication facilities be adequate for the conduct of air operations which will

almost invariably have to commence weeks and possibly months before those of Land and possibly Naval operations. The latter factor is, I suggest, one which must have the fullest possible consideration when determining the location of the Headquarters of the Commanders-in-Chief. Even at the lower Staff levels it is essential for sound planning and development of operations that the staffs of the three Services should be within easy transportation distance of each other, and I will go so far as to recommend within walking distance of each other.

549. Finally, on the more tactical plane, it is essential to have in the field an operational co-ordinating organisation, similar to A.E.A.F. Advanced Headquarters (which was fully mobile), which can keep in touch at one end and at the same time with army headquarters and headquarters of air formations in the forward areas and with the main operational air headquarters in rear. Particularly is this required for the planning of operations in which heavy bombers are used in a tactical role. Only in this way can the bomber forces involved be adjusted smoothly to such alterations in the plan as may be dictated, often at very short notice, by changes in weather and/or in the ground situation.

Footnotes

1. *Appendices not reproduced.*
2. *Maps not reproduced.*
3. *Subject to modification in the light of information subsequently received.*
4. *Appendices not reproduced.*
5. *R.P. = rocket projectile.*
6. *Maps not reproduced.*
7. *R.C.T. = Regimental Combat Team.*
8. *Maps and Appendices not reproduced.*
9. *Maps not reproduced.*
10. *Maps not reproduced.*
11. *Maps not reproduced.*
12. *Maps not reproduced.*
13. *These figures may be liable to review when enemy documents have been subjected to research.*
14. *Apart from the operational factors referred to in paragraphs 505, 506 and 507, it is appreciated that there is a "morale" side to this question. On the one hand there are the fighting troops who maybe kept awake by the effects of minor air action to which they cannot retaliate, and, on the other, the tired crews returning from missions, whose aircraft cannot avoid the prohibited areas, either because of shortage of petrol or because they have been already badly damaged, and who find themselves fired upon and possibly shot down by friendly A.A. defences.*

5

THE FINAL STAGES OF THE NAVAL WAR IN NORTH-WEST EUROPE

The following despatch was submitted to the Lords Commissioners of the Admiralty on the 4th December, 1945, by Admiral Sir HAROLD M. BURROUGH, K.C.B., K.B.E., D.S.O., British Naval Commander-in-Chief, Germany.

British Naval Commander-in-Chief, Germany,
c/o Admiralty.
4th December, 1945.

Be pleased to lay before Their Lordships the enclosed copy of my report to the Supreme Commander, Allied Expeditionary Force, on the Final Stages of the Naval War in North West Europe.

2. As explained in my covering letter to the Supreme Commander, the aim of this report is to supplement the detailed information and statistics in the War Diaries and thus to provide a continuous narrative which is brief, but at the same time contains sufficient detail and references to facilitate research into any particular period or episode.

3. Reports of proceedings were rendered at the time in respect of most of the episodes described in the narrative of this period, but no separate report has been rendered on the naval arrangements for the occupation of Germany.

4. I would bring to Their Lordships' notice, the co-operation and assistance received from the Commanders-in-Chief, The Nore, Portsmouth and Plymouth, in regard to the formation of the Naval Parties destined for Germany which were thus able to move to their destinations with far less delay than had been thought possible. The lion's share of the credit for this must go to the Commander-in-Chief, The Nore, Admiral of the Fleet Sir John C. Tovey, G.C.B., K.B.E., D.S.O., in whose Command the Parties for the most vital ports were formed, and who throughout, by his personal interest in the progress of the planning, had done everything possible to make matters go smoothly.

5. The co-operation and assistance received from the Personnel Departments of the Admiralty and from Plans Division (Q), were also notable.

(Signed) H.M. BURROUGH,
Admiral.

THE FINAL STAGES OF THE NAVAL WAR IN NORTH-WEST EUROPE.

Office of Allied Naval Commander-in-Chief,
Expeditionary Force.
13th July, 1945.

I have the honour to submit the enclosed report, outlining the activities of the Allied Naval Forces under my command from the time of the crossing of the Rhine, to the 13th July, 1945, when your period of command as Supreme Commander, Allied Expeditionary Force, was terminated.

2. The aim of this report is to supplement the information in the War Diaries, which were rendered periodically from D Day onwards, by a narrative which is of sufficient brevity that a busy man might find time to read it, but which mentions all important events so that the historian may find clues for more detailed research.

3. This was a period of widespread and historical activity for all the Sea, Land and Air Forces under, your command. The naval role in these crowning achievements was primarily to ensure the maintenance of the Armies and Air Forces in the field by protecting their lines of communication where they crossed the sea. This had been their primary role since the 6th June, 1944, but with the supplementary operations undertaken during these months, and the preparation of the naval forces of occupation, the period becomes one of greater naval activity than any since the days of maintenance over the beaches.

4. More than the other Services, the United States and British Navies felt the demands of the Naval War in the Far East during this time, with the resultant considerable withdrawals from the naval strength at my disposal. With many unknown commitments ahead and many plans awaiting fruition, this reduction in our naval strength would have caused me more uneasiness had I not had ample evidence that fortitude and hard work would enable the Allied Navies to accomplish all that was required of them, despite reductions in their strength.

5. In these latter days, the French Navy was rapidly gaining in strength and it was a proud moment when French Naval Forces took part in the operation for the liberation of Bordeaux, the first major operation they had undertaken under my command.

6. But it is to the combined work of the United States and British Navies that the future historian will turn for an example of faultless team work and mutual

understanding between nations, that may be equalled in the future but surely never surpassed. Tradition and custom, the parents of procedure, are very deeply rooted in all Navies and when one Navy is placed under the Commander-in-Chief of another nationality, the procedure of his own Service must be paramount in both. No exception occurred in this case, and the United States Navy readily adapted itself to the requirements of a closely knit British Naval organisation.

7. The foundations of this, the most fruitful and harmonious naval combination of all time, were laid by my predecessor, the late Admiral Sir Bertram H. Ramsay, K.C.B., K.B.E., M.V.O., and I am proud to be able to claim that the co-operation between our two Services has grown no less since his passing.

8. As the best expression of my feelings at the time of the termination of our great enterprise, I reproduce the messages made by me on the occasions of the termination of the Supreme Command and the last U.S. Naval Forces leaving the European Theatre of Operations, together with the replies made by yourself and Admiral H.R. Stark, Commander, U.S. Naval Forces in Europe.

(Signed). H.M. BURROUGH,
Admiral.
GENERAL DWIGHT D. EISENHOWER, U.S. Army,
Supreme Commander,
Allied Expeditionary Force.

THE FINAL STAGES OF THE NAVAL WAR IN NORTH-WEST EUROPE.

The direct contribution of the Allied Navies to the crossing of the Rhine was the assistance they provided at the crossing, and to the Armies operating on the western flank in the east Scheldt area.

2. Early in March, 1945, a force of L.C.M.s and L.C.V.(P)s[1], known as Force "U" and under the command of Captain P.H.G. James, R.N., was formed to assist the, 21st Army Group in crossing the Rhine.

A corresponding force of United States landing craft had been formed the previous winter to assist the American Armies, and both British and U.S. craft were transported overland with their crews and all equipment in tank transporters.

In fact, only L.C.V.(P)s were used on account of their greater manoeuvrability and they proved extremely useful for such jobs as towing sections of pontoon bridges. They also did a certain amount of ferrying, notably in the American sector where they did valiant work under fire in the Remagen Bridge area.

3. At the request of the Allied Armies, small boom and asdic parties were supplied at the Rhine crossing with the object of preventing German midget submarines, explosive boats and saboteur swimmers from interfering with our communications. All were of great assistance as the Germans made some determined but fruitless efforts with these weapons.

4. On the lower Rhine and West Scheldt estuary, the naval Force "T", under Captain A.F. Pugsley, C.B., D.S.O., R.N., continued to be responsible for the protection of the seaward flank of our Armies and carried out a constant succession of Commando raids, mostly by L.C.A.[2], on the enemy's positions in the area. These raids were almost uniformly successful.

5. Craft of both Force "T" and Force "U" took part in the final crossings of the Rhine when the Canadian Army was advancing westward into Holland.

Tasks facing the Allied Navies after the Rhine Crossing.

6. With the crossing of the Rhine accomplished, a survey of the wider scene found the Allied Navies charged with the following variety of tasks:-

(a) The provision of specialised seagoing ships and craft required for the maintenance of the Allied Armies in the field, together with the responsibility shared with the Commander-in-Chief, The Nore, for the protection of merchant shipping used for the same purpose.

(b) The working of the ports through which the main stream of military imports flowed. Some 10,000 tons of stores on British account and 20,000 tons on U.S. account were passing through Antwerp daily, while the main personnel traffic passed through Ostend and Calais in the British zone and Le Havre in the U.S. zone.

(c) Preparation of Naval Parties to participate in the occupation of Germany including the provision of an operational Port Party to open the port of Hamburg. Arrangements for naval representation on the S.H.A.E.F. Missions to Denmark and Norway.

(d) The provision of naval assistance for the reduction of pockets of resistance on the west coast of France. Most of these pockets had only nuisance value to the immediate war effort but importance was attached to the early opening of the port of Bordeaux and operations were in train to this end.

(e) The protection of the Scheldt Approaches.

(f) Naval measures to bring speedy relief to Holland.

(g) The planning of operations to occupy the Channel Islands after surrender, and to occupy Norway under a variety of conditions.

Prospects of Opening a North German Port.

7. Of these widespread problems the first one brought into prominence after the Rhine crossing was the opening of a North German port. This project had long been discussed and in the event of prolonged resistance the opening of such a port might become a vital need, though it was agreed that such an early opening was not in the circumstances, as they then were, an urgent necessity; nor in fact was it a feasible

project from the naval point of view to open a port as quickly as Army requirements would prefer, particularly the port most required, Hamburg. It was established that owing to the shortage of minesweepers and the necessity for being prepared to open Dutch ports concurrently for civil relief, only one German port could be opened at a time. Apart from the limitations likely to be imposed by the minesweeping conditions, particularly the difficulties of sweeping our own mines, it was necessary for all resistance to have ceased along the Dutch, and North-West German coasts before minesweeping could be started. The reduction of Heligoland and neutralisation of enemy batteries on Wangerooge[3] were also essential before the Elbe Approaches could be swept.

8. Subject to these considerations naval plans had always been based on the assumption that Hamburg would be the port to be opened on British account, though recent Army opinion had considered Emden as an alternative if enemy resistance was sustained. The opening of Bremen, with the exception of the minesweeping, would be an American responsibility as that port was to work on United States account, and by now the landward and seaward limits of the Bremen enclave had been finally established.

9. Apart from the reduction of Heligoland, which H.M.S. ROBERTS and H.M.S. EREBUS were being held ready to bombard after the major work of neutralisation had been accomplished by Bomber Command, plans were in hand for assaults on the main Frisian Islands on which it was estimated that the German naval personnel alone amounted to over I2,000. With naval assistance, landward assaults were planned as being the more economical and the First Canadian Army was responsible for those on Wangerooge and Alte Mellun, while the Second Army was to be responsible for the reduction of the two islands off the Cuxhaven Peninsula (Neuwerk and Scharhorn) which was considered necessary to enable minesweeping operations to begin in the Weser and Elbe Estuaries.

Protection of Shipping.

I0. Throughout this period much attention and effort were given to reducing the threats to shipping caused by submarines, E-Boats, midget submarines and mines. Especially in the Scheldt Approaches there were almost daily clashes with the enemy either by the naval forces, which were working under Commander-in-Chief, The Nore, or by the local patrol craft operating under Rear-Admiral F.E.P. Hutton, the Flag Officer, Belgium.

II. Despite efforts for their protection a certain number of merchant ships was damaged and sunk by these attacks and due tribute must be paid to the courage and steadfastness of their crews as well as to the efforts made by the escorting warships to prevent casualties.

Operations on the West Coast of France (Operation "Venerable").

I2. Of the German pockets remaining on the west coast of France, most had nuisance value only, but it was considered essential to reduce the pockets astride the Gironde

Estuary so that the port of Bordeaux could be opened. Plans for this operation had originally been made the previous November under the codename "Independence," but the operation had to be postponed on account of the Ardennes push. These were now brought up to date, and it was decided to carry out the operation with a target date of 15th April under the code-name "Venerable."

The naval tasks being:-

(*a*) Bombardment, primarily in the Ponte de Grave area, of enemy armament which could bear on friendly ground and Air Force.

(*b*) To remove sunken blockships and scuttled shipping to clear the Channel to Bordeaux; preliminary work had been in progress since October, 1944, by French contractors with the assistance of the U.S. Navy.

(*c*) The minesweeping necessary to sweep the entrance to the Gironde Estuary and the river.

13. It was later decided that the reduction of the Ile d'Oleron was also essential to the opening of the Estuary and River. A supplementary operation, code-name "Jupiter," was therefore planned to achieve this. It included bombardment of targets on the island and transport of personnel and equipment for the assault.

14. Bordeaux was to be opened by French ground forces under General de L'Arminat. The naval operations were under the command of Commander Task Force 122 (Vice-Admiral A.G. Kirk, U.S.N.) and Contre-Amiral Rue was in command of the French Naval Task Force which consisted of the French ships LORRAINE and DUQUESNE with destroyer and minesweeper support.

15. The bombarding ships arrived in an area to the south-west of Ponte de Grave which had been previously swept for mines, and LORRAINE, DUQUESNE and the destroyers carried out shoots on pre-arranged targets on 15th and 16th April, then withdrawing to Brest.

16. It was considered that the submarine menace did not warrant the risk of LORRAINE taking part in Operation "Jupiter," and DUQUESNE and the destroyers only took part. DUQUESNE had previously embarked at Casablanca a full outfit of ammunition for herself and replenishments for the destroyers, and the assault on the Ile d'Oleron was carried out on 30th April with the French ships bombarding gun batteries and other targets throughout the day. Twenty-four L.C.V.(P) were used as lift for assaulting troops and by nightfall all the southern portion of the island was in French hands, and only one of the L.C.V.(P) was lost.

17. The subsequent clearance of the Gironde and Garonne Rivers was carried out by French naval units, assisted by the 31st Minesweeping Flotilla and the 4th Minesweeping M.L. Flotilla, all the naval units continuing under the command of Commander Task Force 122.

Relief of the Channel Islands.

18. Plans for the occupation of the Channel Islands after a German surrender, had

been started in June, 1944, under the code-name "Nestegg," the operation being mounted from Plymouth. Early in May, 1945, it seemed that the capitulation of the German garrison in the Channel Islands was imminent and on the 2nd May the Supreme Commander asked for a British warship to be at 24 hours' notice to carry his representatives to accept the German surrender. H.M.S. BULLDOG, escorted by H.M.S. BEAGLE, escorted the Supreme Commander's representatives, headed by Brigadier Snow, to St. Peterport on the 8th May and in the early hours of the 9th May the surrender negotiations were completed on the Quarterdeck of H.M.S. BULLDOG.

19. On 8th May, the "Nestegg" convoy, consisting of 3 L.S.T., I0 L.C.T.[4], minesweepers and suitable escort sailed from Plymouth bringing occupational troops and food. Half the convoy went to Jersey and half to Guernsey and a detachment was later sent to Alderney.

20. During the next few days some 22,000 prisoners were evacuated from the Channel Islands in the same ships and craft and on the I6th May naval responsibility for the Islands passed from A.N.C.X.F. to the Admiralty.

The Relief of Holland.

2I. The introduction of food supplies to Holland, where by March, I945, lack of essential food-stuffs was causing both actual starvation and an acute political problem, had long been planned under the code-name "Placket". The Commander-in-Chief, the Nore, and Flag Officer, Holland, under A.N.C.X.F., were mainly responsible for the execution of this project which had to be planned for a variety of circumstances. From the naval aspect, these included the ferrying of food in minor landing craft through the inland waterways, the opening of a route from the Scheldt to Dordrecht by which schuyts and barges could pass, the opening of the main Dutch ports from seaward and the landing of supplies over selected beaches if the enemy concentrated his resistance in "fortresses" commanding the ports. It was always an essential condition that enemy resistance must have ceased before civil relief could begin, but once this condition was fulfilled, the problem became one of providing food and coal with the least possible delay as the people of West Holland had no reserve whatsoever to fall back on. It was therefore necessary to have a considerable number of minesweeping and landing craft at short notice, and to make provision for the latter to be augmented should it be necessary to land over the beaches, which would also have entailed the use of beach clearance and beach parties. A Port Repair Party for Rotterdam under Captain C.D. Maud, D.S.O., R.N., had been held in readiness in Belgium since the previous autumn, and plans were made to introduce this party with the minimum delay.

22. With the realisation that their defeat was imminent, the Germans showed their willingness towards the end of April to come to some agreement whereby food and other necessary supplies could be introduced into Holland under flag of truce. By the Ist May details of the scheme had been agreed with the Germans, and Allied Air Forces commenced dropping emergency food-stuffs to the Dutch population in ten selected areas. Royal Air Force and United States heavy bombers continued to drop

some 1,500 tons of food a day until 8th May, when the first Allied coasters arrived in Dutch waters and were given safe conduct and access to the port of Rotterdam.

Occupation of North German Ports.

23. For several months preparations for the despatch of Naval Parties required for the occupation of North German Ports had been in hand under my Chief of Staff (P.H.)[5], Rear Admiral W.E. Parry, C.B., at his Headquarters in London.

24. As it was not possible to form these Naval Parties in time to enable them to be ready on the Continent to move into their ports when required, extemporised arrangements had to be made for naval representation and advice to be at the disposal of the British and Canadian Army Commanders who would make the advance into the ports.

25. This was done by sending the Naval Officer-in-Charge (designate) to join the Army Formation concerned. Rear-Admiral G.C. Muirhead-Gould, D.S.C. (Flag Officer, Wilhelmshaven (designate)), was appointed temporarily to the staff of the Commander-in- Chief, 21st Army Group. At the same time officers of captain's rank were sent to the Headquarters of the First Canadian and Second British Armies. The officers at these three Headquarters were later relieved by officers appointed specifically as Naval Liaison Officers, Rear-Admiral Muirhead-Gould being relieved on 3rd May by Captain R.S. Warne, C.B.E., R.N.

26. The "Eclipse"[6] Naval Parties moved across the Channel as soon as they were formed and with little or no training. The stores, which it was essential should arrive in the ports at the same time as the Parties, had been sent ahead to Antwerp together with certain harbour craft, and these were assembled with the personnel of the Parties in an ex-Belgian Cavalry Camp at Burg Leopold. The diary of the movements of these Parties shows how these Parties despite their late formation did, with the unstinted help of the Army, reach their destinations soon enough to take timely control of the situations in their ports.

27. The actual surrender of the North German Ports began on 26th April when a Naval Officer of 30 Advance Unit (the naval unit specially formed for the collection of intelligence) reached the Bremen City Hall at 1030 and accepted the surrender of the city from the acting Bergermeister. U.S. Naval Task Force 126 designated for this port was already on the Continent and the Commander of this force (Rear-Admiral A.G. Robinson, U.S.N.), made a preliminary reconnaissance on the 27th April. He found that there was no apparent damage to docks, quays and other harbour installations but that warehouses were totally destroyed and prisoners-of-war stated that many mines had been sown in the enclosed basins and the adjacent river. The capacity of the port was restricted to some extent by sunken ships and in fact no war or merchant ships were found afloat.

28. On the 3rd May the Hamburg garrison surrendered unconditionally, and Commodore H.T. England, D.S.O., who had gone forward with the occupying Army forces entered the port as Commodore-in-Charge. He found the attitude of the port officials cowed but cooperative. The Port Party for Hamburg was not far behind and entered the port two days later.

29. The 5th May saw the surrender of all German Forces in Germany, Holland and Denmark, including the garrisons of Heligoland and Frisian Islands, and with the cessation of offensive operations all the remaining Naval Parties were able to move into their respective ports to establish control and initiate measures for the disarmament of the German Navy.

30. The two British Flag Officers, who were to be in command of the naval forces occupying the ports in the British zone of North Germany, were then moving in to set up their Headquarters. These Flag Officers were:-

Rear-Admiral H.T. Baillie-Grohman, C.B., D.S.O., O.B.E., whose title then was Flag Officer, Kiel. His command included the naval forces in the area eastward of the Elbe to the Russian border, and his title was later altered to Flag Officer, Schleswig-Holstein. He set up his Headquarters first at Kiel and later at Plön so as to be within easy reach of 8th Corps Headquarters.

Rear-Admiral G.C. Muirhead-Gould, D.S.C., whose title then was Flag Officer, Wilhelmshaven. This was changed later to Flag Officer, Western Germany, to indicate better the scope of his command, which included all naval forces in the British zone west of the Elbe, and Hamburg. His Headquarters were first established at Sengwarden near Wilhelmshaven and later moved to Buxtehude about 20 miles from Hamburg.

3I. These two Flag Officers with the staffs and Naval Parties under their commands lived through some adventurous and difficult times and the stories of their early days given in their reports of proceedings make interesting and instructive reading.

32. Admiral Baillie-Grohman reports that VE Day was anything but a public holiday for himself and his staff, for on that day, besides interviews with German senior officers, he had to cope with 4,000 troops who landed at Eckernforde from landing craft unaware that the war was over and full of enthusiasm for continuing it. The influx of refugee ships from the Baltic was a constant source of anxiety to him at the time.

33. Admiral Muirhead-Gould landed at Heligoland and accepted its surrender on the IIth May. He found the island devastated by bombing and almost uninhabitable, but left a British Naval Party on the island under the command of a Lieutenant-Commander, who on the next day found himself compelled to place the German Senior Naval Officer under arrest for his obstructive conduct.

Naval Situation in Norway and Denmark at the Time of Surrender.

34. The S.H.A.E.F. Mission to Denmark of which the naval element was headed by Rear Admiral R.V. Holt, C.B., D.S.O., M.V.O., had arrived in Copenhagen on the 5th May. It was considered important to make an early show of naval strength in Copenhagen and on the 9th May, the cruisers BIRMINGHAM and DIDO with four destroyers arrived there and assisted materially in those early and difficult days which are more fully described by Rear-Admiral Holt in his report. Operation "Crosskeys" was that designed to provide for the early establishment of coastal and minesweeping forces in Danish waters and the "Crosskeys" convoy, consisting of H.M.S. TASAJERA carrying Coastal Force Maintenance Unit No. 2 together with two

Coastal Force Flotillas, four Minesweeping Flotillas, tankers and other craft carrying stores, arrived in Copenhagen on the 22nd May.

35. In Norway the first members of the S.H.A.E.F. Mission arrived at Oslo on the 8th May and Commodore Askin, Royal Norwegian Navy, as representative of the Allied Naval Commander, opened direct negotiations with representatives of the German Naval High Command in Oslo. The British Flag Officer, Norway (Rear-Admiral J.S.M. Ritchie) sailed from Rosyth in H.M.S. DEVONSHIRE, which was carrying H.R.H. Crown Prince of Norway who landed with his suite on the 13th May after scenes of enthusiasm from boats carrying crowds of cheering Norwegians as the ship steamed up the Oslo Fiord.

36. British Naval Officers-in-Charge designated for the main ports in Norway left England in destroyers on 13th May and settled down in their ports to the primary job of organising minesweeping in the approaches to the ports, which was largely carried out by German minesweepers under German supervision.

The Surrender of the German Navy.

37. The Allied Naval Commander-in-Chief had been present at Rheims on the 7th May when General Jodl and Grand Admiral Friedeberg, the plenipotentiaries of the German High Command signed the unconditional surrender of all the German Land, Sea and Air Forces in Europe to the Allied Expeditionary Force and simultaneously to the Soviet High Command. The signature was witnessed by Lieutenant-General W.B. Smith on behalf of the Supreme Commander, General Suslaparoff on behalf of the Russians and General Sevez on behalf of the provisional Government of France. The Allied Naval Commander-in-Chief signed the orders to the German Navy.

38. In Berlin on the 8th May, soon after midnight, Field-Marshal Keitel, Grand Admiral Friedeberg and General Stumph, the plenipotentiaries of the German High Command, signed the unconditional surrender of all the German Land, Sea and Air Forces to the Allied Nations. The Allied Naval Commander-in-Chief was present at the signature which was witnessed by Air Chief Marshal Tedder, Marshal Zukov, General Spaatz and General de Latre de Tassigny.

39. The orders for the surrender of the German Fleet were contained in "Eclipse" Memo. No. I originally issued in July, 1944, and revised and brought up to date since. "Eclipse" Memo. No. I contained the Supreme Commander's orders to the German armed forces for the conduct of their surrender when it came, and besides instructions in general terms contained specialised orders to the German Navy and Air Force. The naval section gave detailed instructions as to the conduct of the German Fleet after surrender and its initial provisions may be summarised as follows:-

(a) The immediate despatch of a responsible German Flag Officer to A.N.C.X.F. with details of all minefields in North-West European waters, of the location of all departments and branches of the German Admiralty (Ober Kommando der Kriegsmarine) and details of locations of all service warships down to and including Elbing Class torpedo boats as well as minesweepers and Sperrbrechers. This Flag

Officer was to bring with him a Communications Officer able to explain all communications matters including particulars of the codes and ciphers in current use in the Germany Navy.

(*b*) The despatch of responsible officers to the Commanders-in-Chief, The Nore and Rosyth, with charts of all minefields and other navigational information on the North Sea. Certain other German naval officers were also to be detailed for specialised duties with British naval authorities.

(*c*) Much more detailed information on the current state of the German Navy was to be supplied by the German High Command to A.N.C.X.F. within I4 days of the surrender.

40. Orders for the surrender of the German U-Boat fleet were issued by the Admiralty and the planning and the co-ordination of the operations necessary to receive the surrender of the U-Boats were the responsibility of the Commander-in-Chief, Western Approaches.

4I. When the surrender occurred the naval special orders (which embodied the basic special orders which had been agreed between the British, United States, Soviet and French Naval Authorities) were issued to the German Admiralty as they stood, and in addition the Admiralty issued orders by signal to German submarines at sea giving them instructions on how to proceed to surrender. One small adjustment to the naval special orders had to be made to include German naval garrisons in the Mediterranean, which was outside the Supreme Commander's sphere of responsibility. As the orders to Ober Kommando der Wehrmacht in respect of all three services were not actually issued and as the naval special orders only dealt with matters of naval import, no instructions were in fact issued to the German Admiralty (O.K.M.) on such general matters as orders for prisoners-of-war, German responsibility for maintenance of armed forces and so on.

Use of German Codes and Cyphers.

42. On the I0th May S.H.A.E.F. (Forward) gave instructions to O.K.W.[7] that no codes or cyphers were to be used except in the case of signals to units of the German Fleet, when codes could be used until 2359 on IIth May. It was then realised that the German naval authorities could not issue instructions in plain language to their U-Boats in the Far Eastern waters to comply with the surrender terms because the U-Boats might not believe the authenticity of the message and the Japanese would probably prevent their leaving. Accordingly instructions were given that codes were to be used for this special purpose of giving orders to U-Boats in Far Eastern waters.

Compliance with naval special orders.

43. The German authorities complied with naval special orders as well as circumstances permitted and O.K.W. broadcast an order against scuttling on the I0th May. The naval representatives arrived at the Headquarters of British naval authorities

in England as instructed and in such numbers that both the Commanders-in-chief concerned asked that the duplicate parties for which provision had been made should not be sent.

44. The naval representatives detailed to proceed to the Headquarters of A.N.C.X.F. arrived at Rheims p.m. on the I0th May and were sent under escort to A.N.C.X.F.'s Headquarters. This delegation consisted of Vice-Admiral Ruge, Rear-Admiral Godt (Submarines) with Commander Koltzer as communications officer. These officers proved most co-operative and gave all the information required by the naval special orders except certain hydrographical information which could only be produced by the various sub-commands and certain information about mines on the western seaboard of the Atlantic. These three German officers left A.N.C.X.F.'s Headquarters a.m. on the I4th May with instructions to provide further information; these instructions were complied with to the best of their ability.

Control of O.K.W. and O.K.M.

45. On the 9th May A.N.C.X.F. nominated Captain G.O. Maund, D.S.O., R.N., and Commander H.C.C. Ainslie, D.S.C., R.N.Z.N., as the naval representatives on General Rook's mission to O.K.W. These officers left for Flensburg by air on the I2th May.

46. Captain Sir John M. Alleyne, D.S.O., O.B.E., R.N., was the senior naval representative on the O.K.M. ministerial control party, and he left Versailles for Flensburg on the I4th May. On the 15 May A.N.C.X.F. placed Captain Alleyne in charge of O.K.M.

47. Captain Maund returned to A.N.C.X.F.'s Headquarters on the I6th May and was then given a directive placing him as A.N.C.X.F.'s representative in charge of the naval element at O.K.W. and of O.K.M.

48. After the dissolution of O.K.W. on the 23rd May and the arrest of Admirals Doenitz and Von Friedeberg amongst a number of other German Senior Naval Officers, command of O.K.M. was assumed by Admiral Backenkohler; he was succeeded on the 25th May by Admiral Warzecha.

49. Captain Alleyne was succeeded on 27th May by Captain E. Hale, R.N., who on Captain Maund's withdrawal became the senior naval representative at O.K.M.

50. The policy for the control of O.K.M. was laid down by the Allied Naval Commander-in- Chief in a message to Captain Maund on the 6th June. The complete dissolution of O.K.M. was envisaged in this message, but during the first phase the main structure of the organisation was to be retained until certain investigations had been completed, transfers of German personnel completed and decisions reached on sailings of War and Merchant ships to the United Kingdom, or Allied ports; and arrangements made for the use of facilities in German naval dockyards. When this programme had been completed, it was envisaged that the operational side of O.K.M. should be disbanded completely and the administrative side reduced to four or five departments.

5I. This phase was achieved on the I2th July, when the dissolution of O.K.M. was started and a new organisation for the administration of the German minesweeping forces employed on mine clearance was established. The new organisation was brought into force on 21st July, a week after the Supreme Commander had laid down his office.

52. It remains to transfer these German minesweeping forces to the Mine Clearance Board which is being established under civil auspices.

53. Apart from the long term tasks of control of the disarmament of the German Navy and the disbandment of its personnel, there were two immediate naval problems to be dealt with after the surrender. One of these was the opening of the sea routes to the North German Ports and the other the collection of intelligence, particularly that which might have a vital bearing on the prosecution of the War against Japan.

The opening of the sea routes to the North German Ports.

54. This problem had to be tackled with energy, as it was essential to open the North German Ports to traffic soon so that warships and merchant ships required by the Allies could be removed, so that British warships could visit German naval ports and so that the import programme could be started. It was clear that unless imports of food were made soon, a large percentage of the German population would starve before long and apart from humanitarian scruples, starvation of the German population would have an immediate effect on the economic life of the lately occupied countries which it was our first aim to rehabilitate, particularly if famine lowered the output of coal from the Ruhr.

55. With this in mind, minesweeping of the North Sea route to Heligoland had begun well before the surrender and by the 9th May a force of 44 ships was based at Cuxhaven for sweeping the Elbe and its approaches.

56. By this time it was clear that the Ems had been mined at Emden and the Weser above Bremerhaven, before the surrender brought about the cessation of the enemy's policy of fouling all ports before abandoning them. The Weser to Bremerhaven, the Elbe, the Kaiser Wilhelm Canal and all the West Baltic Ports were reported clear of enemy mines.

57. It was decided that the risk of enemy mines could be disregarded in order to admit urgent shipping to ports to which reliable intelligence indicated the routes were clear, and urgent traffic was first admitted to Hamburg on the 9th May.

58. British mines had still to be considered but by mid-May, Bremerhaven, Emden and Kiel (via the Canal) were declared open to urgent traffic.

By the 1st June, Hamburg and Kiel (via the Canal) were open to normal traffic and by mid-June Bremerhaven also.

The Collection of Naval Intelligence.

59. Progressively, as the German forces were rolled back, Intelligence objectives were overtaken and exploited until the collapse of the enemy put us in possession of virtually all his naval secrets. The phase was one more of organising the full exploitation of what came into our hands than of seeking the targets themselves, although only the dash and skill of 30 Advance Unit and of the U.S. Naval Technical

Mission in Europe saved many of the more important "finds" from destruction. The work of the Royal Naval Field Intelligence Unit also did much to reveal and preserve these targets.

The Removal of A.N.C.X.F.'s Headquarters to German soil.

60. Since late September, 1944, A.N.C.X.F.'s Headquarters had been located at the Chateau d'Hennement, St. Germain, about six miles from Versailles and thus convenient to the main departments of S.H.A.E.F.

61. It was a natural conclusion that A.N.C.X.F. should move to Frankfurt so as to be alongside the Supreme Commander's Headquarters, and early in May arrangements to this end were well in hand.

62. The intention then was that A.N.C.X.F.'s "Post Hostilities" Staff, under Rear-Admiral W.E. Parry, C.B., should move from London to Minden, where this staff would be best located to put into execution the plans for the control and disarmament of the German Navy. At Minden they would be ten miles from Bad Oeynhausen, where 21st Army Group Headquarters was being established, while Lubbecke to which the British Control Commission was shortly to move is eight miles away.

63. But soon after the surrender it seemed likely that the Supreme Allied Command would terminate somewhat sooner than had been envisaged and with this in mind it seemed preferable for A.N.C.X.F.'s Main Headquarters to go to Minden. It was still necessary, however, for a strong liaison staff to be maintained at Supreme Headquarters and Rear-Admiral Parry was accordingly made head of this staff, which was established at Frankfurt early in June. A.N.G.X.F.'s Main Headquarters opened at Minden on 15th June.

EXCHANGE OF MESSAGES ON THE TERMINATION OF THE SUPREME COMMAND.

The following messages were exchanged on the termination of the Supreme Command:-

From: Admiral Sir H.M. Burrough, K.C.B., K.B.E., D.S.O., Allied Naval Commander-in-Chief, Expeditionary Force.

To: General of the Armies D.D. Eisenhower, Supreme Commander, Allied Expeditionary Force.

Tomorrow, for the first time, the United States Ensign will not be flown over my Headquarters, and the hauling down of "Old Glory" tonight will mark the end of one of the happiest associations in a Combined Command which has probably ever existed.

2. It is with great and sincere regret that I myself and the officers and men of the Royal Navy who have had the privilege of serving under your inspiring leadership realise that our association has drawn to a close. For the rest of our lives we shall

remember this association with great pride in the fine achievements of the United Team which you have led to Victory in Europe.

3. On behalf of all my Command, and all members of the Royal Navy who have had the privilege of serving under you as Supreme Commander, I wish you continued success, lasting good health and happiness in your future, which we know will be as brilliant as has been your past.

From: General of the Armies D.D. Eisenhower.
To: Admiral Sir H.M. Burrough, K.C.B., K.B.E., D.S.O.

With warm personal regard and appreciation and best wishes for your continued success, I truly appreciate your generous message. While I have already sent out a general expression of gratitude to the entire Command, I think it appropriate to record the deep sense of gratification I have felt towards the Royal Navy because of the unvarying efficiency, loyalty and aggressiveness with which its contingents have served under me during the past three years. Both in the Mediterranean and in this theatre I have found nothing among the personnel of the Royal Navy but cheerful cooperation and a determination to see the job through that have made my association with it one of the truly pleasing experiences of this whole war. I regret our separation which, for my part, is a physical one only. In spirit I shall always remain closely associated with all the elements that have worked so effectively together in the tasks assigned us by the Combined Chiefs of Staff.

Combined Command terminates at midnight, I3th July, I945, and brings to a close one of the greatest and most successful campaigns ever fought.

History alone will judge the Allied Expeditionary Force in its true perspective, but we, who have worked and struggled together, can feel nothing but pride in the achievements of the men we have been honoured to command, and sadness at having to be parted now. Whatever history may relate about the exploits of this Allied Force, and the memory of man is short and fickle, it is only we, at this time, who can fully appreciate the merit and due worth of the accomplishments of this great Allied team.

These accomplishments are not limited to the defeat of the Nazi hordes in battle – a continent has been liberated from all that is an antipathy to the ideal of democracy which is our common heritage. Above all, we have proved to the whole world that the British and American peoples can forever be united in purpose, in deed and in death for the cause of liberty.

This great experiment of integrated command, whose venture was cavilled at by some and doubted by many, has achieved unqualified success, and this has only been made possible by the sympathetic, unselfish and unwavering support which you and all other commanders have wholeheartedly given me. Your own brilliant performance is already a matter of history.

My gratitude to you is a small token for the magnificent service which you have rendered, and my simple expression, of thanks sounds totally inadequate. Time and opportunity prohibit the chance I should like to shake you and your men by the hand, and thank each one of you personally for all you have done. I can do nothing more than assure you of my lasting appreciation, which I would ask you to convey to all those under your command for their exemplary devotion to duty and for the most magnificent loyalty which has ever been shown to a commander.

MESSAGES EXCHANGED BETWEEN A.N.C.X.F. AND COMNAVEU ON THE DEPARTURE OF THE LAST U.S. NAVAL FORCES FROM THE EUROPEAN THEATRE OF OPERATIONS.

From: Allied Naval Commander-in-Chief, Expeditionary Force.
To: Commander, U.S. Naval Forces in Europe.

The departure on the 9th July of the remaining United States Landing Ships and Craft from the United Kingdom brings to an end the largest combined amphibious force that has yet been assembled. The work of the L.S.T.s and Landing Craft of both nations during the assault and subsequent build-up has been one long record of harmonious co-operation, the ships of each nation in their turn bearing and being glad to bear as much of the burden as their capacity would allow.

Not only have the L.S.T.s carried immense numbers of vehicles of all sorts and descriptions but they have also carried large numbers of men safely across dangerous waters. I hope you will express the thanks of the Allied Naval Command to the officers and men of all ships now departing from the United Kingdom for the great part they have played in the Liberation of Europe. We are indeed sorry to say good-bye to them.

From: Commander, U.S. Naval Forces in Europe.
To: Allied Naval Commander-in-Chief, Expeditionary Force.

Thank you for your message of farewell to the officers and men of our amphibious forces soon due to leave the United Kingdom. It is with real pleasure that I pass it along to COMPHIBCRAFT 12th to be made known to all hands. The close and happy relationships that have grown up between A.N.C.X.F. and the Amphibious Forces of our two nations have been a source of great satisfaction.

There will be many regrets at saying goodbye but there will also be the realisation that the friendships made will be lasting and the hope that in years to come they will often be revived.

Admiralty footnotes

1. L.C.M. – landing craft for mechanised transport.
L.C.V.(P) – landing craft for personnel.
2. L.C.A. – landing craft for assaulting troops.
3. Wangerooge – the easternmost of the East Frisian Islands.
4. L.S.T. – landing ship for tanks.
L.C.T. – landing craft for tanks.
5. P.H. – "Post Hostilities" Staff.
6. Operation "Eclipse" – the occupation of the North German Ports.
7. O.K.W. – German High Command Headquarters.

6

OPERATIONS IN NORTH-WEST EUROPE

FROM 6TH JUNE, 1944, TO 5TH MAY, 1945.

The War Office,
September, 1946

The following despatch was submitted to the Secretary of State for War on 1st June,
1946, by Field Marshal The Viscount Montgomery of Alamein, G.C.B., D.S.O.

I arrived in England on 2nd January, 1944, after handing over command of the Eighth Army, and immediately started a detailed study of the plans for the assault of the Continent – Operation OVERLORD.

The Commander-in-Chief of the Allied Naval Expeditionary Force was Admiral Sir Bertram Ramsay and of the Allied Expeditionary Air Force, Air Chief Marshal Sir Trafford Leigh- Mallory. There was no parallel appointment of Commander-in-Chief of the Allied land forces, but General Eisenhower decided that I should act in that capacity for the assault, and subsequently until the stage was reached in the development of our operations when a complete American Army Group could be deployed on the Continent. No definite period was stipulated for this, but Headquarters Twelfth United States Army Group were formed in London and prepared to take command of First and Third United States Armies at the appropriate time. This Army Group, when formed, remained under any operational control until 1st September: when the Supreme Commander took over direct control of the land battle.

The assault was an operation requiring a single co-ordinated plan of action under one commander; I therefore became the overall land force commander responsible to the Supreme Commander for planning and executing the military aspect of the assault and subsequent capture of the lodgement area.

In the initial stages, the object of Operation OVERLORD was to mount and carry out an operation to secure a lodgement on the Continent from which further offensive operations could be developed.

The troops under my operational control comprised 2I Army Group and First United States Army (General Omar N. Bradley). 2I Army Group comprised First Canadian Army (Lieutenant-General Crerar), Second British Army (Lieutenant-General Dempsey), the British Airborne Troops (Lieutenant-General Browning), and various Allied contingents. Attached to First United States Army were the American 82 and I0I Airborne Divisions. Ninth United States Air Force planned with First United States Army, while Second British Army worked with Second Tactical Air Force, R.A.F.

THE PLAN.

The intention was to assault, simultaneously, beaches on the Normandy coast immediately North of the Carentan estuary and between the Carentan estuary and the R. Orne, with the object of securing, as a base for further operations, a lodgement area: which was to include airfield sites and the port of Cherbourg. The left or Eastern flank of the lodgement area was to include the road centre of Caen.

Once ashore and firmly established, my plan was to threaten to break out on the Eastern flank – that is in the Caen sector; by this threat to draw the main enemy reserves into that sector, to fight them there and keep them there, using the British and Canadian armies for the purpose. Having got the main enemy reserves committed on the Eastern flank my plan was to make the breakout on the Western flank, using for this task the American armies under General Bradley, and pivoting on Caen; this attack was to be delivered Southwards down to the Loire and then to proceed Eastwards in a wide sweep up to the Seine about Paris. This would cut off all the enemy forces South of the Seine, over which river the bridges were to be destroyed by air action. This general plan was given out by me to the General Officers of the field armies in London on the 7th April, 1944. The operations developed in June, July and August exactly as planned; I had given D + 90 as a target date for being lined up on the Seine; actually the first crossing of the river was made on D + 75.

The Normandy beaches were selected because they offered a better shelter for shipping and were less heavily defended than other possible beach areas along the Channel coast. They satisfied the minimum requirements of the Air Forces, in terms of their distance from home bases, for the provision of air cover.

The absence of major ports was overcome by the gigantic engineering feat of constructing two artificial ports in the United Kingdom; these were towed across the Channel in sections and erected, one in the United States sector and one in the British sector. In spite of considerable damage during the unprecedented June gale, the port at Arromanches in particular proved a great success.

The invasion operations may be said to have begun with the action of the Air Forces. The first stage was the gaining of air superiority, an essential preliminary always to all major offensive operations. This task was admirably accomplished. As

D Day drew nearer, attacks were delivered against, coast defences along the whole length of the Atlantic Wall. Meanwhile, prevention of enemy air reconnaissance during the period of concentration of the invasion forces was highly successful, and contributed towards the gaining of tactical surprise.

Combined naval and air operations were intensified against E-boats and U-boats as the great day approached.

The Enemy Situation.

The German commander in France and the Low Countries was Field-Marshal von Rundstedt; his title was Commander-in-Chief West. Under his command were two Army Groups: the larger comprising more than two-thirds of the operational troops available, was Army Group "B", commanded by Field-Marshal Rommel, which consisted of Seventh Army (Normandy and Brittany), Fifteenth Army (Pas de Calais and Flanders), and 88 Corps (Holland). Rommel was appointed to this command in February, 1944, at the direct instance of Hitler. It was his first operational command since he had left Tunisia nearly a year previously.

Army Group "G", commanded by Blaskowitz, had the First and Nineteenth Armies, stationed on the Biscay coast and in the Riviera respectively.

There was a third headquarters in France of Army Group status, called Panzer Group West: under General Schweppenburg. It was responsible for the administration and training of the Panzer formations while they were operationally under command of the other Army Groups. It was originally intended to command them in battle. This system later led to some confusion in the handling of the enemy armour.

These Army Groups at D Day comprises some sixty divisions, or about one quarter of the field force of the German army. From the end of 1943 their strength was conserved, and even increased in anticipation of the Second Front, and in spite of losses in Italy and Russia. The only formation which left the theatre in 1944 was an S.S. Corps, which was despatched to Russia in April, but returned to Normandy within two months.

There was considerable variation in the quality of the German divisions in the west. The equipment, training and morale of the S.S. and Panzer divisions was of the highest order; the infantry formations varied from low quality static coast defence troops to fully established field formations of normal German type.

For several years the Germans had been developing the coastal defence organisation which was known collectively as the Atlantic Wall. The enemy assumed that an invader would have to secure a port either in the initial assault or very quickly afterwards, in order to land the heaviest types of equipment and organise maintenance and supply. Port areas were therefore given first priority for defences and by 1944 had become virtually impregnable to seaward assault. After the ports, attention was turned to the Pas de Calais, which bordered the narrowest part of the Channel and was considered the most likely area we would choose for the assault.

Elsewhere defences were on a less organised scale, for by the beginning of 1944 the enemy had not had the resources or transport to put the whole coast line in a uniform state of defence. From March, 1944, however, there was a most noticeable intensification of the defences in Normandy: following a tour of inspection by Rommel.

The coastal defence of the Baie de la Seine was based on a system of linear defences arranged in strong points which were manned chiefly by static coastal troops of low category. The gun positions and localities were protected by concrete and armour from naval gunfire and air attack; extensive use had been made of minefields, wire entanglements, and other obstacles to strengthen the layout. Extensive flooding of the low-lying areas in the coastal belt had been effected, particularly in the marshy country round the Carentan estuary. Existing sea walls had been strengthened and prolonged to form anti-tank obstacles behind the beaches, which themselves were extensively mined. On the beaches, and extending over varying distances below high water mark, were belts of under-water obstacles, the purpose of which was to halt and impale landing craft and to destroy or cripple them by means of explosive charges attached to the individual obstacles, types of under-water obstacles included "Element 'C' " with Tellermines on the forward face, the ramp type wooden obstacle with Tellermines on the top of the ramp, wooden posts with Tellermines attached, steel hedgehogs and steel tetrahedra.

The enemy artillery defence consisted of long range coast artillery and field artillery. The former was sited well forward, covering in particular the entrances to Cherbourg, the Carentan estuary and the Seine. Heavy gun batteries located in the Cherbourg area and round Le Havre almost overlapped in range, and presented the gravest danger to the approach of all large vessels to the transport area off the Normandy beaches. Behind the coast artillery, some two or three miles inland, field and medium artillery units of the divisions occupying the coastal sectors were sited; the task of these guns was to bring fire to bear on craft approaching the beaches and on to the beaches themselves. In all there were some thirty-two located battery positions capable of firing on the assault beach areas.

After Rommel's inspection there was an acceleration in the construction of under-water obstacles, and these were developed at increasing distances below high water mark; the number of coastal batteries increased and the construction of casemates and overhead cover was undertaken on a wider scale. Flooding became more extensive. Anti-air-landing obstacles commenced to appear on our air photographs in the most suitable dropping and landing areas; they consisted of vertical poles and stakes, and in some cases were fitted with booby traps.

Rommel and von Rundstedt were not in agreement on the manner in which invading forces should be dealt with. Rommel, who was no strategist, favoured a plan for the total repulse of an invader on the beaches; his theory was to aim at halting the hostile forces in the immediate beach area by concentrating a great volume of fire on the beaches themselves and to seaward of them; he advocated thickening up the beach defences, and the positioning of all available reserves near the coast. Von Rundstedt, on the other hand, favoured the "crust-cushion-hammer" plan; this implied a "crust" of infantry manning the coast line, with a "cushion" of infantry divisions in tactical reserve in close in rear, and a "hammer" of armoured forces in strategic reserve further inland. The cushion was designed to contain enemy forces which penetrated the crust, and the hammer was available for launching decisive counter attacks as required. These differing theories led to a compromise; the armoured reserves were generally kept well back, but the majority of the infantry divisions was committed to strengthening the crust. The result was that, in the event, the Panzer divisions were forced to engage us prematurely and were unable to concentrate to deliver a co-ordinated blow: until it was too late.

In the NEPTUNE sector it was anticipated that the enemy garrison would consist of three coast defence divisions supported by four reserve divisions, of which one was of the Panzer type. In the last weeks before D Day, however, there were indications that some redistribution of enemy forces was taking place in France, but in the event the appreciation of the resistance proved substantially correct.

The estimated rate of enemy build-up and the probable development of his defensive strategy were constantly reviewed during the planning period. The speed of concentration of enemy reserves was largely dependent on the success of our air operations designed to reduce his mobility, together with the effect of sabotage activities of the French Resistance organisation. Events showed that a degree of success was achieved in this direction, far greater than hoped. At this stage of the planning, it was estimated that the enemy could concentrate up to twenty divisions (including eight Panzer divisions), in the Normandy area by D + 6. This contrasted with the previous estimates of twelve divisions. By D + 20, under the worst conditions for ourselves, we might expect opposition from some twenty-five to thirty divisions, of which nine or ten would be armoured formations. It was necessary to anticipate the possibility of the enemy having up to fifty divisions in action by D + 60.

It was appreciated that the Germans would be alerted in the NEPTUNE area on the night D - I as our seaborne forces approached the Normandy coast, and that by the end of D Day the enemy would himself have appreciated that OVERLORD was a major operation delivered in strength. In accordance with his expected policy of defeating us on the beaches, it was probable that he would summon initially the nearest available armoured and motorised divisions to oppose us, and that in the first stages we should have to meet immediate counter attacks designed to push us back into the sea. Having failed in this purpose it was appreciated that the enemy would concentrate his forces for major co-ordinated counter attacks in selected areas; these might develop about D + 4 or D + 5, by when it was estimated that he might have in action against us some six Panzer divisions. By D + 8 it was reasonable to suppose that, having failed to dislodge us from the beaches, the enemy would begin to adopt a policy of attempting to cordon off our forces and prevent expansion of the bridgehead. For this he would require to bring up infantry in order to relieve his armoured formations, which would then be concentrated for a full-out counter-stroke. It was to be expected, then, that there would be an initial concentration against the bridgehead of armoured and motorised divisions, followed by the arrival of infantry formations.

There were encouraging factors in the Intelligence appreciations in April and May. Whereas in January, 1944, it had been appreciated that within two months of the start of OVERLORD the enemy would be able to move as many as I5 divisions into

Western Europe from other theatres, the corresponding estimate in April was six: as a result of the mounting successes of the Soviet forces on the Eastern Front and of events in Italy. By D Day the Allies had captured Rome and Kesselring's forces in Italy were in retreat, while in Russia the Crimea had been cleared and the Germans were nervously predicting an all-out Russian offensive.

Identifications on the Eastern Front and in Italy received in the immediate pre-D Day period gave an increasingly encouraging picture of absorption of German armour on fronts other than our own.

Topography.

The inundations behind the selected beach areas, and particularly in the Varreville sector at the base of the Cotentin peninsula, created a grave problem in ensuring the creation of adequate exits from the beach areas to the hinterland. In the Varreville sector it was of the utmost importance for us to secure the causeways across the flooded areas if we were to avoid being pinned by relatively minor enemy forces to the very narrow beach strip. In the Vierville – Caen sector beach exits tended to canalize through small coastal villages, which were in a state of defence and had been provided with extensive obstacles and which would require speedy clearance by our assaulting troops. The system of water lines, inundations and marshes behind the Carentan estuary was extensive and there were few available routes crossing these barriers; the seizure of these routes intact was of the utmost importance.

The hinterland behind the beaches generally favoured defensive tactics and was on the whole unsuitable for the deployment of armoured forces.

Apart from the open rolling plain to the south-east of Caen, the area was covered to a depth of up to 40 miles inland by "bocage" – pasture land divided by unusually high hedges, banks and ditches into many small fields and meadows. In such conditions, observation was extremely limited, and movement off the road defiles was very restricted: not only for wheeled transport, but often for tanks. On the other hand it was ideal infantry country; there was excellent concealment for snipers and patrols, while defensive positions dug into the banks were well protected from tanks and artillery.

The Normandy highlands ran from south-east to north-west across the assault frontage, at a depth of up to 25 miles inland. The country was broken and irregular in parts, with steep hills and narrow valleys. The dominating feature of the northern ridge was Mont Pinçon, some 18 miles south-west of Caen.

Preliminary Operations.

In the broad strategic sense, preparations for the assault of north-west Europe began at sea and in the air many months before D Day. Winning the Battle of the Atlantic was essential to ensure the passage of the vast volume of personnel and stores from America and Canada to the battle front. The strategic air offensive against Germany had a vital effect on the war by strangling the whole economic structure of the country.

An essential preliminary to the assault was the reduction of the German Air Force to the degree required to ensure mastery in the air over our seaborne forces in the Channel, and over the beaches on the assault coast. The next army requirement was the interdiction of rail and road communications, with the object of delaying the movement of enemy troops and supplies to the battle area. It was desirous also to mislead the enemy about the sector selected for the assault, and, lastly, to pave the way for our actual landing operation by pre-D Day air attacks against coast defences and installations. Other preliminary air tasks of direct importance to the army were the flying of reconnaissance missions over a wide area, and the prevention of enemy reconnaissance over our centres of concentration and embarkation.

So admirably were these commitments carried out by the Air Forces that we were afforded immunity from enemy air reconnaissance during the vital period, a factor of first importance in the design for achieving tactical surprise in our assault operation; moreover, there were only one or two attacks by the German Air Force on the assault forces during the sea passage or at any time on the beaches during D Day.

The interdiction of rail communications was effected as a result of a detailed plan for destroying the servicing and repair facilities which were essential for the operation of railways in northern and western France, the Low Countries and western Germany. In full operation by D-60, the programme brought attacks closer to the NEPTUNE area as time grew shorter, and the result was a shortage of locomotives and stock, repair facilities, and coal over a wide area, while 74 bridges and tunnels on routes leading to the battle area were impassable on D Day. Reports on 7 June showed that all railway bridges over the Seine between Paris and the sea were impassable, and also one of those on the lower section of the Loire. Road bridges were also attacked with most successful results; the 13 bridges between Paris and the Channel, and the five main road bridges between Orléans and Nantes, were either destroyed or damaged.

Attacks prior to D Day on coast defence batteries in the NEPTUNE area were worked into an overall plan of action against the whole length of the assault coast, in order to mislead the enemy about our intentions. These operations retarded the construction of overhead cover for major batteries covering the Baie de la Seine, and at the same time served to increase the enemy's fears that it was intending to assault in the Pas de Calais: astride Cap Gris Nez. This was a matter of first importance in our plans.

Preliminary naval operations included sweeps against enemy U-boats, R-boats and E-boats, and minelaying designed to afford protection to the sea passage across the Channel.

The Assault.

My plan of assault, as approved by the Supreme Commander, provided for simultaneous landings by eight equivalent brigades – of which three were British and two were Canadian brigades, and three were American combat teams. With the assaulting brigades, two battalions of U.S. Rangers and portions of two British

Commando Brigades took part. The Americans assaulted on the right flank as they would ultimately require direct entry of personnel and stores from the Atlantic.

Airborne forces were used on both flanks. On the right, 82 and 101 U.S. Airborne Divisions dropped at the base of the Cotentin Peninsula to assist in capturing the beaches and isolating Cherbourg. 6 British Airborne Division was given the task of seizing the crossings over the Caen Canal and of operating on our extreme left.

First United States Army was to assault astride the Carentan estuary with one regimental combat team between Varreville and the estuary (Utah beach), and two regimental combat teams between Vierville and Colleville (Omaha beach). The initial tasks were to capture Cherbourg as quickly as possible, and to develop operations southwards towards St. Lô in conformity with the advance of Second British Army.

Second British Army assault was to be delivered with five brigades between Asnelles and Ouistreham (Gold, Juno and Sword beaches), with the intial tasks of developing the bridgehead south of the line St. Lô – Caen and southeast of Caen, in order to secure airfield sites and to protect the eastern flank of First United States Army while the latter was capturing Cherbourg.

During the night preceding D Day, while the naval assault forces made the sea passage, the programme of intensive air action against the enemy defences was to begin with operations by Bomber Command, while airborne forces were to be dropped on the flanks of the assault area. At H Hour, supported by naval bombardment and air action, and by the guns, rockets and mortars of close support craft, the leading wave of troops was to disembark and force its way ashore.

The total initial lift in the assault and follow-up naval forces was of the order of 130,000 personnel and 20,000 vehicles, all of which were to be landed on the first three tides. In addition to the basic eight assaulting brigades/regimental combat teams, a variety of attached troops were required in the assault including special assault engineers, amphibious tanks, and other detachments which varied for the different beaches according to the specific "menu" (i.e., composition of the assault wave) decided upon by the subordinate formations.

Priority of air lift was given to American airborne forces owing to the vital tasks of securing the beach exits and facilitating deployment from the Utah beach. Main bodies of both 82 and 101 United States Airborne Divisions were to land in the general area of Ste. Mère Église on the night D – 1/D, the latter to assist the seaborne assault on the Utah sector and the former to guard the landward flank and prevent the movement of enemy reserves into the Cotentin peninsula. The remaining air lift was allotted to Second British Army for 6 Airborne Division (less one brigade) which was to land before H Hour east of Caen, with the tasks of seizing the crossings over the Orne at Bénouville and Ranville and, in conjunction with Commando troops, of dominating the area to the east of Caen in order to delay the movement of enemy forces towards the town.

American Ranger units were to land in the assault on the west of Omaha beach, and had the task of attacking enemy defences on the east side of the Carentan estuary. One British brigade of two Commandos was to link the assaults on the Juno and Sword sectors. A second Commando brigade was to land behind the assaulting division on the Sword Sector and while one Commando dealt with Ouistreham, the remainder of the brigade was to cross the Orne at Bénouville and attack the enemy coast defences of the river up to Cabourg inclusive.

The Assault Technique.

Prolonged study and numerous experiments had been devoted to the development of the technique of assaulting a defended beach. As a result, various types of specialised military equipment were available by D Day, including assault engineer tanks, tank-carried bridges for crossing anti-tank ditches, mat-laying tanks for covering soft clay patches on the beaches, ramp tanks over which other vehicles could scale sea walls, flail tanks for mine clearance, and amphibious assault tanks. These devices were integrated into the specially trained assault teams which led the assault forces.

The development of under-water obstacles on the assault coast has already been mentioned, and it was necessary to include in the assault some teams of sappers and naval obstruction clearance units trained in clearance of this type of obstruction. These obstacles also affected the decision on the tidal conditions required at the time of commencing the assault, because no extensive clearance could take place whilst they were covered by the tide.

The Joint Fire Plan.

The purpose of the Joint Fire Plan was to allocate tasks to the resources of the three Services, with the object of assisting the Army to get ashore. The chief requirements were to destroy or neutralise the enemy coast artillery batteries which might interfere with the approach of the naval convoys or bring fire to bear on the anchorages, and to neutralise the enemy strong points and defended localities that were sited for the immediate defence of our assault beaches.

It has been shown that preliminary air attacks were delivered against enemy coast defence batteries in the preliminary operations prior to D Day. The Fire Plan proper was to begin on the night preceding the assault, when the heavy bombers of Bomber Command were to attack in great strength the ten most important batteries; this operation was to be timed as late as would be consistent with the return of the aircraft to England by daylight. Following the Bomber Command operations, attacks were planned by medium bombers, using special navigational devices, on a further six coast defence targets; this phase was to begin at civil twilight, and about the same time the naval bombardment directed by spotting aircraft and culminating with close support fire from assault craft carrying various types of armament was to commence, and about half-an-hour before H Hour[1] the heavy bombers of the Eighth United States Air Force, and medium bombers of the Ninth United States Air Force, were to begin action against coast defence artillery and enemy beach defences and localities. Included in the naval assault forces was a variety of specially fitted craft carrying 4.7 inch guns, 4 inch mortars, barrages of 5 inch rockets, Centaur tanks fitted with 75 millimeter howitzers, 17 pounder anti-tank guns, as well as ordinary self-propelled field guns of the assaulting divisional artilleries which were to be embarked in tank landing craft and to work as regimental fire units.

The Fire Plan aimed at building up the supporting fire to a tremendous crescendo which would reach its climax at the latest possible moment before the leading troops waded ashore, in order to give the defenders the minimum time to recover before being set upon. The heavy air bombardment was timed to commence on the beach frontages to within ten minutes of H Hour, and from this time fighters and fighter-bombers were to take up the air offensive, and in particular undertake the task of neutralising the enemy field batteries located inland. Air support tentacles were to accompany the assulting troops, and fighter-bomber squadrons were to be at hand to answer calls for close support, while the medium and heavy bombers returned to their bases to refuel and re-arm in readiness for further missions. No fewer than 17I Allied fighter squadrons were to be employed in the overall assault phase, and in the event the Allied Air Forces flew some 11,000 sorties on D Day.

Direct Air Support.

The joint army and air forces organisation for direct air support becomes a complicated machinery in major amphibious operations. Special arrangements were necessary to cover the period before the army and air force headquarters and control staffs were set up on the far shore and the air formations arrived overseas.

For the assault, the problem was complicated by the location of Headquarters Allied Tactical Air Forces at Uxbridge, while the Navy and Army Group Headquarters were at Portsmouth during the assault phase. It thus became necessary to set up the army component of Air Support Control at Uxbridge, together with a special intelligence staff which was charged with supplying the air staff with information concerning the progress of operations. The Anglo-American army staff at Uxbridge was controlled from my main headquarters at Portsmouth, and worked in matters of immediate air support on general directives, which defined the military plan and priorities for the application of the available direct air support. Under the conditions of the initial stage of amphibious operations it was necessary to move the focus of control of army/air operations back to Army Group level, because of the necessary centralisation imposed on the Air Forces and because the normal point of control (Army Headquarters) had no Air Force counterpart with it and no air formations within reach or communication.

Special assault tentacles were allotted to all assaulting brigades and were to provide the initial means for requesting air support, pending the landing of the normal detachments. These tentacles worked to Uxbridge, while on the same network were included Divisional and Corps headquarters ships as well as Army and Army Group headquarters. Army headquarters were to monitor calls for support, but the responsibility for their submission to the Tactical Air Forces rested with the Army Group detachment at Uxbridge.

In order to provide means of immediate response to calls for air assistance during the assault, some squadrons were airborne within wireless range of divisional headquarters ships in anticipation of requests for direct support.

Requests for pre-arranged air support during the assault phase were co-ordinated at main Army Group headquarters, and submitted to the air forces through the Uxbridge staff. The latter also co-ordinated the bomblines and ensured that all concerned were kept informed.

The Build-up.

The general principles upon which the build-up of our forces and material were planned, were, first, the provision of the maximum number of fighting formations on the Continent in the first few days and, secondly, the introduction into the build-up system as quickly as possible of the maximum degree of flexibility; so that changes in priority of troops, administrative, echelons, transport and stores could be made as the situation demanded.

By the end of D Day it was planned that, including airborne forces, the Allies would have eight divisions ashore together with Commandos, Ranger battalions and some fourteen tank regiments. By D + 6 the total forces would rise to some thirteen divisions, exclusive of airborne formations, with five British armoured brigades and a proportionate number of American tank units. Between twenty-three and twenty-four basic divisions were due in Normandy by D + 20. Comparison with the estimated enemy strength was difficult to make; some types of enemy divisions, were organised on a considerably smaller establishment than our own; some were under conversion from training organisations and were known to be deficient of equipment. Our own build-up, moreover, included a considerable proportion of fighting units classed as corps and army troops and which, therefore, were not apparent in the divisional figures of the build-up table.

Planned build-up tables are inevitably suspect; it was impossible to estimate the delaying effect on the enemy build-up of our air action. In our estimates, the effect of weather on cross-channel movement and beach working was a major imponderable.

In order to make our build-up flexible, a special inter-Service staff was organised called "Build-up Control" (BUCO). This body was formed, as a result of Mediterranean experience, to organise the loading and despatch of craft and ships from home ports, and was the agency by which changes in priority were effected.

It is of interest to record that in order to fit the assault force into the available craft and shipping, British divisions were limited to 1,450 vehicles in the initial lift, the corresponding figure for armoured brigades being 320. No formation was to be made up in excess of 75 per cent. of its War Establishment in transport until after D + 14. Similar limitations were imposed on the American units.

Planned Development of Operations.

Once the troops were ashore it was necessary for them to "crack about"; the need for sustained energy and drive was paramount, as it was necessary to link our beachheads and penetrate quickly inland before the enemy opposition crystallized. I gave orders that the leading formations should by-pass major enemy centres of resistance in order to "peg-out claims" inland. I emphasised to commanders on all levels that determined leadership would be necessary to withstand the strain of the first few days, to retain the initiative, and to make sure that there would be no setbacks.

In the planning stages of a major operation it is customary to issue for the guidance of subordinate commanders and staffs, an estimate of the progress of operations. Such an estimate normally takes the form of a series of "phase lines" drawn on an operational map to indicate the positions to be reached by leading troops at intervals of a few days. I was not altogether happy about the phase lines given, because imponderable factors in an operation of the magnitude of OVERLORD make such forecasting so very academic. While I had in my mind the necessity to reach the Seine and the Loire by D + 90, the interim estimates of progress could not, I felt, have any degree of reality. The predictions were particularly complicated by two major divergent requirements. On the one hand the general strategic plan was to make the break-out on the western flank pivoting the front on the Caen area, where the bulk of enemy reserves were to be engaged; on the other hand the Air Forces insisted on the importance of capturing quickly the good airfield country south-east of Caen. Though I have never failed in my operations to exert my utmost endeavour to meet the requirements of the Air Forces, in planning these operations the over-riding requirement was to gain territory in the west. For this reason, while accepting an estimate for seizing the open country beyond Caen at a relatively early date after the landing, I had to make it clear that progress in that sector would be dependent on the successful development of the main strategic plan.

Administration.

The administrative problem facing the British forces was essentially different from that of the Americans. The operational plan demanded the very rapid development of lines of communication behind the American forces, and the administrative requirements for opening up railways and roads from Cherbourg and the Brittany ports were very large. There was no parallel problem foreseen on the British flank.

The limiting factor in the build-up of operational forces appeared likely to be the rate at which maintenance resources could be landed. The problem therefore was to develop the capacity of the beaches to the maximum degree. Since there would be no port facilities at all until Cherbourg was captured and opened, and since in any case Cherbourg would not be able to do more than relieve some of the burden of beach maintenance, it was planned to erect two artificial harbours, together with a number of breakwaters, in the Baie de la Seine. The components which made up these artificial harbours were to be towed across the Channel in special lanes through the minefields, and although the estimated time required for their construction was from I4 to 42 days, it was provided that as far as possible use would be made of the shelter of the outer breakwaters once they had been completed. The subsidiary breakwaters were to be formed by sinking 60 block ships in groups of I2 at suitable sites along the coast.

The British forces were to be maintained over the beaches until such time as sufficient ports were captured and developed, and it was assumed that beach maintenance could cease on the opening of the Seine ports. In the United States sector it was planned to open Cherbourg and subsequently the main ports of the Brittany peninsula, and in this way to dispense gradually with the necessity for beach working.

Special establishments were created for operating the British beaches, comprising Beach Bricks, Beach Groups and Beach Sub-Areas. These special units and headquarters were formed on an inter-Service basis and included detachments of the various arms. In this way the individual beaches were worked by self-contained organisations.

It was planned to maintain Second British Army for the first few days from Beach Maintenance Areas and subsequently from two army roadheads, one of which was ultimately to be handed over to First Canadian Army; a Rear Maintenance Area was to be established as soon as conditions permitted. In view of the damage caused by our bombing, it was considered necessary to be independent of railways for the first three months of the operation; the lines of communication were therefore to be entirely road operated for this period.

The administrative planning for the operations was based on the expectancy of reasonable weather conditions during June, July and August. Some allowance was made in planning the rate of administrative build-up for days when the beaches would be working at low capacity; but the risk had always to be faced that any serious or prolonged break in the weather, particularly during the first two weeks, might have a grave effect on the maintenance of the forces and therefore on their operational capabilities.

Civil Affairs.

Civil affairs planning initially aimed at ensuring that the civil population did not impede troop movements, at preparing for the organisation of local labour and transport, and at setting up the necessary machinery for the control and use of local resources and for the replacement of unacceptable local officials. It was anticipated that there would be a large number of refugees and civilian wounded, and special composite detachments of Civil Affairs personnel were organised in readiness to deal with the problem, while arrangements were made for food and medical supplies for the inhabitants of the bridgehead to be phased in from D + 1 onwards.

THE BATTLE OF NORMANDY.

The Assault.

At 0200 hours 6 June, a "coup de main" party of 6 Airborne Division was dropped near Bénouville, to seize the bridges over the Canal de Caen and the River Orne. Surprise was complete, both bridges were captured intact and a close bridgehead was established. Half an hour later, 3 and 5 Parachute Brigades began to drop east of the Orne.

On the whole, the drop of 6 Airborne Division was more scattered than had been planned, but one repercussion of this was that the enemy was misled about the area and extent of the landings. In spite of enemy counter action the division secured the left flank of the Allied beachheads.

IOI United States Airborne Division began dropping south-east of Ste. Mère Église at about 0130 hours. The division quickly seized the two villages of Pouppeville and St. Martin-de-Varreville, behind the Utah beaches, 82 United States Airborne Division landed west of the Carentan – Cherbourg main road from 0230 hours onwards. The division seized the town of Ste. Mère Église and protected the inland flanks of IOI Airborne Division.

While the airborne landings were in progress, over 1,100 aircraft of Bomber Command commenced the air offensive as planned. Nearly 6,000 tons of bombs had been dropped on the coast batteries by dawn.

Meanwhile, the Allied sea armada drew in towards the coast of France, preceded by its flotillas of minesweepers. Not until the leading ships had reached their lowering positions, some seven to eleven miles offshore, and the naval bombardment squadrons had opened fire on the shore defences, was there any appreciable enemy activity.

During the sea passage heavy seas were running in the Channel, and it was an outstanding feat on the part of the naval forces that in spite of this every main essential of the plan was carried out as intended.

The cloud conditions were not very favourable for bombing when over 1,300 heavy bombers of the Eighth United States Air Force and eight medium divisions of the Ninth United States Air Force, swept over the target area. Meanwhile the heavy ships of the naval bombardment squadrons opened on the coast defence batteries, while gradually the destroyers and the great number and variety of supporting craft successively came into action as the assault craft ran into the beaches and the troops stormed ashore.

On Utah beach, VII United States Corps assaulted on a front of one regimental combat team. The progress of the assault was greatly assisted by thirty amphibious tanks, launched five thousand yards offshore, which arrived on the beach with the loss of only one. Casualties were not excessive, and movement ashore proceeded well; a second Regimental combat team was soon disembarked, and a beachhead was secured on a four thousand yard front. During the day in some places the troops made contact successfully with IOI Airborne Division.

On Omaha beach, H Hour for the assault had been fixed at 0645 hours. V United States Corps assaulted on a broad front with two regimental combat teams, with the initial objective of Vierville-sur-Mer, and Colleville-sur-Mer, some three miles to the east.

By nightfall V United States Corps had secured a beachhead about a mile in depth on the line Vierville – Colleville, and some forward elements were already pushing towards the high ground near Formigny, some two miles inland.

Second British Army assaulted on the fight in the Gold sector with 50 Division of 30 Corps. In the centre sector, designated Juno, was 3 Canadian Division, and on the left 3 British Division (Sword sector): both of which were under I Corps.

50 Division assault was made on a two brigade front. The intention for D Day was

to penetrate the beach defences between Le Hamel and La Rivière, and to secure a covering position which would include the town of Bayeux and the high ground in the area of St. Léger, astride the main road from Bayeux to Caen. The division had under command 8 Armoured Brigade, of which two regiments were amphibious, assault teams of 79 Armoured Division, and a Royal Marine Commando; which was to land immediately behind the leading right hand brigade and move west along the coast to seize Port-en-Bessin.

As on Omaha beach, the weather was extremely unfavourable; it was considered too rough to launch the amphibious tanks. The leading infantry touched down within a few minutes of H – Hour – which was 0725 hours. The leading brigade moved quickly inland to its objective on the Bayeux – Caen road. Meanwhile reserve brigades were landed successfully and by last light the forward positions of 50 Division were roughly on the line Manvieux – St. Sulpice – Vaux – Brécy – Creully. At Creully contact was made with patrols of 3 Canadian Division, but touch had not been gained with V United States Corps on the right.

In I Corps sector, 3 Canadian Division assaulted with two brigades, and 3 British Division on a frontage of one brigade. The initial task of these formations was to secure a covering position on the general line Port-en-Bessin – Caen – River Orne to the sea, joining up with 6 Airborne Division on the left. With 3 Canadian Division there was 2 Canadian Armoured Brigade (including one amphibious regiment), while 27 Armoured Brigade (with two amphibious regiments) was under command 3 British Division; both formations were supported by appropriate detachments from 79 Armoured Division.

The two leading Canadian brigades assaulted astride Courseulles-sur-Mer about 0800 hours.

Due to the rough sea the landing was behind schedule (H Hour was 0735 – 0745 hours).

The task of 3 British Division was to assault the beaches just east of Lion-sur-Mer and advance on Caen to secure a bridgehead there over the River Orne. The leading brigade was to secure a firm base on the Périers-sur-le-Dan feature, through which the following brigades were to advance on Caen. The division was to link up with 6 Airborne Division on the bridges over the canal and river at Bénouville. The plan provided for troops of 4 Commando Brigade clearing up the area between 3 Canadian and 3 British Divisions, I Commando Brigade was made responsible for capturing enemy posts on the left flank of the Corps sector and the port of Ouistreham.

H Hour for 3 British Division was fixed for 0725 hours and the assault waves reached the beaches well on time. The leading brigade was soon a mile inland attacking Hermanville, Colleville, and battery positions on the southern outskirts of Ouistreham. The follow-up brigade came ashore shortly after 1000 hours and reached its assembly positions near Hermanville quickly and pushed on southwards. The reserve brigade of 3 British Division landed soon after midday; it was moved to the left of the divisional area owing to the heavy opposition which had been encountered at Douvres-la-Délivrande.

By nightfall, the division was well established with forward elements on the line

Bieville – Bénouville, where contact was made with 6 Airborne Division. Ouistreham had almost been cleared, but the Commandos had not succeeded in capturing the heavily fortified strong point at Douvres.

East of the River Orne, 6 Airborne Division withstood repeated attempts by enemy infantry and tanks to capture Ranville and to wipe out the Bénouville bridgehead. The division was joined during the afternoon by Commandos of I SS Brigade. At 2100 hours the gliders of 6 Air Landing Brigade arrived and served to strengthen our positions on the left flank.

As a result of our D Day operations a foothold had been gained on the Continent of Europe.

Surprise had been achieved, the troops had fought magnificently, and our losses had been much lower than had ever seemed possible.

Linking up the Beachheads.

At first light on 7th June the Omaha beaches were still under close fire from enemy weapons of all calibres, but the American troops fought steadily and gradually extended their initial holding. Patrols eastwards along the coast made contact with British troops, who captured Port-en-Bessin.

By 9th June American troops captured Isigny with a bridge over the River Vire about one mile to the south-west. Further east crossings were effected over the River Aure, and Colombières was reached. 2 United States Division came into action in the centre of the Corps bridgehead, reaching Rubercy on 9th June. Meanwhile, on the left of the beachhead I United States Division made good progress and linked up with 50 British Division just west of Bayeux on 8th June.

By 10th June V United States Corps secured the Fôret-de-Cerisy and pushed patrols into Balleroy. Patrols of 29 United States Division were in contact with 101 United States Airborne Division and, two days later when Carentan was finally captured, the beachheads had been securely linked. With the joining of V and VII United States Corps, our bridgehead was made continuous throughout the assault frontage.

The operations for the capture of Caen were continued from the North by 3 British Division, and from the North-West and West by 3 Canadian Division; but it quickly became apparent that the enemy was concerned for the security of this nodal point, and to prevent the expansion of our bridgehead South of the Caen – Bayeux road.

While I Corps operations were developing round Caen, 30 Corps were engaged in heavy fighting in the Tilly-sur-Seulles sector. The intention was to thrust South through Tilly-sur-Seulles towards Villers Bocage, employing initially 8 Armoured Brigade, which was to be followed by 7 Armoured Division (then coming ashore).

In the morning of 12th June the 30 Corps advance had reached the general line La Belle Epine – Lingèvres – Tilly – Fontenay-le-Pesnel – Cristot – Brouay. In these villages the enemy had established strong points with a co-ordinated system of anti-tank defences, backed up by detachments of infantry and armour.

East of the River Orne our troops were concerned in maintaining the bridgehead in face of continuous counter attacks, and took heavy toll of the enemy.

By I2th June the beachheads had now been firmly linked into a continuous bridgehead on a front of over fifty miles, varying in depth eight to twelve miles.

Development of the Bridgehead.

My orders on I8th June, which were finalized the following day, instructed First United States Army to capture Cherbourg and clear the peninsula of enemy. Moreover, operations were to be developed against Le Haye du Puits and Coutances at the earliest possible moment without waiting for the fall of Cherbourg. As additional American troops were available, First United States Army was to break away to the South directed on Granville, Avranches and Vire. Second Army was to capture Caen and provide a strong Eastern flank for the Army Group: continuing the policy of absorbing the enemy reserve divisions in its sector.

Following the isolation of Cherbourg, VII United States Corps continued Northwards on a front of three divisions. On 20th and 2Ist June the Corps closed in on the defences of Cherbourg itself and began preparations for the final assault, which commenced in the afternoon of 22nd June. On 27th June the garrison of the arsenal surrendered. The task of opening the port was energetically tackled by the allied navies, but it was to be late August before Cherbourg was in a fit state to receive heavy lifts alongside berths.

To implement my instructions for the development of the pincer movement on Caen, Second Army regrouped in order to launch 30, 8 and I Corps into this operation. I was determined to develop this plan with the utmost intensity with the whole available weight of the British forces. I wanted Caen, but realised that in either event our thrusts would probably provoke increasing enemy resistance: which would fit in well with my plan of campaign.

In fact, enemy resistance increased and there were now elements of no fewer than eight Panzer divisions on the twenty mile stretch of the Second Army front between Caumont and Caen.

While VII United States Corps was completing the capture of Cherbourg during the last week in June, the rest of the American Army was building up and regrouping. The attack Southwards started on 3rd July with a thrust by VIII United States Corps employing 82 Airborne, 79 and 90 Divisions. The object was to converge on Le Haye du Puits, and on the first day 82 Airborne Division secured Hill I3I about two miles North of the town. Further progress was made on the following day against stubborn enemy resistance.

Meanwhile on 4th July, VII United States Corps attacked South-West of Carentan with 83 Division. Again progress was very difficult owing to the numerous water obstacles and bocage, but by 5th July the edge of the flooded area North of St. Eny was reached.

Further East, XIX United States Corps captured St. Jean-de-Daye on 7th July, and continued its advance to within four miles of St. Lô.

On Ist July the S.S. formations made their last and strongest attempts against the Second Army salient. All of these attacks were engaged by our massed artillery with devastating effect, and all but one were dispersed before reaching our forward infantry positions.

Second Army intention now was to continue the battle for Caen by a direct assault from the North. As a preliminary 3 Canadian Division attacked Carpiquet on 4th July with the object of securing the airfield and of freeing the Western exits from Caen.

For the direct assault on Caen, I Corps employed three divisions with two armoured brigades in immediate support, and a third readily available.

In order to help overcome the strong enemy positions I decided to seek the assistance of Bomber Command, R.A.F., in a close support role on the battlefields. The Supreme Commander supported my request for the assistance of Bomber Command, and the task was readily accepted by Air Chief Marshal Sir Arthur Harris.

The plan was for the three attacking divisions to converge on Caen, clear the main part of the town on the West bank of the Orne and seize the river crossings. The air bombardment was designed to destroy enemy defensive positions and artillery, and to cut off the enemy's forward troops from their lines of supply in rear.

It was planned that the bombing attack should immediately precede the ground assault but, owing to the weather forecast, it was decided to carry out the bombing on the evening before the attack; aircraft were therefore timed over the target between 2150 and 2230 hours 7th July, while the ground attack was to commence at 0420 hours on the following morning.

By nightfall, 8th July, 3 Canadian Division had secured Franqueville, while tanks and armoured cars closed in on the western outskirts of Caen. In the centre 59 Division cleared St. Contest and La Bijude, while 3 Division got into the north-east corner of Caen and directed 33 Armoured Brigade to the bridges.

On the morning of 9th July, 3 Division reached the dock area and met troops from 3 Canadian Division who had entered the town from the west. The bridges over the river in the city were either destroyed or completely blocked by rubble, and the enemy remained in occupation on the suburb of Faubourg-de-Vaucelles on the east bank.

My aim remained to launch the break-out operation on the Western flank as soon as possible, and meanwhile to hold the main enemy forces on my Eastern flank.

During the period 10th-18th July, Second Army delivered a series of thrusts, with the primary object to make progress Southwards towards Thury Harcourt: all operations were related to this task and to the maintenance of pressure on as broad a front as possible.

Meanwhile First United States Army continued its advance Southwards; by steady pressure and hard fighting it gradually overcame the difficulties of terrain and the increased enemy opposition.

On the right VIII Corps made good progress, and by 14th July had reached the general line of the north bank of the River Ay, with patrols west of Lessay.

In the centre sector VII Corps made ground west of the River Taute, and XIX Corps pushed on between the Taute and the Vire. On 16th July XIX Corps mounted a strong attack with two divisions against St. Lô and by the 19th July the town was captured. On the extreme left V Corps improved its positions in conjunction with the XIX Corps operation towards St. Lô.

Thus by 18th July First United States Army was in possession of St. Lô, and of the ground west of the River Vire which was required for mounting the major break-out assault operation to the south.

While 12 and 30 Corps operations were in progress west of the River Orne, preparations for a major thrust east of the river were completed with all possible speed. 2 Canadian, 8 and I Corps were employed in this operation.

As a result of these operations the situation on the eastern flank was now greatly improved, and the German armour had been drawn east of the Orne again and heavy losses caused to the enemy.

My orders on 21st July were for First Canadian Army and Second British Army to develop operations in order to secure the line along the River Dives from the sea to Bures, thence along the Muance to St. Sylvain, and on through Cauvicourt, Gouvix and Évrecy to Noyers and Caumont.

Headquarters First Canadian Army (General Crerar) was to take the field on 23rd July, when it would assume responsibility for the extreme left flank sector, taking I Corps under command. 2 Canadian Corps was to remain under Second Army for the moment. On 24th July, Second Army was to take over the left divisional sector of First United States Army, thus releasing American troops for operations elsewhere.

The Break-out.

On 25th July the weather conditions improved and the break-out operations began.

First United States Army plan was to deliver a break-in assault against the enemy defensive positions with VII United States Corps employing three infantry divisions. The American attack started in the sector between Périers and St. Lô. The Eighth U.S. Air Force was employed in the tactical role and dropped a carpet of bombs immediately in front of the leading troops, as a preliminary to their advance. Twenty-four hours after the VII Corps assault, VIII Corps in the coastal sector was to advance South. XIX United States Corps was also to launch attacks in the St. Lô sector, beginning simultaneously with VIII United States Corps.

On 27th July the decisive actions of the operation took place. The enemy began to withdraw along the entire front, and Lessay and Périers were occupied. In the central sector, mobile columns were sent within two miles of Coutances. On XIX Corps front the enemy was cleared out of the loop in the River Vire immediately South of St. Lô.

On the eastern flank, an attack by 2 Canadian Corps southwards along the Falaise road started at 0330 hours on 25th July. Steady progress was made but as the advance continued enemy opposition hardened and it was necessary to discontinue our thrust during the night 25/26th July.

While Second British Army was switching its main weight to the Caumont sector, the progress of the break-out operation proceeded apace. On 28th July, 4 and 6 U.S. Armoured Divisions passed through the infantry on the western sector and thrust South towards Coutances. The town was captured in the afternoon and firm contact was established there between VIII and VII Corps. To the South-East, troops of VII and XIX Corps had got to within five miles of the main Avranches – Caen road. All reports indicated that West of the River Vire to the coast the enemy was completely disorganised. Avranches was taken on 31st July.

VIII U.S. Corps, under command of Headquarters third U.S. Army (General Patton), was then directed into the Brittany Peninsula. With the entry into the field of the Third U.S. Army, Headquarters Twelfth U.S. Army Group (General Omar Bradley) assumed command of both American armies. The Twelfth U.S. Army Group remained under my operational control.

The enemy was trying to recover his balance as the powerful American attack pushed back his left flank and began to swing South-East and East. He tried to stabilise a front on "hinges" at Caumont, on the Orne, and on the high ground between Caen and Falaise. One by one the hinges, or "key rivets," were successively knocked out by the British armies working from West to East as the attack of the American armies on the West flank gathered momentum.

Second Army regrouped with creditable speed, and it was found possible to commence the thrust southwards from the Caumont area on 30th July.

The main weight of the attack was to be developed by 8 and 30 Corps on a narrow front. 30 Corps was to wheel South-West, initially to the line Villers Bocage – Aunay-sur-Odon, while 8 Corps, in a wider sweep on its right, swung down to Bény Bocage and on the Vire – Tinchebray – Condé triangle.

The attack started on 30 Corps front at 0600 hours 30th July.

The initial attack was supported by heavy and medium bombers which carried out their attacks in spite of low cloud and bad weather.

Progress on the 8 Corps flank proved easier than on 30 Corps front. By 31st July 8 Corps had secured crossings over the River Soulevre and 30 Corps had cleared Cahagnes. Heavy fighting continued though progress was slow in both 8 and 30 Corps owing to enemy counter attacks and the great difficulty of the country. During the first days of August 2 Canadian Corps mounted three attacks, east of the Orne as part of the general programme of maintaining pressure in that area.

By 6th August the area Laval – Mayenne – Domfront had been reached by the Americans. On the following day First Canadian Army, which had now extended its front to include the Caen sector, was to begin a series of major attacks astride the Caen – Falaise road, which had so long been the fundamental aim of our policy on the Eastern flank.

I was still not clear what the enemy intended to do. I did not know if the enemy would stand and be defeated between the Seine and the Loire, or whether he would endeavour to withdraw his forces behind the Seine. There was no evidence to show on what line he was intending to reform his front; it was evident from the British and Canadian troops in close contact with the Germans east, south-east and south of Caen, that he was definitely holding his ground in this sector; he was evidently trying to pivot on the Caen area.

On 6th August I issued orders for the advance to the Seine.

I instructed First Canadian Army to make every effort to reach Falaise itself in the forthcoming attack; in the subsequent advance to the Seine the main Canadian axis was to be the road Lisieux – Rouen. On its right I intended Second British Army to advance with its right directed on Argentan and Laigle, whence it was to reach the Seine below Nantes. Twelfth United States Army Group was to approach the Seine on a wide front with its main weight on the right flank, which was to swing up towards Paris.

Between 7th and IIth August it became clear that the enemy had decided to fight the battle of France on our side of the Seine. On the 7th a major counter attack, employing up to six armoured divisions, was launched on Hitler's orders against the American forces in the area of Mortain. The brunt of it fell on 30 United States Infantry Division which held the onslaught sufficiently long to enable two American divisions who were moving south between Avranches and Mortain to be switched to the danger area. The counter attack was designed to cut off the forces operating south of Avranches by a drive to the sea. In the face of this counter-attack the Americans, assisted by the full weight of the tactical air forces, stood firm.

I ordered the right flank of the Twelfth U.S. Army Group to swing North towards Argentan, and intensified the British and Canadian thrusts southwards to the capture of Falaise.

First Canadian Army was ready to launch its thrust southwards in the direction of Falaise on the night of 7th August. The object was to break the enemy defences astride the Caen – Falaise road, and to exploit as far as Falaise.

The attack was to take place under cover of darkness after a preliminary action by heavy bombers; the infantry was to be transported through the enemy's zone of defensive fire and forward defended localities in heavy armoured carriers. At first light on 8 August the infantry debussed in their correct areas after a four miles drive within the enemy lines, and proceeded to deal with their immediate objective. The first phase of the operation had been successful.

While VII United States Corps and 8 British Corps were held up in their respective sectors, the right wing of Twelfth United States Army Group proceeded with its planned operations.

On 7th August XV Corps continued to make progress and on the following day entered Le Mans.

In Brittany, Third United States Army units were engaged in heavy fighting at the approaches to St. Malo, Brest and Lorient.

My plan was to make a wide enveloping movement from the southern American flank up to the Seine about Paris, and at the same time to drive the centre and northern sectors of the Allied line straight for the river. In view of the Mortain counter attack, I decided to attempt concurrently a shorter envelopment with the object of bottling up the bulk of the German forces deployed between Falaise and Mortain. It was obvious that if it was possible to bring off both these movements the enemy in Normandy would be virtually annihilated.

On 8th August I ordered Twelfth United States Army Group to swing its right flank due north on Alençon at full strength and with all speed. At the same time I urged, all possible speed on First Canadian and Second British Armies in the movements which were converging on Falaise.

By I2th August, on Second Army Front heavy fighting was in progress on the high ground three miles south-east of Vire, and at the same time leading troops were only a few miles short of Condé. East of the River Orne the bridgehead was extended to the south-east, and also to the north-east to link up with elements of 2 Canadian Division who had crossed the River Laize.

After four days' fighting, on I2th August reconnaissance reports clearly showed a general trend of enemy movement to the east from the Mortain area through the corridor between Falaise and Argentan and on towards the Seine ferries.

The Allied Air Forces were pounding the enemy in the pocket but the problem of completing the encirclement was no easy one; the Germans realised that their existence depended on holding open the corridor, and bitter fighting ensued as a result of our attempts to frustrate them. On the north side of the corridor it must be recalled that the enemy had long been in possession of the vital ground north of Falaise, and had thus had ample opportunity for the development of strong, well sited defences.

Strenuous efforts continued to close the corridor between Falaise and Argentan. British and American forces pressed in from all sides of the pocket to annihilate the enemy which it contained. XV United States Corps was well established in the Argentan area on I3th August.

VIII United States Corps advanced north from Mayenne to positions on the western flank of XV United States Corps. Meanwhile V and XIX United States Corps pressed on in the extreme western and north-western sectors of the pocket.

The main Canadian thrust on Falaise from the north was resumed on I4th August, and the town fell to the Canadians on I6th August.

The battle of the pocket continued, but by I6 August the enemy lost almost all cohesion: divisions were hopelessly jumbled up and commanders were able to control no more than their own battle groups. The Allied Air Forces were presented with targets probably unparalleled in this war: aircraft formations were engaging endless columns of enemy transport, packed bumper to bumper and rendered immobile by the appalling congestion.

On I9 August the neck of the pocket was finally closed when American troops from the south linked up at Chambois with the Polish Armoured Division fighting with First Canadian Army.

The next day the enemy made his last co-ordinated attempt at forcing our cordon. After this attack, which was unsuccessful, the battle of the Mortain – Falaise pocket was virtually at an end, though the process of mopping up took some time.

Speedy regrouping on the Twelfth U.S. Army Group front, combined with outstanding administrative improvisation, enabled the advance eastwards of the Third U.S. Army to continue while the battle of the Falaise Pocket was still in progress. By 20 August, troops of General Patton's army reached and crossed the Seine in the area of Mantes and began to work westwards along the river towards Elbeuf.

The other armies of 2I Army Group then began the race to the Seine. The Allied Air Forces throughout the drive to the river had carried out relentless attacks against the ferries which provided the only means of escape to the enemy.

Second Army crossed the River Seine in the vicinity of Vernon, and the leading troops were across the river on 25 August. On First Canadian Army front, 2 Canadian

Corps secured crossings about Port de l'Arche and Elbeuf, astride a sharp bend in the river about eight miles south of Rouen on 26 August. The crossings were made in most cases without serious opposition.

In the Twelfth United States Army Group sector, Third United States Army swept forward to Troyes, Chalons-sur-Marne and Rheims. First United States Army began crossing the Seine on 26 August between Melun and Mantes Gassicourt.

The break out was now complete and the drive across the Pas de Calais was about to commence.

The outstanding point about the Battle of Normandy is that it was fought exactly as planned before the invasion. The measure of our success was, in the event, far greater than could ever have been foreseen, because of the faulty strategy of the enemy.

The only sound military course open to the Germans at the end of July, would have involved staging a withdrawal to the Seine barrier and with it the sacrifice of north-western France. Instead he decided to fight it out between the Seine and the Loire.

In planning to break out from the bridgehead on the western flank, a prerequisite was the retention of the main enemy strength on the eastern flank. The extent to which this was achieved is well illustrated in the following table, which shows the estimated enemy strength opposing us in the eastern and western areas of our front during June and July.

This result was achieved by the retention of the initiative and by very hard fighting, which enabled us to expand our territorial gains in the West and to engage and wear down the enemy strength along the whole of the Allied front.

	Estimate Enemy Strength Opposite Caumon-Cotentin Sector			Estimated Enemy Strength Opposite Caumont-Caen sectors		
	Panzer Divisions	*Tanks*	*Infantry Battalions*	*Panzer Divisions*	*Tanks*	*Infantry Battalions*
15 June	-	70	63	4	520	43
25 June	1	190	87	5	530	49
30 June	½	140	63	7½	725	64
5 July	½	215	63	7½	690	64
10 July	2	190	72	6	610	65
15 July	2	190	78	6	630	68
20 July	3	190	82	5	560	71
25 July	2	190	85	6	645	92

The mounting of the break-out operation suffered considerable delays. One of the main reasons was the weather, which not only upset the schedule of our beach working, causing delay in the arrival of troops and stores, but also hampered the action of the air forces.

The development of the bridgehead to the South-East of Caen was a slow and difficult matter. The success of the plan involved pulling the enemy's reserves against our Eastern flank, and this was achieved to such a degree that in spite of all our efforts it was impossible to make rapid headway in the sector which the enemy obviously regarded as the most vital.

THE DRIVE ACROSS THE PAS DE CALAIS
TO ANTWERP AND THE RHINE.

On 26th August, I issued detailed orders for the conduct of the advance North of the Seine. Twelfth Army Group was to operate on the right flank of 2I Army Group, and directed First United States Army along the general axis Paris – Brussels, with the object of getting established in the general area Brussels – Maastricht – Liège – Namur – Charleroi.

On Ist September the Supreme Commander assumed command and direction of the Army Groups himself, and I was no longer, therefore, his overall land force commander. From now on my despatch will be primarily concerned with 2I Army Group proper, that is, with the British and Canadian forces, together with the various Allied contingents which served with them.

In considering the development of the strategic plan after crossing the Seine the primary object, of course, was the destruction of the German Army.

As a result of discussions between the Supreme Commander and myself, from now on the eventual mission of 2I Army Group became the isolation of the Ruhr.

The urgent problem was to prevent the enemy's recovery from the disaster sustained in Normandy. A major consideration was the administrative situation created by our ever lengthening Lines of Communication. My administrative staff had, however, been building up reserves during August in order to support the pursuit. Imports were out by 60 per cent. in order to release a considerable quantity of transport from beach and port clearance for forward maintenance purposes.

The immediate tasks of 2I Army Group were the destruction of the enemy in North-East France, the clearance of the Pas de Calais with its V-bomb sites, the capture of aiifields in Belgium, and the capture of Antwerp.

Between 25th and 30th August, Second British Army and First Canadian Army crossed the Seine, and the four Allied armies now started advances which were eventually to bring them to the Rhine on a very broad front.

On the right, Third United States Army, having concentrated East of Paris (which was liberated on 25th August), was striking Eastwards during the first week of September to Nancy and Verdun. Shortly afterwards another column was directed South-East towards the Belfort area, to join up with the Seventh United States Army approaching from Marseilles.

The First United States Army advanced over the Aisne with its right flank directed on the Duchy of Luxembourg and its left flank on the general axis Mons – Liège.

Second British Army advanced North-East on Central Belgium, while First Canadian Army was about to sweep up the Channel coast.

On the left, 2 Canadian Division drove straight through Tôtes on Dieppe; the division entered the port towards the evening of Ist September. 2 Canadian Corps continued to advance rapidly North of the Somme which was crossed on 3rd September. 3 Canadian Division closed in on the defences of Boulogne and Calais on 5th September; reconnaissance revealed that the enemy was intending to fight in defence of both these ports.

Meanwhile, I Corps advanced North of the Seine on Ist September. While the 49 Division swung left into the Havre peninsula, the 5I Division went straight for St. Valery and liberated the town on 2nd September. Probing on the 3rd September showed that the elaborate defences of Havre were fully manned. 5I Division was ordered to take over the Northern sector of the perimeter and preparations for the assault were put in hand. On the I2th September the garrison commander surrendered.

30 Corps was the spearhead of the British drive to the North. Amiens was reached on 3Ist August, Brussels was entered on 3rd September, and the city of Antwerp on the following day. This advance imposed a considerable strain on administration. Our spearheads were being maintained some 400 miles from the temporary base in Normandy. The greatest strain was thrown on road transport, because only short stretches of railway were available owing to the widespread demolitions. But all difficulties were overcome, and the pace of the pursuit was maintained.

The Advance to the Meuse and Rhine.

The Supreme Commander directed that our immediate aim should be the establishment of bridges over the Rhine throughout its entire length, and that we should not go beyond this until Antwerp or Rotterdam could be opened. In view of the time factor it was agreed that 2I Army Group should launch its thrust to the Rhine before completing the clearance of the Scheldt estuary.

My intention now was to establish bridgeheads over the Meuse and Rhine in readiness for the time when it would be possible to advance eastwards to occupy the Ruhr. I ordered the resumption of the Second Army advance from the Antwerp – Brussels area for 6th September, and by IIth September a bridgehead was established over the Meuse-Escaut Canal. It was already noticeable that the enemy was beginning to recover his balance, so that the urgency of launching the thrust to the Rhine was underlined.

On Sunday I7th September the battle of Arnhem began. The purpose was to cross the Meuse and the Rhine, and to place Second Army in a suitable position for the subsequent development of operations towards the northern face of the Ruhr and the North German plains. The thrust to Arnhem outflanked the northern extension of the West Wall, and came very near to complete success.

The essential feature of the plan was the laying of a carpet of airborne troops across the waterways from the Meuse-Escaut Canal to the Neder Rijn, on the general axis of the road through Eindhoven to Uden, Grave, Nijmegen and Arnhem. The airborne carpet and bridgehead forces were provided by 82 and I0I United States Airborne Division and I British Airborne Division, and a Polish parachute brigade. Along the corridor, or airborne carpet, 30 British Corps was to advance and establish itself North of the Neder Rijn with bridgeheads over the Ijssel facing East. From the start, however, adverse weather conditions prevailed, and indeed, during the eight vital days of the battle, there were only two on which the weather permitted even a reasonable scale of offensive air support and air transportation. As a result, the airborne formations were not completed to strength (indeed 82 Airborne Division was without a complete gliderborne Combat Team). It had moreover been the intention to fly in 52 Division, but this project had to be abandoned. Resupply missions were repeatedly cancelled, and when flown were often on a greatly reduced scale.

Had reasonable weather conditions obtained, I believe the Arnhem bridgehead would have been established and maintained.

Full success at Arnhem was denied us for two reasons. First: the weather prevented the building up of adequate forces in the vital area. Second: the enemy managed to effect a very rapid concentration of forces to oppose us, and particularly against the bridgehead over the Neder Rijn. In face of this resistance the British Group of Armies in the North was not strong enough to retrieve the situation created by the weather, by intensifying the speed of operations on the ground. It was not possible to widen the corridor sufficiently quickly to reinforce Arnhem by road.

On 25th September I ordered withdrawal of the gallant Arnhem bridgehead.

The vital crossings at Grave and Nijmegen were retained, and their importance was to be amply demonstrated.

On the central sector of the Allied front, by the middle of September the First and Third U.S. Armies were fighting on the Siegfried Line from the Aachen area through the Ardennes to the region of Trier, and southwards along the general line of the upper Moselle.

By the third week in September the Sixth U.S. Army Group which had landed at Marseilles was firmly deployed on the right of Twelfth U.S. Army Group; the Allied front was continuous to Switzerland.

Operations to open up Antwerp.

The enemy had achieved a measure of recovery. This was clear not only in the Arnhem operation, but also in his reaction to American thrusts in the Siegfried Line. It was necessary to prepare for a hard killing match before it was possible to secure the Ruhr and advance into Germany. There was also the task to open the approaches to Antwerp before winter set in.

The immediate intention therefore became the clearance of the Scheldt Estuary.

This task was given to the First Canadian Army and lasted through October to the first week in November. The enemy resistance was vigorous, and some very hard fighting took place, leading up to the final operation for the capture of Walcheren. The reduction of this fortress presented many novel problems which were overcome principally by very remarkable precision bombing by Bomber Command, which breached the dykes and submerged large areas of the island. The extensive use of special amphibious devices enabled our troops to operate in the resulting floods. The naval craft put up a very fine performance in this battle, in spite of severe casualties from the coast defences and the rough seas. Walcheren was eventually cleared of the enemy by 8th November.

While the First Canadian Army were clearing the banks of the Scheldt, I Corps on its right wing, together with 12 Corps of Second Army, were engaged in clearing south-west Holland up to the River Maas; at the same time I Corps was protecting the right flank of 2 Canadian Corps operating in Beveland and Walcheren.

As soon as the Scheldt and south-west Holland operations were completed, First Canadian Army took over the northern sector of 21 Army Group as far east as Middelaar, which included assuming responsibility for the Nijmegen bridgehead.

This was to facilitate the Second Army operations which were to line up facing east for the drive to line the Meuse. This regrouping had a further object: First Canadian Army was required to plan the battle of the Rhineland, which was to be launched from the Nijmegen area; Second British Army was to plan the subsequent assault across the Rhine.

By early December, Second British Army was lined up along the River Meuse as far South as Maeseyck, whence the front crossed the river to the area of Geilenkirchen and joined the Ninth United States Army.

Plans for the regrouping of 21 Army Group for the Rhineland battle were completed by early December. In fact some divisions were actually on the move to their new concentration areas, when, on 16th December, the German counter-offensive in the Ardennes broke.

The Battle of the Ardennes.

The full weight of the German counter-offensive in the Ardennes was not immediately apparent; extremely bad weather had precluded satisfactory air reconnaissance, and the German concentration had been carried out with a high degree of secrecy. However, on the 18th I was considering the possible effects of a major enemy thrust towards Brussels and Antwerp on our dispositions – for the Army Group was at that time transferring the bulk of its weight to the extreme Northern flank. I ordered the concentration for the Rhineland battle to stop, and had plans prepared for switching some divisions from the Geilenkirchen sector to the west of the Meuse.

By the 19th the full implications of the German attack were established. It was known that the Sixth S.S. Panzer Army was thrusting in a North-Westerly direction towards Liège, with the Fifth Panzer Army in a wider wheel on its left. Seventh German Army was in support. On the same day the Supreme Commander entrusted to me temporary command of the First and Ninth U.S. Armies (with effect from the 20th), as they were at that time on the Northern side of the German salient, and therefore remote from the Twelfth U.S. Army Group axis.

On the 19th I ordered General Dempsey to move 30 Corps west of the Meuse, to a general line from Liège to Louvain, with patrols forward along the Western bank of the river between Liège itself and Dinant. This Corps was thus suitably placed to prevent the enemy crossing the river, and could cover the routes from the S.E. leading into Brussels. It subsequently became necessary in connection with the regrouping of American First Army to send some British divisions east of the Meuse. But throughout the battle I was anxious to avoid committing British forces more than was necessary. Had they become involved in large numbers, an acute administrative problem would have resulted from their Lines of Communication crossing the axis of the two American armies. Moreover, it was foremost in my mind that as soon as the German attack had been defeated the business of the Rhineland battle should be returned to as quickly as possible.

The battle of the Ardennes was won primarily by the staunch fighting qualities of the American soldier, and the enemy's subsequent confusion was completed by the intense air action which became possible as weather conditions improved. Sixth S.S. Panzer Army broke itself against the Northern shoulder of the salient, while Fifth Panzer Army spent its drive in the fierce battle which centred on Bastogne. Regrouping of the First and Ninth U.S. Armies, assisted by British formation, made possible the rapid formation of a reserve corps of four U.S. divisions under General Collins. The action of this corps, co-ordinated with the drive from the south by General Patton's Third U.S. Army, pinched the enemy forces out of the salient and began the bitter struggle which was to push them out of the Siegfried Line.

The enemy had been prevented from crossing the Meuse in the nick of time. Once the Meuse crossings were secure it became increasingly apparent that the opportunity had come to turn the enemy's position to our advantage. Hitler's projected counter-offensive ended in a tactical defeat, and the Germans received a tremendous battering. As soon as the situation had been restored I was able to order the British divisions north again to the concentration areas which had been made ready in December.

The Battle of the Rhineland.

The main objective of the Allies on the Western front remained the Ruhr. Once the Ruhr had been isolated from the rest of Germany, the enemy's capacity to continue the struggle would quickly peter out. Beyond this, the object of our operations was to force mobile war on the enemy by developing operations into the northern plains of Germany. It was necessary first to line up on the Rhine; then to bridge the river and gain a suitable jumping off position for a mobile campaign in the Spring.

The enemy was in a very bad way; he had suffered another major defeat with heavy losses in men and equipment. Moreover, the great Russian winter offensive was now under way, and we did not wish to give the enemy the chance to switch forces to the east.

The Supreme Commander's orders to 2I Army Group provided for a line-up on the Rhine from Düsseldorf northwards. Ninth U.S. Army remained under my operational control.

First it was necessary to eliminate the enemy salient west of the R. Roer between Julich and Roermond. Second Army completed this task by 28 January. The divisions concerned, less defensive troops left holding the river line, immediately started north to join the concentration for the Rhineland battle.

The battle of the Rhineland was based on two converging offensives between the Rhine and the Meuse, with the object of destroying the enemy forces masking the Ruhr. It was intended, by interdiction from the air and by employing the maximum available forces on the ground, to prevent the enemy withdrawing to the east bank of the Rhine; in this, success was largely achieved.

First Canadian Army was ordered to launch an attack S.E. from the area of the Nijmegen bridgehead to meet the Ninth U.S. Army, whose thrust was developed from the Julich – Roermond sector northwards.

It was originally planned to launch the two operations almost simultaneously, but the southern thrust was delayed. In the event this proved to our advantage.

The date by which the Ninth U.S. Army could attack was dependent on the rate at which U.S. divisions could be released from other sectors of the Allied front, as the strength of that Army was to be increased to 12 divisions. Release of these divisions depended on the situation on the rest of the front. Twelfth U.S. Army Group was still involved in the Ardennes, particularly in thrusting towards the system of dams on the River Roer which control its flood waters. As long as the enemy held these dams he was in a position to impose flood conditions likely to impede the crossing of the river. Further south, the heaviest fighting was in the Saar and in the Colmar pocket – in both areas the enemy had achieved local successes.

The weather remained an anxious uncertainty. The thaw was beginning and, apart from the floods, it was playing havoc with our road communications.

The concentration of divisions for the Canadian Army attack was completed in the first week in February. Elaborate arrangements were made to assemble the forces employed into the very confined concentration areas, and also to mislead the enemy about our intentions.

On 8 February the northern wing of the pincer movement started. 30 Corps, under command of First Canadian Army, launched its attack into the Reichswald Forest and the northern extension of the West Wall, on a front of five divisions, supported by very considerable Air Forces and over 1,000 guns. This began the memorable battle which, in intensity and fierceness, equalled any which our troops have experienced in this war.

The Germans quickly built up to about eleven equivalent divisions, including four parachute divisions and two armoured divisions; in particular their paratroops fought magnificently. Meanwhile the situation was improving in other parts of the Allied Front. Operations in the Colmar area had been successfully concluded and the Germans thrown back across the Rhine at the southern extremity of the Allied front; the Saar sector had been stabilised. More important still, Sixth S.S. Panzer Army was transferred to the eastern front, to oppose the mounting Russian offensive. The concentration of American divisions into the Ninth U.S. Army was achieved remarkably quickly, over long distances, using shocking roads and tracks, and in appalling weather.

The launching of the American thrust had been planned to start between 10th and 15th February but at the last minute, before abandoning the Roer dams, the enemy carried out demolitions which loosed the flood waters. There followed an anxious period of waiting, with all the troops teed up for the battle, while the water subsided sufficiently to enable the crossing to be launched. On 23rd February the Ninth U.S. Army, under command of General Simpson, commenced its attack northwards towards the area where First Canadian Army was fighting a most intense battle. Owing to the delay in starting the southern thrust, the Reichswald battle had drawn enemy strength from the Ninth U.S. Army sector. The Americans took every advantage of this opportunity and advanced with admirable speed; their action in its turn eased the pressure in the North.

As Ninth U.S. Army swung North, the First U.S. Army was made responsible by the Supreme Commander for the security of its southern flank; the thrusts towards Cologne were thus related directly to our operations.

The keynotes of the battle of the Rhineland were the intense and fanatical opposition of the enemy who, as we had hoped, accepted battle West of the Rhine, and secondly the appalling weather conditions. The northern flank of the Reichswald operation was conducted mainly in various types of amphibious vehicles; in general, the mud and slush were indescribable and greatly hampered the movement of troops and supplies through the heavily wooded areas which are so lacking in roads.

On 3rd March the two armies linked up; the Americans were in Geldern, and 35 Division of XVI Corps made contact with 53 Division in the northern outskirts of the town. But it was not until the 10th that the enemy bridgehead covering Wesel was liquidated.

21 Army Group was now lined up on the Rhine as far South as Düsseldorf.

The enemy had suffered yet another heavy defeat. He had lost nearly 100,000 men in killed, wounded and prisoners. Eighteen divisions and a large number of hastily formed units had been battered.

THE BATTLE OF THE RHINE.

On 7th March, following a swift break through, First United States Army secured intact the railway bridge at Remagen and immediately began forming a bridgehead on the East bank.

The importance of this bridgehead to our subsequent operations cannot be overestimated; the enemy reaction to it was immediate, and a considerable number of surviving enemy formations soon became committed in the sector.

Meanwhile, Third United States Army thrust to the Rhine at Coblenz and subsequently established a bridgehead south-west of the city over the River Moselle. On 15 March American troops thrust southwards from this bridgehead and eastwards from Trier, while Seventh United States Army attacked northwards between the Rhine and Saarbrucken. While Seventh Army fought steadily through the Siegfried defences and pinned down the German troops, armoured columns of Third Army drove into the rear of the enemy positions. Resistance east of the Moselle crumbled, the Saar was enveloped, and the Rhine cities of Mainz and Worms were captured. By the third week in March the Allied Armies had closed to the Rhine throughout its length.

While the battle of the Rhineland was proceeding, the details for the crossing of the Rhine were being worked out. Many engineering and administrative preparations had been initiated back in December, before the Ardennes counter-offensive. In particular, work had started on the roads and railways necessary to establish our lines of communication across the Meuse and Rhine. Furthermore the Second Army depots had been stocked with some 130,000 tons of stores for the coming operations. And so 21 Army Group launched the operation for crossing the Rhine a fortnight after completion of the battle of the Rhineland.

The fortnight between the end of the battle of the Rhineland and the crossing of the Rhine was one of intense activity. Formations were regrouped and lined up in their correct positions, covered by a screen of troops holding the river bank. Dense and continuous clouds of smoke were employed to hide our intentions and final preparations.

On 9 March I issued orders for crossing the Rhine north of the Ruhr. My intention was to secure a bridgehead: prior to developing operations to isolate the Ruhr and to thrust into the northern plains of Germany.

Outline Plan.

In outline, my plan was to cross the Rhine on a front of two armies between Rheinberg and Rees, using Ninth American Army on the right and Second Army on the left. The principal initial objective was the important communications centre of Wesel. I intended that the bridgehead should extend to the south sufficiently far to cover Wesel from enemy ground action, and to the north to include bridge sites at Emmerich; the depth of the bridgehead was to be made sufficient to provide room to form up major forces for the drive to the east and north-east. I gave 24 March as target date for the operation. The battle of the Rhineland was not completed until 10 March, so that the time available for preparing to assault across the greatest water obstacle in Western Europe was extremely short. The all important factor was to follow up the enemy as quickly as possible, and it was possible to achieve this speed of action mainly because of the foresight and preliminary planning that had been devoted to this battle for some months.

The width of the Rhine on our front was between four and five hundred yards, but at high water it was liable to increase to between seven and twelve hundred yards. The mean velocity of the current was about three and a half knots. The river bed itself was composed of sand and gravel and was expected to give a good bearing surface for amphibious tanks and trestles. The course of the river was controlled by a highly developed system of dykes; the main dyke was generally sixty feet wide at the base and some ten to sixteen feet high, and formed a formidable obstacle. Although our operations in February had been severely handicapped by flooding, the waters were subsiding rapidly and the ground was drying remarkably quickly.

Ninth United States Army comprised XIII, XVI and XIX Corps with a total of three armoured and nine infantry divisions. In addition to 8, 12 and 30 Corps, Second Army included for the initial stages of the operation 2 Canadian Corps and XVIII United States Airborne Corps; the latter comprised 6 British and 17 American Airborne Divisions. The total forces in Second Army were four armoured, two airborne and eight infantry divisions, five independent armoured brigades, one Commando brigade and one independent infantry brigade. 79 Armoured Division was in support of the operation with all its resources of specialised armour and amphibious devices.

A tremendous weight of day and night heavy bombers, medium bombers and Allied Tactical Air Forces was made available in support of the operation.

At I530 hours on 23rd March I gave orders to launch the operation, as the weather was good.

The attack began on the night of 23rd March, and by the next morning, all four assaulting divisions (5I Division, I5 Division and 30 and 79 United States Divisions) and I Commando Brigade (British) had accomplished their initial crossings between Rheinberg and Rees. The key to the crossing was the important communicating centre of Wesel, which was captured by the Commando Brigade after an intense air attack by Bomber Command. On the morning of the 24th, XVIII United States Airborne Corps, with 6 Airborne Division and I7 United States Airborne Division, dropped on the East bank of the Rhine within supporting distance of our guns on the West bank.

The enemy reaction was initially strongest on the Northern flank, where three parachute divisions had been concentrated. But, generally speaking, his power of manoeuvre was greatly limited by the very heavy air interdiction programme which had been originated several days before the assault. The airborne troops took full advantage of his failure to launch any effective counter-attack against them, and rapidly made contact with the formations crossing the river. The British and American bridgeheads were quickly joined. Some remarkable engineering feats were accomplished in working ferries and bridging the river, and it is interest to note that the Royal Navy was well to the fore with craft which had been dragged by road all across Belgium, Southern Holland and the Rhineland.

We were now in a position to drive into the plains of Northern Germany. It was a matter of great satisfaction to see how plans which had been maturing back on the Seine were reaching their fulfilment.

The Advance to the Elbe and Baltic.

Within four days our bridgehead over the Rhine had been established, and on 28th March the advance to the Elbe began.

On the right flank Ninth United States Army was directed to the sector Magdeburg – Wittenberge. In the centre Second Army was to advance with its left flank on Hamburg. On the left, 2 Canadian Corps, after crossing through the Second Army bridgehead, swung North along the Rhine to outflank Arnhem and open up the routes leading Northwards from that area. Later, I Canadian Corps assaulted across the river at Arnhem and turned into western Holland to establish a protective flank between the Rhine and the Zuider Zee.

The enemy tried desperately to assemble his remaining forces in opposition to our advance. The core of his resistance formed on the Ems-Dortmund Canal, facing the left and centre of Second Army. Bitter fighting ensued; in the meantime in the Ninth U.S. Army sector, and on the right of Second Army, progress was rapid.

By 3rd April, Ninth U.S. Army had reached the Weser in the Minden area, and had linked up with First U.S. Army advancing from the Remagen bridgehead. The Ruhr was enveloped. Ninth U.S. Army reverted to command Twelfth U.S. Army

Group. The two U.S. armies proceeded with the clearance of the Ruhr, and at the same time pushed forces Eastwards to the Elbe.

The subsequent action of 2I Army Group may be compared with the drive across N.W. France. The German East-West lines of communication to the coast were progressively cut and a series of right hooks were delivered to round up the enemy. The left flank formations drove up towards the coast to complete the task.

8 Corps of Second Army crossed the Weser near Minden on 5th April, followed a few days later further North by I2 Corps, which then worked its way along the East bank in an advance which brought it to the outskirts of Hamburg. This wide turning movement loosened the enemy on the left, and while Bremen was masked from the South by 30 Corps, a hook further up river came in on the city from the East. Bremen fell at the end of the month.

First Canadian Army made steady progress, and by mid-April had liberated most of Northern Holland. By the same time I Canadian Corps had safeguarded our flank in Western Holland and isolated the large enemy garrison there.

The main drive to the Elbe continued towards Luneburg, which was reached on the I8th, and our forces began to line up on the Southern bank of the river masking the city of Hamburg. The Elbe was crossed on 29th April and spearheads made straight for Lubeck in order to seal off the Schleswig-Holstein peninsula. At the same time, moving by road, a U.S. airborne corps of two divisions, together with 6 British Airborne Division, formed a defensive flank facing East on the line Darchau – Schwerin – Wismar. Once across the river our operations were virtually unopposed. The plan for outflanking Hamburg by a manoeuvre similar to that used at Bremen was actually under way when, on 2nd May, the Germans came out to negotiate its surrender. Across the Elbe the countryside was packed with a mass of German soldiers and refugees, fleeing from our own advance and from that of the Russians: with whom we established contact on 2nd May.

The negotiations which began in Hamburg led on 3rd May to the despatch by Doenitz of envoys to my Tactical Headquarters, then at Luneburg Heath. By this time I had ordered a pause in our advance to be made on a line which would cover Hamburg and Lubeck. Some fighting was still in progress with German remnants in the Cuxhaven and Emden peninsulas. The German delegation which came to my Headquarters was headed by General-Admiral von Friedeburg, Commander-in-Chief of the German Navy. He was accompanied by General Kinzel, Chief of Staff to Field Marshal Busch, and by Vice-Admiral Wagner. I quickly established that they had not in fact come to negotiate the unconditional surrender of the troops on my front, and at once made it clear that I would not discuss any other matters. I did, however, take the opportunity to show von Friedeburg a map of the current operational situation of which he was apparently not properly aware, and this helped to convince him of the hopelessness of the German position. He then returnd to recommend to Doenitz the unconditional surrender of all German naval, land and air forces opposite 2I Army Group. On the evening of 4th May, von Friedeburg returned to my Headquarters and signed the instrument of unconditional surrender of those forces.

Cease Fire was ordered on 2I Army Group front as from 0800 hours 5th May.

REVIEW AND COMMENTS.

I have described the part played by 2I Army Group and the Armies under my command from 6th June, I944, to the 5th May, I945, and I should like to take this opportunity of expressing my appreciation of the tremendous tasks accomplished by the Navy, Army and Air Forces throughout the campaign.

Before the operation was launched it was the task of the Air Forces to create conditions favourable to a successful landing and to the subsequent development of operations inland. Both the Army and the Navy relied on this being done, and it was done; the heavy bombers of Bomber Command and of the American Air Force did magnificent work in weakening Germany generally, and in particular in destroying the enemy railway system, which enormously reduced the mobility of the enemy once operations began.

Until the Army stepped ashore it was completely in the hands of the Navy and Air Forces for its sea and airborne landings.

Once the Army was on shore all military operations became combined Army/Air operations; the mighty weapon of air power enabled the Army to conduct its operations successfully and with far fewer casualties than would otherwise have been the case. The Army relied on the Navy and on the Air Forces for secure communications across the sea from our island base in Britain.

I would like to say that the Army owes a great debt of gratitude to the Navy and the Air Force and realises fully its complete dependence on them in all military operations.

In addition I would like to add some remarks concerning the handling of the various arms within the Army, with particular reference to the campaign itself.

Administration.

In the early stages of the campaign much depended on the successful issue of the administrative planning. The task was a formidable one, and in plain terms meant the export overseas of a community the size of the population of Birmingham. Over 287,000 men and 37,000 vehicles were pre-loaded into ships and landing craft prior to the assault, and in the first thirty days I,I00,000 British and American troops were put ashore.

There, was the necessity to foresee and provide all that is required for a major static battle quickly followed by a rapid advance of some 400 miles, which entailed the landing of some 200,000 vehicles and 750,000 tons of stores during the corresponding period. And I can say that, even in these exceptional conditions, planned operations were never held up even for a single day by any lack of administrative resources.

In the early stages the vast quantities of stores required were landed over open beaches, a task which was greatly assisted by the MULBERRY. The stores were directed into a number of field depots, whence they were despatched to the troops. As soon as conditions permitted, these field depots were concentrated into a single organisation called the Rear Maintenance Area.

When the break out from Normandy occurred, considerable problems arose because the L. of C. became stretched in a short time from Bayeux to Antwerp – that is some 400 miles; all bridges over the Seine were demolished, and the railway facilities extensively damaged. In order to maintain the advance, shipping and the discharge of material were cut well below the figure necessary for the daily maintenance of the force, so as to release every lorry possible for ferrying stores forward to the troops. This meant eating into the reserves built up in the Rear Maintenance Area, and it became a matter of urgency to get bases further forward and shorten the Lines of Communication. We had both feet off the ground, relying on opening up the Channel ports, particularly Dieppe, before our accumulated stocks became exhausted. But administrative risks have to be taken in war as well as tactical ones; the point to realise is that a commander requires a nice judgment to know when risks are justifiable and when they are definitely not so.

Gradually the railway systems were re-established, and when eventually the port of Antwerp was opened to shipping, it was possible to base ourselves firmly on depots established between there and Brussels. Subsidiary tonnages were continued to be handled through the Channel ports.

I would mention one very important feature of administration which has been confirmed during the campaign. It is that there is a reasonably constant figure covering the combined ammunition and petrol tonnages required, though, of course, the split between these commodities depends on the type of battle that is being fought.

It is not possible in this dispatch to go into any detail concerning the vast and complicated machinery necessary for the support of a modern army in the field. I will, however, mention the tremendous importance of Movements and Transportation. Their problems in this campaign were immense. There were the numerous technical and engineer problems of repairing and operating the damaged or demolished ports, railways, and inland water transport systems, of four European countries. Bridges had to be built over such obstacles as the Seine and the Rhine. Possibly even more important was the problem of coordinating and allocating traffic over the various means of carriage, and of setting up organisations for operating through services over the different national systems.

The "A" services too, were confronted with special problems. The calculations of reinforcements required, together with a correct balance for every arm and trade, called for considerable foresight and experience, and had a very direct effect of the success of operations. I will also mention Welfare, which had reached a standard in the Army probably never previously approached.

Very great praise is due to the various Services and Departments which so successfully overcame their problems and difficulties, and carried out their functions in such an efficient manner.

Specialised Equipment.

Early in the planning for D Day it became evident that specialised armoured equipment would be necessary to overcome the beach defences. One of the recommendations made as a result of the Dieppe raid had, in fact, been that engineers should be carried behind armour up to the concrete obstacle which had to be breached. This idea was developed so that mechanical means could be used for placing or projecting charges from tanks without exposing the crews. Tank-carried bridges for crossing anti-tank ditches were developed as well, and were launched mechanically from behind armour.

The study of the particular problems presented by the Normandy beach defences led to the preparation of further specialised equipment. Mats laid from tanks were used to cross soft patches of clay on the beaches; a turretless tank was used as a means of providing a self-propelled ramp over which other vehicles could scale sea-walls; flail tanks for mine clearing and amphibious tanks to lead the assault were employed, and were integrated with the engineer tanks into well trained assault teams.

Specialised armour made an important contribution to the success of the landings. The beach defences were quickly overcome and the new technique of landing a great weight of armour early in the assault paid an excellent dividend.

As the campaign progressed the need for special armoured devices became increasingly apparent. Against fixed defences such as existed around the ports, mine-sweeping tanks, flame-throwers and engineer tanks were invaluable. The Churchill flame-thrower was outstandingly successful throughout the campaign. It had a very great moral effect on the enemy and saved us many casualties.

The D Day technique for the early landing and quick build up of armour was also applied at the crossings of the Rhine and the Elbe. This was made possible by the use of amphibious tanks and amphibious assault craft carrying infantry, light vehicles, and supporting weapons. It was largely the use of these craft which allowed operations to be continued throughout the winter over the flooded areas between the Maas and the Rhine.

Armoured personnel carriers were also found to be necessary, and were improvised from tanks with the turret removed. Their use gave armoured mobility to infantry and enabled them more closely to accompany armour in the assault and pursuit. The vehicles, known as "KANGAROOS," I shall mention again later.

All these various equipments were concentrated, for training and administration, in a special formation: the 79 Armoured Division. They were sub-allotted in support of formations and units as operations required. The divisional commander was responsible for providing competent advisers in the use of the equipment at all levels. It was found that centralisation under him was essential in order to achieve flexibility and provide a controlled programme of workshops overhaul, rest and relief.

The R.A.C.

The R.A.C. lived up to its highest traditions in this campaign. It was really properly equipped with adequate scales of reserves, and the fighting gave full scope to its flexibility and adaptability.

The outstanding point which emerges once more is that we require only two basic types of tank – the capital tank (for fighting) and the light tank (for reconnaissance).

The capital tank must be a weapon of universal application, suitable not only for working with the infantry in the attack and in the dog-fight battle, but also capable of operating in the spearheads of the armoured division in pursuit. I am convinced, as a result of experience from Alamein to the Baltic, that it is fundamentally unsound to aim at producing one type of tank for co-operation with the infantry and another for the armoured division. We require *one* tank which will do both jobs. I have learnt that the ubiquitous use of armour is a great battle-winning factor.

Artillery.

The Gunners have risen to great heights in this war and I doubt if the artillery has ever been so efficient as it is to-day.

In considering the future of the artillery, it is very important that we should get the organisation right, with the correct balance between tracked guns and towed guns, and so on. The expenditure of ammunition in this campaign has been tremendous, and as a result of the experience gained, certain facts have emerged. It has been found that a large number of small shells over a given time produces a greater effect on the enemy than the same weight of larger shells. It is moreover, important to remember that there is a time limit for bombardment, after which enemy morale gets no lower and further expenditure of ammunition is wasted. It has been found that our own casualties rise in direct proportion to the distance of the infantry behind the artillery supporting fire.

All these facts point to the need for relatively small shells for close support of infantry, where neutralisation and not destruction is the immediate object. The 25 pounder meets the case; it must have good fragmentation.

I would mention the fuze problem as this requires study and development. It is necessary to have a good proximity fuze and a good time fuze.

Lastly, the Air O.P. The Air O.P. has proved its value in this campaign. It has become a necessary part of gunnery and a good aeroplane is required for the job. Very good R.A. officers are required for duty in the Squadrons, and they must be selected with this in view. Primarily, an Air O.P. officer must be a good gunner – it is not difficult to teach him to fly.

The Engineers.

The Engineer problems were unusually formidable, and had to be executed at a great speed.

In the early days the clearance of beach obstacles and mines gave rise to great anxiety and called for prolonged and detailed study. The armoured vehicles R.E. (A.V.R.E.'s) armed with a petard shooting a heavy demolition charge, were landed very early and operated with great dash and success against obstacles and pillboxes. The problem of placing the MULBERRIES or artificial ports was solved by the excellent co-operation between the Royal Navy and the Engineers on both sides of the Channel. As the beachhead began to expand, demolitions on a grand scale had to be overcome – demolition of ports, railways, bridges and airfields – combined with extensive and very skilful mine laying.

The repair of well blitzed and intentionally demolished airfields, or more often construction of new ones, was in itself a major task: upon which depended our support from the air.

Twin petrol pipelines were laid from Cherbourg across the Seine at Rouen, and from Boulogne stretching across the Rhine. These were supplied from ships pumping ashore, and later in particular from the famous "PLUTO." The pipelines transported during the campaign more than a million tons of petrol.

Nearly two thousand Bailey bridges were erected, including spans across the Seine, the Meuse, the Rhine and the Weser – some of which were nearly a mile long. It has once more been shown that rivers, even very big rivers with complete demolition belts, do not hold up an army, in spite of the weight of modern traffic.

Armour and the mass of lorries assisting the Army played havoc with the roads, and the maintenance of them in conditions of continual traffic, especially in low-lying districts in severe winter conditions, was perhaps the most heartrending task that faced the Engineers. They were greatly assisted by the Pioneer Corps, which in this task, as in so many others, did a very excellent job.

The most determined demolitions were in the ports. But it has been proved that it is impossible to destroy a port so badly that it cannot be put into some sort of operation by the time the Navy have cleared the mines obstructing its entrance.

The Sappers were very well equipped; but it is important to remember that it is the human element – the resourceful officers and skilled and willing men – which is the major factor in engineering in war. We were often very short of Sappers, particularly during the big river crossing operations.

Signals.

It is fundamental that successful operations demand really efficient communications. It is therefore worth emphasising that a commander, at whatever level, must take his R. Signals adviser into his confidence from the earliest stages in preparing a plan.

Much of Signals' work was of the unspectacular, slogging variety which the provision of a vast network of communications involves. The constant aim of Signals was to build up the solid cable head as far forward as possible, to provide reliable jumping-off places for communications in the battle area. To serve my own Tactical Headquarters, which frequently moved at intervals of every two or three days, use was made of an ultra high frequency wireless of an entirely new type (No. I0 set). This method gave me secure speech communication with my armies and my Main Headquarters.

I think that one of the main Signals lessons has been the necessity for insisting that the officers reach a really high standard of technical ability. Modern equipment becomes increasingly complicated and diverse, and the officers must know all about it, if they are to get the best results.

The Infantry.

In spite of predictions to the contrary, the Infantry has lost none of its importance on the battlefield.

Modern infantry is a master of more weapons than ever before, and the infantryman's life depends primarily on the skill with which he uses them; he must reach an increasingly higher standard of training. It has been a war of movement, but although the infantry man may motor into battle, his training must keep him hard and tough – a point which must never be overlooked in these days of troop carrying transport.

The introduction of the armoured personnel carrier is an important innovation in the employment of infantry. It enables infantry to be transported across bullet-swept zones in order to arrive fresh at the vital part of the battlefield. The development of this technique has already gone far, and done much to enlarge the scope of infantry tactics. For example, in the first major attack by the Canadian Army astride the Falaise road on 7 August, infantry carried in "Kangaroos" were moved by night a distance of five miles to their off-loading point; the last four miles of this advance were actually within the enemy positions, and the troops debussed almost on the edge of the enemy gun areas. They then fanned out to overrun the belt of country they were attacking.

The tendency to do more and more by night has been greatly facilitated by the provision of "artificial moonlight". Artificial moonlight, provided by Searchlight batteries, has now become a standard part of our military organisation and has greatly assisted the activities of the infantryman. It has also proved its value in more rearward areas to the bridge builders and administrative echelons.

It has again been the Infantry who suffered the heaviest casualties. I cannot praise too highly the stamina and persistence which the Infantry displayed in the campaign. Divisions were called upon to remain continuously in action for many months on end – to this they responded admirably, even during the very bitter winter we experienced.

Airborne Forces.

Airborne forces must now form an essential part of the Army, as there will often be occasions in which they can play a vital role. Apart from their participation in the battle, the threat of their use can be turned to important advantage, for experience has shown that thereby the enemy can be led to make considerable and even vital dispersions of his front line forces. This is in addition to the need to lock up troops in rear areas for guarding vital zones and installations when the opponent is known to have airborne troops at his disposal.

The use of airborne forces in highly mobile operations is limited, because the time required for planning their descents frequently results in the ground troops over-running the projected dropping zones. But in deliberate operations, such as the seaborne assault, or the assault across a major river obstacle, airborne troops have proved to be a battle winning factor.

The threat of an airborne operation, in conjunction with other factors, was material in causing the Germans to retain major formations in the Pas de Calais during the initial period after our landing in Normandy. Nearer the battlefield, uncertainty as to our intentions, combined with the use of dummy paratroops, caused alarm and despondency to the enemy. This delayed the arrival on the battlefield of portions of his forces at a vital time.

There are a number of limitations in the use of airborne troops, chief of which is the uncertainty of weather. But I believe this factor will become less important in the future, as scientific methods are developed to facilitate the use of aircraft under adverse weather conditions.

The Medical Organisation.

No account of this campaign would be complete without some mention of the truly remarkable success of the medical organisation. But it must be remembered that there were two factors which contributed greatly to the results achieved; probably no group of doctors has ever worked on better material, and secondly, they were caring for the men of a winning army. The men of 21 Army Group were fully immunised and fully trained; their morale was at its highest; they were well-clothed and well-fed; they were fighting in a climate to which the average British soldier is accustomed; hygiene, both personal and unit, was exceptionally good; welfare services were well organised. The exhilarating effect of success also played its part in reducing the rates of sickness.

Commanders in the field must realise that the medical state of an army is not dependent on the doctors alone. Their efforts are immeasurably facilitated when morale is at its highest, and of all the factors which ensure a high state of morale, there is none more important than success.

The sickness amongst troops was almost halved as compared with the last war. It is striking that, as we swept through Germany, liberating prison camps such as Belsen and Sandbostel where thousands of persons were dying of typhus, only twenty-five British troops contracted this disease. None died of it. This was due to preventive inoculations and to the adequate supply and use of a powder called D.D.T.

Air transport has been of great importance in the evacuation of casualties. By this means over a hundred thousand wounded men were evacuated to base hospitals from front line units. In the sphere of transfusion, great quantities of blood and blood plasma were used. A co-ordinated service of air transport and refrigerator trucks ensured that fresh blood was always at hand for surgeons working directly behind the lines – even during the rapid advance into Belgium.

Another interesting fact is that, in the last war, two out of every three men wounded in the belly, died. Field Surgical Units, operating close behind the lines, greatly reduced this danger. In the Normandy campaign two out of every three men wounded in the belly recovered.

The healing of war wounds has been revolutionised by the use of penicillin. Many men who in the last war would have been permanent invalids, were fit and ready to go back to the line within a month of being wounded.

To sum up, the doctors were prepared to lay 15 to I that once a man got into their hands, whatever his injury, they would save has life and restore him to health. It is a fine thing that these odds were achieved with a handsome margin.

Conclusion.

I must emphasise that my despatch has been primarily concerned with 2I Army Group; but it is well to remember that any complete history of the campaign in North-West Europe would tell more of the tremendous efforts of the United States and of the fighting on the more Southerly sectors remote from the 2I Army Group zone.

I would also say that the scope of my despatch has permitted only the briefest reference to our great Russian ally.

Events have amply shown that a splendid spirit of co-operation was established between the British and American services, and that, under General Eisenhower a strong, loyal team was quickly brought into being, while the various components of the great invasion force were welded into a fine fighting machine.

It has been brought home to me, not only in this campaign but throughout the war, that the soldier on the battle front, and the worker on the home front are closely linked members of the same team – neither can achieve any success without the other; both have to stand firm under fire and both have to see that their job is carried out in spite of all the enemy can do.

I do not propose in this despatch to record the names of those who have deserved my personal and official gratitude for their services in the campaign. To name any might seem to imply some lack of appreciation of others; where all did so well it seem invidious to mention names.

I record my deep appreciation and gratitude to all who served with me in this historic campaign: from the highest commander to the most junior private soldier.

In conclusion I wish to pay tribute to the splendid fighting spirit, heroism and endurance of the ordinary soldier. And if I were asked what is the greatest single factor which contributed to his success, I would say morale. I call morale the greatest single factor in war. A high morale is based on discipline, self-respect and confidence of the soldier in his commanders, in his weapons and in himself. Without high morale, no success can be achieved, however good may be the strategic or tactical plan, or anything else. High morale is a pearl of very great price. And the surest way to obtain it is by success in battle.

Footnote
1. On the day ultimately selected H hour varied between 0630 for the Western Task Force to 0745 on the Eastern sectors.

ABBREVIATIONS

LIBERATING EUROPE: D-DAY TO VICTORY

A/C	Aircraft
A/S	Anti-Submarine
A/U	Anti-U-boat
AA	Anti-aircraft
Act.	Acting
ADGB	Air Defence of Great Britain
AEAF	Allied Expeditionary Air Force
AF	Air Force
AFC	Air Force Cross
AFV	Armoured Fighting Vehicle
Air OP	Air Operations
ALC	Assault Landing Craft
ALG	Advanced Landing Ground
ANCXF	Allied Naval Commander-in-Chief, Expeditionary Force
AOC	Air Officer Commanding
AP	Armour Piercing
APIS	Army Photographic Intelligence Section
ASR	Air Sea Rescue
ASV	Anti-Surface Vessel
AVRE	Armoured Vehicle Royal Engineers
BUCO	Build-Up Control Organisation
C. in C.	Commander-in-Chief
CATOR	Combined Air Transport Operations Room
CBE	Commander of the Order of the British Empire
COMINCH	Commander-in-Chief, U.S. Navy
COREP	Control Repair Organisation
COSSAC	Chief of Staff to the Supreme Allied Commander
COTUG	Control Tug Operation
CTF	Commander, Task Force

DD	Duplex Drive
DFC	Distinguished Flying Cross
DSC	Distinguished Service Cross
DSO	Distinguished Service Order
E-Boat	*See S-Boot*
ETO	European Theater/Theatre of Operations
ETOUSA	European Theater of Operations, United States Army
FDT	Fighter Direction Tender
FFI	*Forces Françaises de l'Intérieur*
FOB	Forward Observer, Bombardment
FOBAA	Flag Officer, British Assault Area
FOO	Forward Observer Officer
FOsB	Forward Observers, Bombardment
GAF	German Air Force (*Luftwaffe*)
GCB	Knight Grand Cross of the Most Honourable Order of the Bath
GCC	Group Control Centre
GCI	Ground Control Intercept/ Ground Control Interception
GP Bomb	General Purpose Bomb
HE	High Explosive
HMS	His Majesty's Ship
IAZ	Inner Artillery Zone
IFF	Identification Friend or Foe
KBE	Knight Commander of the Most Excellent Order of the British Empire
KCB	Knight Commander of the Most Honourable Order of the Bath
L. of C.	Line(s) of Communication
LCA	Landing Craft Assault
LCC	Landing Craft Control
LCF	Landing Craft Flak
LCG	Landing Craft Gun
LCI	Landing Craft Infantry
LCI(L)	Landing Craft Infantry (Large)
LCM	Landing Craft Mechanized
LCP	Landing Craft Personnel
LCP(L)	Landing Craft Personnel (Large)
LCS	Landing Craft Support
LCT	Landing Craft Tank
LCT(R)	Landing Craft Tank (Rocket)
LCVP	Landing Craft, Vehicle, Personnel
Lieut.	Lieutenant
LRCP	Licentiate of the Royal College of Physicians
LSD	Landing Ship Dock
LSI	Landing Ship Infantry
LST	Landing Ship Tank

MC Bomb(s)	Medium Capacity Bomb(s)
MEW	Ministry of Economic Warfare/Minister of Economic Warfare
MGB	Motor Gun Boat
ML	Motor Launch
MLC	Mechanized Landing Craft/Motor Landing Craft
MOVCO	Movement Control
MP	Military Police/Military Policeman(men)/Member of Parliament
MRCS	Member of the Royal College of Surgeons
MT, M/T	Motor Transport
MTB	Motor Torpedo Boat
MV	Motor Vessel
MVO	Member of the Royal Victorian Order
NFC	Naval Forces Commander
OKM	*Oberkommando der Marine* (Germany's Naval High Command)
OKW	*Oberkommando der Wehrmacht* (Germany's supreme command of the armed forces)
OP	Observation Post
ORP	*Okręt Rzeczypospolitej Polskiej* (Ship of the Republic of Poland)
POL	Polish
POW, PoW	Prisoner of War
QM	Quartermaster
R Boat	*Räumboote* (a type of small naval vessel, built as a minesweeper but which could be used for several purposes during the Second World War)
RA	Royal Artillery
RAAF	Royal Australian Air Force
RAC	Royal Armoured Corps
RAF	Royal Air Force
RAF BC	Royal Air Force Bomber Command
RANVR	Royal Australian Naval Volunteer Reserve
RASC	Royal Army Service Corps
RCAF	Royal Canadian Air Force
RCM	Radio Counter Measures
RCN	Royal Canadian Navy
RCT	Regimental Combat Team (US)
RDF	Radio Direction Finding
RE	Royal Engineers
Ret.	Retired
RM	Royal Marines
RN	Royal Navy
RNR	Royal Naval Reserve
RNVR	Royal Naval Volunteer Reserve
RNZN	Royal New Zealand Navy
RNZNVR	Royal New Zealand Naval Volunteer Reserve

RP	Rocket Projectile
S-Boot	*Schnellboot* (meaning "fast boat")
SAS	Special Air Service
SFCP	Shore Fire Control Party
SGB	Steam Gun Boat
SHAEF	Supreme Headquarters, Allied Expeditionary Force
SS	Steamship
TAF	Tactical Air Force
TF	Task Force
TURCO	Turn Round Control Organisation
US	United States
USAAF	United States Army Air Force
USN	United States Navy
USS	United States' Ship
VC	Victoria Cross
VHF	Very High Frequency
VIP	Visits of Important Personages
VLA	Very Low Altitude
W/T	Wireless Telegraphy/Wireless Telephony

INDEX OF NAVAL AND MILITARY UNITS

INDEX OF PEOPLE